Rethinking International Development Series

Series Editors:

Andy Sumner, Co-Director of King's International Development Institute, King's College London, UK.
Ray Kiely, Professor of International Politics, Queen Mary University of London, UK.

The *Rethinking International Devsssselopment* series publishes cutting-edge titles that focus on the broad area of 'development'. The core aims of the series are to present critical work that:
– is cross disciplinary;
– challenges orthodoxies;
– reconciles theoretical depth with empirical research;
– explores the frontiers of development studies in terms of 'development' in both North and South and global inter-connectedness;
– reflects on claims to knowledge and intervening in other people's lives.

Titles include:

Anthony Ware (*editor*)
DEVELOPMENT IN DIFFICULT SOCIOPOLITICAL CONTEXTS
Fragile, Failed, Pariah

Andrew Shepherd and Julia Brunt (*editors*)
CHRONIC POVERTY
Concepts, Causes and Policy

Katie Wright
INTERNATIONAL MIGRATION, DEVELOPMENT AND HUMAN WELLBEING

Caroline Harper, Nicola Jones, Ronald U. Mendoza, David Stewart and Erika Strand (*editors*)
CHILDREN IN CRISIS
Seeking Child-Sensitive Policy Responses

David Alexander Clark
ADAPTATION, POVERTY AND DEVELOPMENT
The Dynamics of Subjective Well-Being

Xiaoming Huang, Alex C. Tan and Sekhar Bandyopadhyay (*editors*)
CHINA AND INDIA AND THE END OF DEVELOPMENT MODELS

Erik Lundsgaarde (*editor*)
AFRICA TOWARD 2030
Challenges for Development Policy

Sara C. Motta and Alf Nilsen Gunvald Nilsen
SOCIAL MOVEMENTS IN THE GLOBAL SOUTH

Rachel Sabates-Wheeler and Rayah Feldman
MIGRATION AND SOCIAL PROTECTION

Sue Kenny and Matthew Clarke (*editors*)
CHALLENGING CAPACITY BUILDING
Comparative Perspectives

Jens Stilhoff Sörensen (*editor*)
CHALLENGING THE AID PARADIGM
Western Currents and Asian Alternatives

Niamh Gaynor
TRANSFORMING PARTICIPATION?
The Politics of Development in Malawi and Ireland

Andy Sumner and Meera Tiwari
AFTER 2015: INTERNATIONAL DEVELOPMENT POLICY AT A CROSSROADS

Simon Feeny and Matthew Clarke
THE MILLENNIUM DEVELOPMENT GOALS AND BEYOND
International Assistance to the Asia-Pacific

Eric Rugraff, Diego Sánchez-Ancochea and Andy Sumner (*editors*)
TRANSNATIONAL CORPORATIONS AND DEVELOPMENT POLICY
Critical Perspectives

Rethinking International Development Series
Series Standing Order ISBN 978–0230–53751–4 (hardback)

You can receive future titles in this series as they are published by placing a standing order. Please contact your bookseller or, in case of difficulty, write to us at the address below with your name and address, the title of the series and the ISBN quoted above.

Customer Services Department, Macmillan Distribution Ltd, Houndmills, Basingstoke, Hampshire RG21 6XS, England

Cash Transfers and Basic Social Protection

Towards a Development Revolution?

Moritz von Gliszczynski

Lead Researcher, LAG Soziale Brennpunkte Niedersachsen, Germany

First published 2015 by
PALGRAVE MACMILLAN

Palgrave Macmillan in the UK is an imprint of Macmillan Publishers Limited, registered in England, company number 785998, of Houndmills, Basingstoke, Hampshire RG21 6XS.

Palgrave Macmillan in the US is a division of St Martin's Press LLC, 175 Fifth Avenue, New York, NY 10010.

Palgrave Macmillan is the global academic imprint of the above companies and has companies and representatives throughout the world.

Palgrave® and Macmillan® are registered trademarks in the United States, the United Kingdom, Europe and other countries.

ISBN: 978–1–137–50568–2

This book is printed on paper suitable for recycling and made from fully managed and sustained forest sources. Logging, pulping and manufacturing processes are expected to conform to the environmental regulations of the country of origin.

A catalogue record for this book is available from the British Library.

Library of Congress Cataloging-in-Publication Data
Gliszczynski, Moritz von, 1983–
    Cash transfers and basic social protection : towards a development revolution? / Moritz von Gliszczynski.
        pages cm.—(Rethinking international development series)
    Includes bibliographical references.
    ISBN 978–1–137–50568–2 (hardback)
    1. Transfer payments – Developing countries. 2. Economic assistance, Domestic – Developing countries. 3. Income maintenance programs – Developing countries. 4. Public welfare – Developing countries. I. Title.

HC59.72.P63G55 2015
332′.04246091724—dc23   2015003644

Contents

List of Illustrations

Figures

Tables

Acknowledgements

My research into cash transfers was funded by the German Research Foundation (DFG) as part of the FLOOR research group at Bielefeld University.

This book would not have been written without the support of many dear colleagues and friends.

First and foremost, I thank Lutz Leisering for long years of sage advice and guidance, first as my teacher, then as my supervisor. Without him, this book would not have been possible.

I am equally indebted to my colleagues in the FLOOR research group, especially Michael Leutelt, Katrin Weible, John Berten, Tobias Böger and Elsbe Lück. I could not have wished for better co-workers and friends.

Last but not least, I am grateful to my family, for believing in me even at times when I found it hard to do so myself.

List of Abbreviations

ADB	Asian Development Bank
BIEN	Basic Income Earth Network
BIG	coalition basic income grant coalition
CCT	conditional cash transfer
CHR	Commission on Human Rights
DFID	Department for International Development
FIAN	Food First Information and Action Network
GTZ	Gesellschaft für technische Zusammenarbeit (German technical cooperation)
GIZ	Gesellschaft für internationale Zusammenarbeit (German international cooperation)
HAI	HelpAge International
IADB	Inter-American Development Bank
ICESCR	International Covenant on Economic, Social and Cultural Rights
IDPM	Institute for Development Policy and Management
IDS	Institute of Development Studies
IFPRI	International Food Policy Research Institute
ILO	International Labour Organisation
MCDSS	Ministry of Community Development and Social Services (Zambia)
NREGA	National Rural Employment Guarantee Act
ODI	Overseas Development Institute
OECD	Organisation for Economic Cooperation and Development
OECD-DAC	Organisation for Economic Cooperation and Development – Development Assistance Committee
PEP	public employment programme
SEWA	Self Employed Women's Association
SKAD	sociology of knowledge approach to discourse
SCT	social cash transfer
StC	Save the Children
UDHR	Universal Declaration of Human Rights
UN-CEB	United Nations Chief Executives Board
UNDP	United Nations Development Programme
UNICEF	United Nations Children's Fund
WHO	World Health Organization

Introduction

Around the world the turn of the New Millennium in 2000 was perceived as a chance to begin anew and face the global challenges that had arisen since the fall of the Iron Curtain ten years before. A new leaf was turned over by many crucial institutions and organisations, both nationally and internationally, including the United Nations and its specialised agencies. The Millennium Development Goals (MDGs) were created as a promise that the global policy community would do its utmost to eradicate the most severe forms of poverty, hunger and disease that had been plaguing developing countries for so long. However, the MDGs did not clarify how to actually face the problems of the developing world and left global organisations to search for their own solutions.

The result of this search was a surprising departure from more traditional instruments of development policy such as infrastructural policies and the promotion of economic growth. The early 2000s saw a strong resurgence of interest in social protection in global development policy, especially basic social protection in the form of non-contributory benefits to the poor. Prominent development organisations, including the World Bank and the International Labor Organisation, published strategies that espoused social protection as the perfect instrument to alleviate poverty, promote growth and employment, and stabilise the ailing states of the Global South. In time, the majority of global development organisations, from NGOs to specialised UN organisations, began to advocate the implementation of social protection, including non-contributory benefits.

Supporting social protection in the Global South was a departure from a decades-long divide between developed and developing countries in the minds of development experts. Until the early 2000s it had been widely assumed that developing countries lacked the administrative and financial capacity to implement sustainable measures of social protection until they had reached a threshold of economic development on par with developed countries. Meanwhile, the nation states of the Global North were taken for granted as exemplary providers of social protection.

When perceptions on social protection shifted in the early 2000s, the change in global policy was swift. Today virtually all significant development organisations support the implementation of social protection with technical and financial assistance, while research on the practice of social protection and advocacy for further extension has increased exponentially in the past decade.

There is, however, a lack of research on the shift of global policy towards social protection in and of itself. Which changes in global ideas led development policy to completely change its stance on social protection? How exactly did the process of change take place? In this book I attempt to answer these questions by looking at an especially interesting case of basic social protection that has emerged as a staple of global policy in spite of traditionally strong reservations: non-contributory benefits to the poor or social cash transfers (SCT).

But why are social cash transfers an especially interesting case of social protection in the Global South? While cash transfers are fairly common in the welfare states of Europe, they have never been a favoured instrument of social protection in public debates. Political forces both on the right and the left have long treated cash transfers as a necessary evil, citing concerns of causing dependency and stigmatisation. Traditionally these concerns were also transposed to global development policy and compounded by the lack of cash transfers in developing countries and the specific ideas of development organisations: the very idea of development long relied on the perception that poor people in developing countries would have to help themselves and that any support should focus on creating favourable background conditions. With the exception of food aid in emergencies, direct handouts of goods, let alone cash, were strongly rejected – indeed, an attempt to promote cash transfers as development policy in the early 1990s failed quite clearly and swiftly. It is especially surprising and interesting to observe that cash transfers have emerged as a crucial component of recent approaches to social protection in development policy. Currently, the majority of development organisations claim that basic social protection via cash transfers is not only affordable to developing countries, but in fact a prerequisite of sound economic development and social progress, as exemplified by the ILO's concept of a 'global social floor'.

Similar to the emergence of social protection in general, the shift towards cash transfers was quick: following a phase of intense research and advocacy in between 2000 and 2005, the most significant development organisations began to support the implementation of cash transfers and made them part of their strategies on social protection. This was mirrored by a significant increase in new cash transfer programs in developing countries in the mid-2000s – some observers have even called the emergence of cash transfers a 'development revolution' (Hanlon et al. 2010).

This book critically examines whether such assertions are true. Even though taking up cash transfers has naturally been a significant change in global development policy, it remains to be seen to what extent the fundamental ideas of development have really changed. Throughout the following chapters I will analyse whether the emergence of cash transfers is really a revolution or rather part of a gradual shift in the ideas behind development.

An analysis of cash transfers also has implications for the future development of social protection in the Global South because the ideas that legitimise non-contributory benefits contain the basic concept of social responsibility that shape the way social policy is done by nation states and global organisations. In other words, it is worth checking if cash transfers are connected to a general model of social protection and what the nature of this model may mean for the future development of social policy in the Global South. A more residual model of social protection that focuses on basic instruments like cash transfers may indicate that social policy in the Global South will remain focused on the poor – in all likelihood leading to low benefit levels and weak or limited systems of social insurance in a nation state that only takes responsibility for alleviating severe poverty (see Korpi and Palme 1998). Conversely, a model of social protection that embeds cash transfers into a wider context of other means of protection, both basic and advanced, may indicate that developing countries are on the way to building complex welfare states of their own that combine basic support for the poor with social insurance and other social policies, in a nation state that takes responsibility to protect its citizens from a range of social problems and risks besides poverty.

In the following analysis, I illustrate that cash transfers, while not a 'revolution' of development in the narrow sense of the term, have indeed been part of a gradual change in development policy that has maintained some traditional ideas while introducing new concepts to legitimise non-contributory benefits. On the one hand, cash transfers are legitimised as instruments that promote economic growth, a goal of development policy that has remained stable since the inception of the field after the Second World War. On the other hand, cash transfers have also been legitimised with reference to new ideas of human development which contain different policy goals such as the alleviation of poverty, the promotion of human capabilities and protection from risks, crises and shocks.

The combined legitimisation of cash transfers with both economic development and human development emerged from a long-term process of change starting with shifts in four major global discourses on poverty, development, risk and human rights. Each of these four discourses underwent shifts in between the late 1980s and late early 2000s which opened up a discursive window of opportunity. In short, these shifts mainly led to a change in perceptions of the poor: where the poor had earlier been regarded as passive beneficiaries of development, they were now seen as potential contributors to social progress; and as long as they received sufficient support, that is, protection from risk and social rights, they could develop agency. The discursive window of opportunity that opened up in the early 2000s favoured the construction of new policies that directly transferred resources to the poor and could be attributed to the ability to foster human capital and economic agency. Indeed, the early 2000s saw the emergence of a new paradigm in global development policy that can be circumscribed as 'growth through redistribution'. The majority of policy actors agreed on the idea that both the reduction of poverty and the promotion of economic growth could be achieved by measures of basic social protection that gave cash directly to the poor. This culminated in the active construction of four variants of non-contributory benefits – family allowances, conditional cash transfers, social pensions and general household assistance – as policy models under the umbrella term 'social cash transfers' in the mid-2000s. These variants of cash transfers have since enjoyed nearly unquestioned legitimacy in global policy and are being advocated by many global organisations.

Last but not least, social cash transfers can in fact be regarded as part of a wider model of social protection. Even though this model of social protection was strongly focused on social cash transfers in the early 2000s, it is not a residual model of welfare that merely focuses on the alleviation of poverty. While the concept of social protection behind cash transfers strongly relies on the economic agency of the poor and cash transfers are only intended to support the poor enough to participate in markets, policy actors envision the implementation of social protection *systems* in the Global South that cover a wide range of life cycle groups and life risks with cash transfers, social services and social insurance. Therefore, an implementation of current concepts of social protection would likely end in the emergence of genuine welfare in the Global South.

However, the model of social protection behind cash transfers does have specific limits that distinguish it from the welfare states of the Global North. First and foremost, the benefit levels of cash transfers are generally left vague and undetermined but evidently aim at bringing the poor to the threshold of economic agency – poverty is rather intended to be alleviated in the short term, not counteracted entirely.

Second, because economic growth and efficiency are core principles of the current model of social protection, basic social protection is focused on those groups who are most vulnerable and who promise to have the most impact on economic growth in the future. Therefore, policy actors generally propose to extend cash transfers first and primarily to older persons and children. Working-age poor, in turn, are expected to contribute to the economy and are meant to be covered by means of basic social protection other than cash transfers, for example, public employment programs. In the end, the model of social protection behind cash transfers, while not residual, is markedly different from concepts of welfare in the Global North. The goals and the design of basic social protection are clearly shaped by ideas of development, leading to a focus on those instruments that are perceived to best facilitate economic growth – in short, a developmental model of social protection.

I.1 Perspective, scope and aim of this book

- To conclude, this book examines a specific dimension of the career of cash transfers from a particular observational standpoint:It adopts a constructivist *perspective*. That is to say, it examines the global discourses and ideas behind cash transfers, not actual schemes as they are implemented in developing countries. The national practice of cash transfers can and does differ from global ideas.
- The *scope* of the analysis is limited to the donor community, that is, those global organisations that began to advocate and finance cash transfer schemes in the early 2000s. This excludes national governments and purely national organisations.
- In consequence, the *aim* of this book is to clarify what global ideas legitimised cash transfers and motivated the donor community to advocate such policies. The intention is not to point out faults in

this legitimisation, but to clarify inconsistencies and tensions in the complex global discourses behind cash transfers that explain political conflicts on cash transfers and have shaped the way they are being implemented.

In the following chapters, I analyse the processes of social construction that led to the legitimisation of cash transfers in global policy and provide an analysis of policy models, policy paradigms and global discourses in their current state, illustrating how exactly cash transfers were part of a gradual change in development policy and in what way they are part of a developmental model of social protection. First, I explain my theoretical approach to the analysis of global ideas and discourses and their impact on policies such as cash transfers (Chapter 1). Then, I begin my analysis by examining which variants of cash transfers have become successful in global policy and what factors facilitated their recognition as development policy (Chapter 2). In the final two chapters, I explore which major shifts in background ideas prepared the rise of cash transfers. I identify the emergence of a new global policy paradigm (Chapter 3) and a number of shifts in four major global discourses (Chapter 4) as the root causes behind the career of cash transfers in global policy.

1
Theory: A Multi-level Analysis of Global Policy Ideas

In this introductory chapter, I attempt to delineate a tentative theoretical framework for the analysis of the discursive background of global policies, based on three eminent strands of research: ideational approaches to policy analysis, the sociology of knowledge approach to discourse (SKAD) and world society theory. These three strands of research will not only serve as the basis of my analytical approach, but also provide hypotheses and guiding questions regarding the career of cash transfers that will guide my empirical analysis.

Why have I chosen to combine ideational approaches, SKAD and world society theory specifically to guide my analysis? An adequate analysis of the career of cash transfers requires a theoretical approach that is equally sensitive to the emergence of new policy solutions, the role of ideas and discourses in this process and offers concepts that facilitate an analysis of policy at the global level.

In this respect, current theories of policy analysis and discourse analysis have a significant gap: there is no single theory that covers policies, discourses and the global level at the same time and gives equal weight to each. However, there are single theories or approaches that cover one or two of the three mentioned fields in depth.

Ideational approaches to policy analysis focus on the way in which new policies emerge and offer a range of concepts that describe the roles that ideas can play in policy. The sociology of knowledge approach to discourse offers a modern variant of discourse analysis with a firm focus on the impact of discourse on social action, including policies. While none of these two approaches covers the global level, world society theory proposes that all social actors and their actions worldwide are influenced by a global culture and specifies concepts that facilitate the analysis of social action at the global level.

Because ideational approaches to policy and SKAD are theoretically open at the global level – without covering it explicitly – and world society theory is compatible with the in-depth analysis of policies and discourses – without offering own concepts for doing so – I assert that a combination of these three complementary strands of research into a single analytical framework can greatly facilitate the analysis of policies like cash transfers in so far as they emerged at the global level.

In the following, I review in short each of the three approaches in order to derive the most significant concepts and theoretical assumptions that can be of use in an analysis of global policy and discourses. I then combine these concepts and assumptions into a coherent multilevel approach to the analysis of global policy and the impact of global discourses. Finally, I derive more specific research questions that guide my empirical analysis later on.

1.1   Ideational approaches in political science

There is a wide variety of approaches in political science which attempt to explain policy by recurring to the influence of knowledge and ideas. For the most part, these approaches belong to the institutionalist tradition, which was amongst the first strands of political science to introduce ideas as an explanatory factor (Peters 2005). Thus, in the following, I will concentrate on the most eminent institutionalist approaches in order to derive central concepts of ideational policy analysis (Béland 2009; Blyth 2001; Campbell 2002; Hall 1993; Schmidt 2008), complemented by a critical perspective on such approaches, as proposed by Nullmeier (2006).

Ideational approaches in general are portrayed as an attempt to balance out the shortcomings of older theories such as rational choice which used causal models that treated ideas as peripheral besides the factors of interests and institutions (Campbell 2002:21–22). The major innovation of ideational approaches is that they grant 'ideas' independent causal influence, in order to better explain policy change and the content of policy programmes (Béland 2005b:29; Blyth 2002:8; Schmidt 2008:304). However, they retain a causal mode of explanation and introduce ideas as a further explanatory factor besides institutions and the interests of policy actor. A central point of inquiry is how an interaction between these three factors influences the political process and which relative weight each factor should be given (Béland 2005b:35; Blyth 2002:44; Schmidt and Radaelli 2004:184).

However, most ideational scholars do not conceptualise this interaction as a balanced concurrence of ideas, interests and institutions. Even though ideas are attributed with potential influence, the other factors are thought to have stronger causal effect, except under very specific circumstances.

Blyth (2001:3; 2002:8–11) gives a characteristic example with his conception of 'uncertainty'. The gist of this position is that ideas will mirror social structures as long as institutional stability is maintained. Under a stable institutional order, institutional rules and the interests of actors determine policy choices. As soon as a crisis de-stabilises the given order, the situation changes: actors become 'uncertain' of their own interests and employ new ideas to re-interpret their situation, de-legitimise the old order and construct a new set of stable institutions (Blyth 2002:37–41). In short, ideas only have an independent causal effect in a phase of 'uncertainty' in between two stable institutional equilibria. The new equilibrium is achieved as soon as a new set of ideas has gained social acceptance and has been stabilised in the form of new institutions – then, the influence of ideas is again superseded by the other factors.

Nullmeier (2006:290) asserts that approaches which employ such a strict causal model are unsatisfactory, since research indicates that ideas, that is, socially constructed knowledge, play a role at all stages of the policy process, irrespective of institutional equilibria. Therefore, concepts which account for the constructed character of social reality and the basal role of ideas in policy are necessary. Nullmeier suggests that 'knowledge' is an appropriate general term for the constructs that constitute social reality, while more specific concepts may designate structures within the general pool of socially shared knowledge (292–297). Such structures can be conceptualised at different levels of abstraction (296–297). At a 'micro' level, one would look for specific policy ideas and arguments that apply to particular issues – which is concurrent with Blyth's usage of the term 'ideas'. The 'meso' and 'macro' levels would be characterised by more overarching structures that constitute and influence entire policy fields or political cultures.

Since the object of this book is the ideational background of social cash transfers in the field of development policy, concepts at the 'meso' and 'macro' level are necessary.

Indeed, some approaches to policy analysis employ such concepts, most notably Schmidt's (2008) 'discursive institutionalism'. Schmidt (2002:210) defines the guiding concept of 'discourse' as 'both a set of policy ideas and values and an interactive process of policy construction and communication'. In contrast to 'idea', this more abstract meso- to macro-level concept of 'a set of ideas' allows Schmidt to examine the relations between different ideas, including contradictions (227–230), or the embedding of ideas into the wider context of knowledge (215). Besides, Schmidt's approach emphasises processes of construction and communication, which are a primary object of this book.

However, Schmidt also agrees with many of the fundamental assumptions of ideational approaches regarding the role of ideas in policy. First and foremost, discourse is conceptualised as one possible causal factor besides interests and institutions (Schmidt 2002:212; 2011:62; Schmidt and Radaelli 2004:184). Second, discourse is only thought to have an independent causal effect on policy under specific conditions of crisis and 'uncertainty', as proposed by Blyth (Schmidt 2002:225, 251).

To summarise, ideational approaches in political science do not seem sufficiently sensitive to the fundamental role of knowledge in policy to ensure an adequate analysis of the discursive background behind social cash transfers. Nevertheless, ideational scholars have developed a number of useful concepts which serve to describe different types of ideas on the three levels of abstraction suggested by Nullmeier. What is more, policy analysis provides useful concepts that describe structures on the level of policy actors. I propose that these basic theoretical elements can be picked up without following the associated causal model of explanation.

In the following, I will shortly review those concepts which appear most useful to my analysis, in order to incorporate them into my own analytical framework.

The placement of ideas on different levels of abstraction can be traced back to Hall's (1993) classic work on policy paradigms. Hall distinguishes between policy change on three levels: the parameters of policy instruments, the instruments themselves and the overarching political 'paradigms' – roughly corresponding to the micro, meso and macro levels of knowledge. In general, these levels of abstraction are present in most typologies of ideas, and there is some agreement on their specific qualities and impact on policy, even though the terminology may differ.

The difference between the levels of abstraction is the way in which policy change takes place. Hall asserted that change on the lower two levels is a routine part of the policy process and happens nearly constantly. In contrast, paradigms remain stable over long periods of time and paradigm change is a disruptive process which is most likely to occur when policy fails unexpectedly (Hall 1993:278–280). In other words, the likelihood of shifts in policy-relevant knowledge decreases with the level of abstraction (Nullmeier 2006:295–297).

A multitude of concepts and terms has been developed to describe the types of ideas which can be found at the three levels. The lowest level in Hall's schematic, the operational parameters of policy instruments, is of limited interest within the scope of this book, which focuses on the middle level of abstraction.

Ideas on the middle level are conceptualised as 'blueprints' (Blyth 2001:3), 'programmatic ideas' (Campbell 1998:386) or 'policy solutions' (Mehta 2011:28), that is, specific programmes of action to solve a political problem – or, simply put, policy ideas. I alternatively suggest the term 'policy model' in reference to world society theory (see later). Social cash transfers can be understood as such a programme of action, as analysed in Chapter 2.

At that highest level of abstraction, scholars usually conceptualise broad sets of general ideas, causal assumptions and norms such as a 'discourse' (Schmidt 2002:210), a 'zeitgeist' (Mehta 2011:40–42) or a 'paradigm' (Hall 1993). In the following, I will employ the terms 'paradigm' or 'policy paradigm', as they are most widely used. These abstract structures of knowledge function as fundamental conceptions of social structures, shaping the goals and strategies of actors within specific fields of policy – including which programmes of action are advocated and implemented and how they are legitimised. Thus, its seems feasible to explore whether a policy paradigm exists in the case of social cash transfers and in how far it may have contributed to their increased usage.

In addition, ideational scholars have conceptualised further types of ideas which appear in Hall's original schematic and do not fit the differentiation between levels of abstraction as neatly.

Firstly, 'problem definitions' are often regarded as an important part of the policy process. It is pointed out that the social problems which policies are meant to solve are not to be taken as given, but are socially constructed by policy actors (see, e.g., Blyth 2002:37–38; Béland 2009:701–702; Mehta 2011:32). Such definitions are clearly more abstract than programmatic ideas and determine the range of policy solutions that is perceived as acceptable (Mehta 2011:32–40). Nevertheless, it is implausible to place them on the highest level of abstraction, since they do not constitute fundamental conceptions of social structures by themselves. Therefore, I define problem definitions as a type of idea which bridges between the high and middle levels of abstraction. I argue that definitions of social problems are a specific element of paradigms that translates them into policy by identifying

issues which conflict with the underlying conception of social structures. Accordingly, policy actors should only accept specific policy ideas
as feasible if they can be constructed as the solution to a pre-defined
problem.

Secondly, 'frames' have been identified as a crucial type of idea
(Campbell 2002:26–28; Béland 2005a:12). Frames are defined as ideas
which actors use to legitimise their policy ideas to the general public or
other actors within policy debates. To this end, political actors creatively
and strategically put their policies into the context of socially recognised
knowledge, for example, by showing how they help to achieve shared
norms and values (Béland 2005a:10–11; Campbell 1998:394).

Again, I propose that frames can be defined as a type of idea which
bridges the middle and high levels of abstraction. Specific elements of
a paradigm become frames as soon as they are utilised to legitimise or
de-legitimise a policy idea. In so far as both problem definitions and
frames are part of paradigms and serve to construct the range of feasible
and legitimate policies, they may have played a role in the career of cash
transfers.

Ideational approaches and policy analysis in general also employ
concepts which describe structures on the level of actors. Since extant
research points out that such structures play a significant role in the
construction and dissemination of ideas on the national and global
level, they are of interest to this book.

The most basic concept is certainly that of a 'policy community'. It
circumscribes a dense and stable network of actors that are involved
in a certain policy field like development policy, that is, who co-ordinate to construct, advocate and implement problem definitions and
programmatic ideas (Kingdon 2003; Béland 2005a:8). The term 'policy
community' implies that the interaction between different actors has
been institutionalised to a certain extent, for example, via fixed channels of communication (Berner 2009:189–191). Such communities may
potentially contain smaller sub-networks in the shape of 'issue communities', which form around specific subjects in the wider policy field. The
policy actors in such an issue community co-ordinate to make policy
regarding the specific subject and thus gain more influence on it than
policy actors outside the sub-network (ibid.). In addition, established
policy communities may contain a fixed 'inner circle' of the most well-
connected and knowledgeable actors in the field. These powerful actors
exercise the most significant influence on policy-making because they
closely co-ordinate to make policy over long spans of time and share
basic ideas (ibid.).

In respect to cash transfers, these concepts raise an interesting question: because social cash transfers are a relatively recent addition to development policy, it is not clear whether a specific policy community with distinct issue communities or an inner circle has already emerged (see Leisering 2009; 2010). The existence of an inner circle would mean that specific policy actors have come to dominate the new policy field of cash transfers and can strongly influence the way in which SCT policy is made, to the exclusion of other actors. To a lesser extent, the same applies to the existence of issue communities. The incidence of such sub-networks would imply that specific sets of actors are particularly influential regarding particular issues of SCT policy.

1.2 Sociological discourse analysis

While ideational approaches to policy analysis offer a range of concepts that facilitate the analysis of single types of ideas, they lack an adequate concept of overarching structures of knowledge and concepts to examine processes of social construction, such as found in discourse analysis. Because of this, discourse analysis well complements ideational policy analysis and can serve to extend the scope of my analysis.

The concept of discourse has become widely used in the social sciences and other disciplines since it was popularised by Foucault. More traditional variants of discourse analysis rather focus on broad historical processes on the level of knowledge and treat social action and policies as their determined outcome (e.g., Foucault 1974). Because I am interested in the construction of cash transfers as policies and intend to emphasise the active role of global organisations, I choose to incorporate the sociology of knowledge approach to discourse, as developed by Keller (2008; 2012), which explicitly focuses on the interaction between discourse and social action.

Crucially Keller defines discourses as an inter-related set of cognitive constructs or ideas that constitute social reality at the most basic level, as well as the social practices which produce these social constructs (Keller 2008:185, 192, 205, 235–236). This constitutes a modification of Nullmeier's arrangement, which places both discourses and paradigms on the third and highest level of abstraction. I propose that sociological discourse analysis in fact covers even more basic structures of knowledge than paradigms on a fourth level of abstraction; if paradigms are sets of ideas in a field of policy, then discourses are structures of wider, more abstract ideas which transcend single policy fields and help to construct paradigms.

What is more, SKAD proposes three concepts to describe the internal structures of discourse that can be of use to the analysis of cash transfers.

Firstly, SKAD conceptualises the most basic structures of discourses as 'schemes of interpretation' (Keller 2008:240–243). Such schemes of interpretation are abstract ideas which construct the basic properties of the subject matter of a discourse and are shared by its participants. Thus, schemes of interpretation shape the perceptions of social actors who participate in a discourse concerning that discourse's specific subject matter, for example, the nature of poverty as a social problem (see Chapter 4).

Secondly, it is possible to re-construct the 'phenomenon structure' of a discourse (Keller 2008:248). This concept rests upon the observation that discourses constitute social reality by constructing different schemes of interpretation for different dimensions of their subject and then connecting them into a structured constellation – resulting in the discursive production of a coherent phenomenon in social reality. For instance, a discourse which constitutes poverty as a social problem may construct the nature of the problem, its consequences, victims of the problem and social actors which are responsible for finding a solution. I will employ the concept of a phenomenon structure to analyse global discourses in Chapter 4 and use it to discover the basic schemes of interpretation which shape the perceptions of policy actors in the field of cash transfers.

Thirdly, another structure which brings elements of a discourse into a coherent whole can be found in the form of 'narratives' (Keller 2008:240, 251–252). Such structures are literally story-lines revolving around specific actors who follow a specific plot from introduction to finish, for example, by solving a social problem. Essentially, narratives function to construct causal connections between different elements of a discourse and enable their presentation as part of a dynamic process. This can serve to dramatise situations and construct a need to act. Chapters 3 and 4 demonstrate that policy paradigms and global discourses rely on certain narratives in order to construct social problems and tie them to common causes.

Finally, three assumptions of SKAD on types of discourses, discursive practices and discursive shifts are also relevant to the study of cash transfers.

First and foremost, discourses in general can fall into two different categories. Keller (2008:228–232) distinguishes between 'public' and 'specialised' discourses. These two types of discourses mainly differ in their audience. Public discourses circumscribe conflictive processes of social construction led via the mass media and democratic fora of debate which involve civil society in general. In contrast, specialised discourses refer to the construction of social reality in partially closed institutional fields which involve only a select group of actors.

This distinction may help to clarify the object of this book. To reiterate, the main research interest is to describe the spread of social cash transfers as a policy idea amongst global organisations in the field of development policy – the focus of research are the specialised discourses carried by global development organisations, not public discourses.

The limitation to specialised discourses is based on the initial assumption that global development policy is a specific social field with proper rules for the production of knowledge and specific social practices which exclude many of the social actors. The character of development policy as a field of practice is emphasised: I focus on discourses among policy actors who actually intend to directly influence the social practice of development by advocating and/or implementing specific policies. This excludes specialised discourses in academia which revolve around the study of such policies but have no direct impact implementation. However, this distinction is rather analytic; empirically, the lines between academic discourses and policy discourses are blurred. The specialised discourses among global organisations often refer to academic knowledge, and some academics actively advocate or implement certain policies. Nevertheless, the focus of this book is on discourses among actual policy actors, that is, those organisations whose primary purpose is to 'make' policy, by both formulating and realising programmes of action.

Secondly, it is assumed that discourses are distinguished not only by their content, but also by specific rules and practices for the production of socially recognised knowledge. In general, such practices signify methods of producing knowledge and/or particular modes of communication which actors have to follow to participate in a discourse (Keller 2008:207–208, 226, 228). Accordingly, I ask which discursive practices may have facilitated the career of cash transfers and which practices characterise the global discourses behind cash transfers. World society theory allows the formulation of several hypotheses on discursive practices that may be common in global discourses (see further).

Thirdly, SKAD makes crucial assumptions about the relationship between discourse and social actors, which leads to conclusions on discursive shifts. It is essential that access to discourses as an active participant is normally regulated. The range of actors who can contribute to discourse is limited in so far as only carriers of certain institutionalised roles are recognised as legitimate producers of knowledge – SKAD defines such roles as privileged 'speaking positions' (Keller 2008:215–217, 255). In general, the performance of such roles requires social actors to know and implement pre-existing discursive practices – in consequence, they are not entirely free to shape discourse, but always have to reproduce any given discourse to a certain extent.

However, this regulation of discursive processes does not mean that social actors are completely determined or controlled by discourse. SKAD emphasises that there is a dialectic relationship between the structural effects of discourse and agency (Keller 2008:255; 2009): the regulations and ideas inscribed within discourse enable and constrain agency, but at the same time social actors actively re-interpret these rules when reproducing discourse in new acts of communication. Since social actors thus have a certain degree of freedom, discourses have an intrinsic dynamic of change. What is more, there is an interaction between the level of discourse and that of 'practice', that is, practical social action as opposed to communication (266). While such practice involves the implementation of ideas, for example, in the form of policies, this does not imply that there is an exact correspondence between the two levels of discourse and practice. That is to say, the two levels can have independent dynamics of change, and developments on the level of practice can influence discourse and lead to discursive shifts – in fact, I argue that perceived failures of development policy in the 1980s which preceded the rise of cash transfers may be an example of such a process.

In addition, SKAD recognises that different social actors may be actively involved in discursive struggles and attempt to influence discourse to establish their view of things as socially recognised truth. Crucially, several approaches to discourse analysis point out that social actors may attempt to exercise such influence by forming 'discourse coalitions' based on similar discursive positions and/or narratives (Keller 2008:254; Nullmeier 2006:297–302). In the case of cash transfers, my analysis illustrates that this field of policy is in fact characterised by the existence of two major discourse coalitions that propose a different legitimisation and different goals for cash transfers (see Section 4.5).

In sum, a sociological approach to discourse analysis provides a more thoroughly constructivist approach than ideational policy analysis by emphasising the impact of knowledge on all aspects of the policy process. Analysing the career of cash transfers from this perspective promises to reveal the most basic ideas and assumptions which led policy actors to construct cash transfers as a policy idea. Keeping the long-standing rejection of such policies in mind, the question then becomes which changes or shifts in discourse may have prepared the ground for the rise of social cash transfers.

1.3 World society theory

The advantages of sociological discourse analysis aside, it is not specifically adapted to the global level of policy and does not contain assumptions on specific structures or discursive elements which may be crucial to global policy and thus the analysis of cash transfers.

In consequence, I turn to John W. Meyer's world society theory, which is highly compatible with approaches that seek to explain policy change via changes in socially shared knowledge (Heintz and Greve 2005; Meyer et al. 1997). Meyer's central assumption is that social actors and their activities worldwide are shaped by an inter-related set of 'global models'. These models are part of a coherent and independent 'world culture', which explains the puzzling similarity or 'isomorphism' between social and political structures in most modern nation states (Meyer et al. 1997:145–150).

Crucially, Meyer asserts that this culture is not just internalised by actors, but has become objectified in the form of global institutions (Heintz and Greve 2005:102). Global models, that is, 'diffuse functional models [...] about actors, action, and presumed causal relations, are centrally constitutive of world culture'. (Meyer et al. 1997:149) and represent the primary mode of institutionalisation – the most important example being the nation state as the central political actor (151–157).

Meyer (1997:148, 161–162) implies that the essential traits of global models are their claim to universal applicability and their widely recognised legitimacy: any deviations need to be justified, while actions that can be framed as implementations of global models are generally taken for granted as normal and appropriate. Regarding the analysis of cash transfers, the concept of global models allows a further clarification of the object of research: I propose that the recent popularity of social cash transfers may mean that they have become institutionalised as global models. These models not only encompass constructions of social actors but also of certain courses of action – policies as scripts of action fall under this definition. Accordingly, it can be hypothesised that certain policy ideas may become institutionalised as global *policy models* (I continue to use this term in the chapter). This allows a better understanding of the career of social cash transfers: their wide acceptance as universally applicable instruments by policy actors after decades of rejection indicates that cash transfers may have become institutional-ised as *legitimate* global models, at least to a certain extent (see later).

World society theory, however, does not elaborate upon the processes which produce global models. It is generally claimed that world culture began to spread significantly during the mid-20th century, but the exact mechanisms are left unclear (Meyer 1997:156–157). An essential role of actors that present themselves as 'disinterested others' by framing them-selves as advocates of global models without vested interests is implied, especially scientists, professionals and global organisations (Meyer 1997:160, 165; Boli 1999). In this way, they gain recognition as the legiti-mate administrators of world culture and (re-)produce the global models which make up world culture. The role of disinterested others can also be conceptualised from the perspective of discourse analysis. It can be assumed that they have privileged speaking positions in discourses on the global level, due to their assumed objectivity – therefore, I expect that not only global organisations but also scientists and other experts took signifi-cant part in the construction of social cash transfers as a global model.

However, there is little elaboration on how disinterested others may construct or transform global models. World society theory has been crit-icised for a narrow macro-deterministic perspective, since it postulates that social action is unilaterally shaped by world culture (Heintz and Greve 2005:111). Heintz suggests that a micro-sociological perspective may complement extant theorisation by uncovering which mechanism creates and reproduces global structures and by clarifying variations in their stability or grade of institutionalisation. This might also draw attention to more weakly institutionalised areas of world society or to processes of institutionalisation that are currently taking place. Such a perspective would explore how social actors actively use and interpret the institutionalised scripts of world culture.

In my analysis, I attempt to adopt such a micro-sociological perspec-tive in order to fill the indicated gap in world society theory. The recent rise of social cash transfers to widespread legitimacy in development policy implies that a process of institutionalisation may have crossed a critical threshold and/or may still be ongoing. The degree of institution-alisation, that is, in how far cash transfers have indeed become global models, is an open question – my analysis demonstrates that different variants of SCT may in fact be institutionalised to different extents.

There are few hypotheses on potential mechanisms which may play a role in such a process of institutionalisation. However, Heintz (2010) proposes that communicative acts of comparison, especially those which use statistics, are especially important to the construction of a global culture. At its most basic, an act of comparison means that different units or events are conceptualised as at least partially commensurable, that is, fundamentally the same. Yet, in the same act, at least one criterion is formulated, which illustrates remaining differences between the objects of comparison (164). Heintz emphasises that the construction of objects as comparable is a social process – it does not originate from their inherent qualities.

Crucially, Heintz (2010) argues that the medium of communication which is used to construct a comparison has an impact on its chance of success (in terms of being understood and answered by the addressee). The hypothesis is that acts of comparison which employ numbers and statistics to construct the similarities and differences of certain units have a higher chance of success than purely verbal or textual communication (167).

To be precise, several qualities of numbers as a medium of comparison ensure that they are understood even across cultural differences: (1) their rules of production are clear and explain themselves; (2) they can be traced back to their empirical origin by the appropriate numerical operations; (3) since the 'language' of numbers follows universal, non-culture-specific rules, they can be produced, transformed and comprehended by anyone, regardless of individual background; (4) numbers as a medium of communication are hard to attribute to subjective opinions or interests; (5) their inherent properties enforce a direct attribution of their information to the factual circumstances that they represent (Heintz 2010:171–174). Therefore, they are particularly able to bridge the cultural distances which prevail at the global level (167, 174) – information that is transmitted via statistical comparison can theoretically be understood and checked by anyone and does not seem to contain any partisan bias, cultural or otherwise.

It is essential to this book that a specific importance of such comparisons to processes of globalisation is suggested (Heintz 2010:175,–177). The basic hypothesis is that comparisons help to construct a 'global consciousness' by enabling a mutual process of observation and description between different social units across the world. In so far as different nation states, cultures or the like are then perceived as similar parts of a global whole, this process of 'cultural globalisation' facilitates the development, diffusion and institutionalisation of globally applicable ideas.

This insight can be applied to my primary research question: if quantitative comparisons can facilitate the construction and spread of globally applicable ideas, it should be asked if they have played a role in the relatively rapid spread of cash transfers in development policy. From the perspective of discourse analysis, the usage of statistical comparisons may be conceptualised as a specific practice of global discourses, which have to transcend cultural and national differences in order to produce universally acceptable knowledge or scripts of action.

1.4   Analytical framework

With this, I conclude the preliminary review of relevant theoretical strands and combine select elements into an analytical framework. The analytical approach which I describe in this section was developed inductively in parallel to the first steps of my empirical work. While the basic elements are theoretically derived, their exact definition and combination was slightly adapted during the course of the analysis.

The framework is based upon the assumption that a world culture of institutionalised models, as proposed by John W. Meyer, does indeed exist. Drawing on discourse analysis and ideational approaches in political science, I conceptualise world culture as the institutionalised part of a universe of socially shared, global knowledge which is shaped by structures at various levels of abstraction. I further posit that ideas from this universe of global knowledge can become institutionalised as global models in world culture, including policy models. Therefore, a global policy analysis should aim to retrace the process through which specific policies become institutionalised as policy models and what degree of global legitimacy they have achieved – that is, to what extent they are taken for granted by policy actors.

I suggest that such processes of institutionalisation are processes of social construction which take place within broad global discourses. Therefore, I define discourses – as conceptualised by SKAD – as the most abstract and fundamental structures within world culture.

Combining world society theory and sociological discourse analysis leads to the assumption that global discourses revolve around broad themes like, for example, poverty or development and contain abstract ideas which form the background of global knowledge behind policy and produce global models. As mentioned earlier, SKAD describes these abstract ideas as schemes of interpretation which shape the perceptions of social actors (Keller 2008:240–243).

I propose that global discourses are thematically broad and vague and do not shape policy directly, since the schemes of interpretation construct social reality for broad subject matters which transcend any single policy field. Instead, various discourses which are relevant to a specific field of policy combine into a more concrete policy paradigm which shapes the specific perceptions of actors in that field. Since the concept of policy paradigms was originally developed in reference to national polities, it is an open question in how far global paradigms may be structurally different. Indeed, Chapter 3 will demonstrate that they take a different shape, at least in the case of cash transfers.

In any case, a global policy paradigm can be conceptualised as a relatively fixed and coherent set of ideas which are recognised by a majority of policy actors. Similar to a paradigm at the national level, a global paradigm should function as a fundamental conception of social structures which shapes the perception of policy actors and, in consequence, policy is made.

I argue that the internal structure of a paradigm can be conceptualised using the different types of ideas which are specified by ideational approaches to political science. From the perspective of discourse analysis, these types of ideas can be regarded as specific types of schemes of interpretation that fulfil a particular function in a policy paradigm. I propose that these specific ideas in a global paradigm are based on more abstract and general schemes of interpretation in global discourses. These general schemes of interpretation provide the foundation of socially shared knowledge from which the specific paradigm is constructed – in so far as a global paradigm is the product of global discourses.

In the case of cash transfers, empirical analysis indicated that the paradigm contained two specific types of ideas: problem definitions and frames – global policy paradigms in other fields may well contain other types of ideas.

Firstly, problem definitions: as indicated earlier, this type of idea constructs tangible social problems that demand intervention and thus guides policy actors to seek solution which conform to the perceived nature of the problem, that is, policies with certain effects and goals. In so far as the problem definitions which are part of a paradigm have significant influence on the design of policy models, they prescribe which specific functions they need to fulfil in order to solve a problem.

Secondly, frames: that is, a type of idea which policy actors use to legitimise policy models by portraying them as normatively appropriate, or as fitting with widely shared policy goals, but without defining a problem which needs to be solved. Policy models are portrayed as having a positive relationship to ideas which function as frames because these ideas are widely recognised by policy actors. But in contrast to problem definitions, they do not influence the design of policy models, because they only function to construct their basic legitimacy without specifying necessary effects.

The distinction between the two types is analytical; as indicated earlier both can be regarded as specific types of schemes of interpretation. Nevertheless, they should be distinguished in the case of cash transfers, since they fulfil particular functions in the paradigm.

Ultimately, the range of policies which is constructed and legitimised within a global paradigm is of primary interest to the analysis of cash transfers. I assume that a paradigm indeed suggests a limited range of policy models, based on the specific set of problem definitions and frames.

Figure 1.1 illustrates how the framework conceptualises the discursive structures defined earlier. Note that the chart only displays a single paradigm, even though the theoretical framework is hypothetically open to the co-existence of several within the same field. I have chosen to reduce the complexity of the chart because only a single paradigm exists in the case of cash transfers (see Figure C.1).

According to Hall (1993) and Nullmeier (2006), the three inter-linked levels of abstraction visible in Figure 1.1 – political discourses, policy

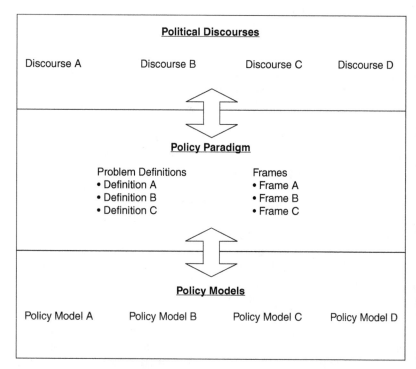

Figure 1.1   A multi-level framework of policy analysis

paradigm and policy models – are mainly distinguished by different probabilities of change. I propose to extend this argument in reference discourse analysis: as mentioned, SKAD proposes a potential inter-action between practice and discourse, in so far as social actors re-in-terpret and transform elements of discourse by translating them into action. Since ideas on the micro-level of abstraction, for example, policy models, concern single issues or policy fields, I would argue that they directly shape social action. In fact, such ideas are often conceptualised as 'precise causal ideas' or clear scripts of action (Campbell 2002:28). Therefore, they should be direct subject to the conscious reflection of actors who attempt to apply them and face the problem of translating an idealised construct into concrete practice. This would be an explana-tion for the higher probability of change – policy actors are constantly adapting their scripts of action to changing circumstances.

The decreasing probability of change at higher levels of abstraction would then imply a similar decline in the level of conscious reflec-tion. Indeed, it seems unlikely that policy actors would directly and consciously modify the paradigms and discourses which fundamentally shape their perceptions. However, this does not imply that paradigms and discourses are immune to change, keeping in mind the proposed interaction between discourse and practice. After all, policy ideas on the micro-level are constructed and legitimised by the structures on the meso- and macro-level. In consequence, I posit that conscious modifi-cations to micro-level ideas can retroactively and indirectly affect the discursive background.

If practice were to lead to modifications in policy models which conflict with the discursive background this may conceivably facilitate shifts at the meso or macro level. This matches with Hall's (1993:280) assumption that the failure of policy is a major cause for paradigm shifts. However, I further propose that even gradual modifications of policy or their perceived success can affect the more abstract discursive background. In fact, as my empirical analysis demonstrates, the prac-tical implementation of social cash transfers and their perceived success have had some effect on discourse – notably, discursive shifts which originally facilitated the legitimisation of cash transfers were furthered by their successful application.

All in all, the framework is thus based on the proposition that policy models emerge from a wide, abstract and variegated background of global knowledge in an interactive process spanning all levels of abstraction. The career of such policies remains the focus of research, that is, the macro- and meso-level are analysed to explain changes on the micro level. In consequence, the following research strategy suggests itself:

1. Starting on the lowest level of abstraction, specific policy models in a given field should be identified. These models are analysed with regard to the problem definitions and frames which are used to construct and legitimise them.
2. A closer look at problem definitions and frames should reveal whether they are systematically connected in the form of a policy paradigm.
3. If a paradigm exists, a detailed analysis of its elements should reveal the underlying global discourses. In a final step, these discourses are systematically analysed in order to examine the most fundamental schemes of interpretation which aided in the construction of the paradigm and the policy models.

Because the focus of this framework is on policy change, each step of the analysis follows a longitudinal perspective – the assumption is that shifts in global discourses may lead to shifts in policy paradigms, finally causing the emergence of new policies or changes in existing policy models. Since the agency of individuals and organisations is recognised, attention is paid to strategic action which has influenced this process.

To summarise, I posit that global knowledge exhibits a complex structure of multiple and inter-linked levels. The three main levels analysed here – political discourses, policy paradigm and policy models – are situated on a spectrum between abstract and concrete, with discourses being the most abstract and policy models the most concrete level of knowledge. In addition, discourses, paradigms and policy models also demonstrate different probabilities of change: my main hypothesis is that change on the more abstract levels of knowledge is significantly slower and rarer than on the concrete levels. Since the multiple levels of knowledge are strongly inter-linked, I assert that the relatively rapid changes in policy models have to be preceded by more ponderous shifts in global discourses and policy paradigms.

1.5   Guiding questions

Based on the tentative framework of analysis designed earlier, I can now formulate more detailed questions which guide my empirical analysis. To reiterate, the scope of this book is limited to the specialised discourse among global organisation in the field of development policy. That is to say, I focus on those global actors who were active in designing, advocating and implementing social cash transfers in developing countries.

The individual questions can be roughly categorised into questions concerning global knowledge and questions concerning the role of policy actors. While the former category aims at uncovering discursive shifts and discursive dynamics which prepared the legitimisation of cash transfers, the latter aims at networks between different policy actors which may have influenced the career of cash transfers.

Firstly, questions concerning global knowledge and discourses:

- How far have shifts in global discourses prepared and influenced the rise of cash transfers as a policy model? If so, what is the nature of these shifts?
- Which specific discourses shape the policy field of cash transfers, and what was their impact?
- Has a policy paradigm emerged from these global discourses? If so, which ideas does it contain, and how have they legitimised cash transfers?
- How far have cash transfers become institutionalised as a policy model? If one or several models exist, what are their characteristics?

Secondly, questions concerning the role of policy actors in the career of cash transfers:

- Is there a policy community in the case of cash transfers? If so, who participates and what are the roles of specific actors?
- Are there specific sub-structures like issue communities or discourse coalitions? If so, which ideas or policy models do they support?
- Are there conflicts between different actors or groups of actors? If so, in how far have they influenced the career of cash transfers?

These questions will guide my analysis in the following chapters, where I analyse policy models, global paradigms and global discourses in that order. The more specific questions listed here will also serve to answer the two major questions of my analysis: how far the rise of cash transfers constitutes a development revolution, and what model of welfare is connected to the idea of cash transfers. While I will attempt to answer my guiding questions as I go along with my analysis, the two major questions of this book are answered comprehensively in the conclusion.

1.6   Methods

The research on which this book is based was conducted using multiple complementary methods: documentary analysis, expert interviews and participant observation. Documentary analysis was the primary method used to analyse global discourses and the ideas of global actors. I collected a large sample of significant policy documents by global organisations ranging from the late 1970s until today, which were then analysed using standard qualitative methodology based on Grounded Theory (Bryant and Charmaz 2007).

In several ways, the analysis of documents was complemented by interviews with international experts in development policy and basic social protection and participant observation at international conferences (see the appendix for a list of interviews and conferences visited). Firstly, interviews and conferences provided an opportunity to check on the current state of the global debate on social protection and test the results of document analysis for their validity. Secondly, both methods also provided invaluable information on the relationships between different policy actors, as well as their activities in the field of cash transfers, including research, advocacy and implementation of cash transfers in developing countries. Finally, both interviews and observation helped to find further pertinent policy documents (especially 'grey literature') to expand the sample for analysis.

2
Constructing Global Models of Cash Transfers (2000–2012)

In this chapter, I begin my empirical analysis by identifying four major variants of cash transfers – family allowances, conditional cash transfers, social pensions and general household assistance – and trace their career as global policy models. In particular, I analyse to what degree each variant of cash transfers was institutionalised as a global model and name three factors that have facilitated the career of each model in some way: advocacy by one or several global organisations, the availability of national examples for the given variant of cash transfer and, finally, the production of statistical evidence on the positive effects of the model.

I also analyse three additional models of basic social protection – public employment programmes (PEPs), transfers in kind and universal basic income – that cannot be classified as cash transfers in the strict sense, but are nevertheless important to the global debate on social protection and cash transfers. Public employment programmes, for instance, are a preferred option for the working-age poor, which are not intended to be covered by cash transfers, while universal basic income play a surprisingly small role in the debate on cash transfers, even though there is a vibrant global discourse on this policy model.

It should be noted that I am employing a constructivist perspective and analyse the *ideas* of global actors or *concepts of* cash transfers. Since these concepts are highly idealised, their practical implementation in developing countries can – and does – deviate from global models (on the implementation of cash transfers, see Leisering 2009:257–258).

I begin my analysis by describing the general idea of cash transfers as policy, whose basic characteristics all variants of cash transfers share, even though the specific policy models differ from it to various degrees.

Then, I move on to a detailed analysis of each major variant of cash transfer, tracing their careers as global models, followed by a brief analysis of alternative models of basic social protection.

For reference, Table 2.1 provides a historical context to my analysis in Chapters 2–4 by listing the most significant events in basic social protection policy at the global level.

2.1 The idea of social cash transfers

In the following, I shortly describe several important aspects of the general idea of cash transfers which characterises all four variants of cash transfers analysed here. Firstly, I examine the *semantics* associated with cash transfers as a general idea and describe the emergence of 'social cash transfers' as an umbrella term for non-contributory benefits to the poor. Secondly, I analyse basic *design features* which are attributed to cash transfers, including their perception as both *flexible* and *regular* benefits, as well as efficiency as a core principle of policy. Thirdly, I describe five major *effects* which policy actors expect cash transfers to achieve and which legitimise them as a policy model.

2.1.1 Semantics

Since 2005, global policy actors have interchangeably used the terms 'social transfers', 'cash transfers' or 'social cash transfers' to refer to non-contributory benefits to the poor. To be precise, the terms 'social transfer' and 'cash transfer' were first used as an umbrella term for all variants of cash transfers in the Department for International Development's (2005:9–13) seminal 'practice paper' on 'social transfers'. In the following years other organisations began to pick up this terminology to circumscribe the general model of cash transfers and the composite term 'social cash transfers' emerged (see references in this chapter).

This is the outcome of a gradual process. The term 'cash transfer' was first used to designate benefits to the poor in the late 1980s and early 1990s, when the German development consultant Bernd Schubert attempted to establish this model in global policy (GTZ 1989; Schubert 1987, 1990; Schubert and Antezana 1991; see Section 2.2.4 for a detailed account). However, this attempt failed, and designation of non-contributory benefits as cash transfers partially fell out of use. Since the mid-1990s, global organisations, primarily the World Bank and the ILO, sparingly used 'cash transfers' and, to a lesser extent, 'social transfers', as umbrella terms for all forms of monetary social security. This included both non-contributory transfers to alleviate poverty and contributory

Table 2. 1 A chronology of basic social protection policy

1985–1992: Bernd Schubert, a German development researcher, initiates the first global debate on SCT. As a result, the GTZ and the World Bank set up a pilot project in Maputo, Mozambique (1990–1992).

1987: The UNICEF publishes the eminent study 'Adjustment with a human face', criticising the structural adjustment policies of the World Bank and the IMF for causing social problems.

1990: The World Bank's World Development Report 1990 takes up the reduction of poverty in the developing world as a primary policy goal. The Bank also establishes the absolute poverty line of 1$ as the first global numerical measure of poverty (Hulme 2010). The UNDP publishes the first report on human development.

1994: The World Bank publishes the seminal study 'Averting the old age crisis', initiating a global wave of pension reforms. Social security first becomes an issue of global policy.

1994–1997: Mexico and Brazil begin setting up new social programmes which develop into PROGRESA and Bolsa Familia.

1995: United Nations World Summit for Social Development in Copenhangen.

2000: The Millennium Development goals are officially adopted by the United Nations. The first goal is to halve global poverty until 2015.

2001: The World Bank publishes its first Social Protection Sector Strategy. The ILO begins its 'Global Campaign for the Extension of Social Security'.

2003: A cash transfer pilot project is set up in Kalomo, Zambia, attracting strong global attention.

2004: The ILO's 'World Commission on the Social Dimension of Globalisation' first uses the term 'global social floor'. The concept is further developed in ILO papers.

2005: DFID publishes 'Social transfers and chronic poverty', the first encompassing overview on SCT.

2006: The 'Livingston Conference' in Zambia declares SCT to be part of the official development agenda for Africa.

2008–2009: The World Bank issues new major publications on safety nets and CCT.

2009: The United Nations Chief Executives Board officially adopts the 'global social floor' as an instrument against the global financial crisis, with the ILO and the WHO as lead organisations.

2010: The ILO publishes a guide on 'Extending Social Security', specifying the concept of a 'global social floor'.

2011–2012: The International Labour Conference discusses and adopts a new 'Social Protection Floors Recommendation'.

2012: The World Bank publishes its second Social Protection Sector Strategy, affirming social protection and cash transfers as central elements of Bank policy.

insurance systems (1997; ILO 2001; Subbarao et al. 1997; World Bank 2001a,c).

The exact origin of both terms is unclear. An analysis of relevant documents suggests that both had a mostly descriptive character. 'Cash transfer' evidently referred to the core principle of (re)distributing of money. 'Social transfer', in contrast, seems to have referred to the fact that these schemes were usually administered by the government. In any case, between 2002 and 2004, both 'cash transfers' and 'social transfers' increasingly became associated with non-contributory benefits to the poor (Barrientos and DeJong 2004; ILO 2004a:109; Tabor 2002).

Interestingly, this was also the phase in which the four major variants of cash transfers were constructed as policy models. Indeed, social pensions were occasionally described as 'cash transfers' during this time (DFID 2004; HAI 2004; HAI and IDPM 2003; ILO 2004b:381). Then, in 2005, the DFID practice paper was published, treating both 'social transfers' and 'cash transfers' as umbrella terms for all variants of non-contributory benefits. Crucially, the composite term 'social cash transfer' was first used in reference to a pilot project which implemented general household assistance in Kalomo, Zambia (GTZ 2005; see Section 2.2.4).

In the following years, most relevant policy actors began using 'social transfers', 'cash transfers' and 'social cash transfers' as umbrella terms for non-contributory benefits – cash transfers seem to have become institutionalised as a global model around this time (e.g., DFID 2011; HAI 2006a; ILO 2005; Künnemann and Leonhard 2008; ODI and GTZ 2005; OECD-DAC 2009; UNDP 2010; UNICEF 2007; World Bank 2008). Because 'cash transfers' and 'social cash transfers' are currently the most widely used terms and encompass all major variants of non-contributory benefits, these two terms are also used to refer to such programmes in the scope of this book.

Analysis does not reveal clear causal factors behind the changes in terminology, but I would argue that the increasing legitimacy of the four variants of cash transfers in the early 2000s led to a gradual shift of meaning for 'cash transfer' and 'social cash transfer'. 'Cash transfer' at least had already been used as an umbrella term for non-contributory benefits to the poor – therefore, policy actors merely excluded social insurance (i.e., contributory transfers) from the scope of the terms.

2.1.2 Design features

Based on global policy literature, social cash transfers in general are defined as regular financial benefits to poor households or individuals. These transfers are usually designed to be non-contributory. Thus, policy actors usually see national governments as being mainly responsible for their implementation (DFID 2005:24–26, 2006a:2; ILO 2001:68; UNICEF and ODI 2009:13–14; World Bank 2006:149). Such transfers are intended to support the general living expenses of beneficiaries. That is, they are not conceptualised as a grant to buy specific goods or services, like food or education, but can be freely dispensed by beneficiaries (DFID 2005:9; ODI and GTZ 2005:8; UNICEF 2012:34; UNICEF and ODI 2009:54; World Bank 2006:151, 2008:25, 256, 264).

Furthermore, they are meant to be 'targeted' in some form, that is, the benefits should go to a pre-defined group of people. The exact methods are a matter of debate (see later).

Document analysis shows that the majority of actors emphasise the crucial importance of three further characteristics: *flexibility*, *regularity* and *efficiency*.

Flexibility is often mentioned as a specific attribute of cash payments which makes them superior to other forms of aid, particularly the distribution of food. At first glance, any form of food aid seems to be of limited use to the recipients because food is evidently intended for consumption. Comparatively, cash is seen as a very variable form of aid. According to general opinion, the beneficiaries of cash transfers can autonomously spend the money to satisfy their individual needs and wants. This is judged to be an advantage, since a variety of recipients in different situations can theoretically profit from the same scheme (DFID 2005:9; ODI and GTZ 2005: 8; UNICEF 2012:34; UNICEF and ODI 2009:54; World Bank 2008: 25, 256, 264).

Regularity is perceived as a similarly fundamental advantage: cash transfers are potentially paid for an unlimited span of time, at least as long as the beneficiary retains the characteristics that made him or her eligible. What is more, benefits are supposed to be paid as fixed sums of cash at regular intervals. Again, this is seen as a huge advantage in comparison to traditional development or emergency aid. In contrast to cash transfers, traditional aid was usually handed out in varying amounts for a limited period of time or in irregularly spaced intervals. Policy actors contrast this with a sense of security and long-term planning capacity which regular cash transfers supposedly offer (DFID 2005:5, 2011:5, 2006a:2; ILO 2010b:23; UNICEF and ODI 2009:13–14).

In addition, *efficiency* is widely promoted as a core principle in the management of cash transfers, specifically cost-efficiency. Most policy actors agree that cash transfers should be designed in a way that allows for the most impact with the given amount of funding (DFID 2006a:5, 2005:20–21, 2011:86; ILO 2009a:31; ODI and GTZ 2005:8; World Bank

2008:2–3, 2009a:81). In practical terms, this means that the benefits are supposed to be targeted on those who need them most, that is, the poorest or at least those who would benefit most from the cash (DFID 2005:27–29, 2011:53–54; ILO 2010a:37–39; UNICEF 2012:24–26; UNICEF and ODI 2009:37–38; World Bank 2008:85–105, 374–375, 2009a:67–71; see further). However, the best method of targeting has been a matter of debate among policy actors as long as cash transfers have been recognised as development policy. There is a consensus that predominant economic and social conditions in the Global South – for example, cash-less economies and scarcity of individual bank accounts – make means-testing infeasible, if not impossible. A large number of alternative targeting methods have been suggested and checked against empirical evidence, but policy actors have not agreed on a best practice.

Some actors, for example, UNICEF or HelpAge International, claim that 'universal' benefits are the best option, that is, a benefit paid to a pre-defined categorical group (e.g., the elderly or children) and does not test income or assets against a poverty line (e.g., HAI 2006c:6; UNICEF and ODI 2009:28–32, 49). It is argued that such universal benefits are preferable since targeting in itself is perceived as an expensive, error-prone process. Thus, universal cash transfers are regarded as superior, since they do not target benefits and theoretically avoid high administrative demands. Conversely, other organisations like DFID and the World Bank argue that universal benefits are too expensive and inefficient in comparison to strictly targeted benefits because they need extensive funding to cover relatively large groups of beneficiaries and do not focus on the most needy (e.g., DFID 2005:27, 2006a:5; World Bank 2008:85–105, 374–375, 2009a:67–71). In short, even though policy actors agree on the importance of efficiency as a core principle, it is somewhat contested how efficiency is best achieved at the level of individual programmes – through a demanding process of precise targeting or by covering categorical groups to avoid exclusion errors.

In addition, it is widely agreed that different social cash transfers programmes should be part of social protection *systems* which cover a wide range of target groups and social problems. Especially the ILO and the World Bank are promoting this 'systemic' approach to cash transfers as an essential guideline of policy. The goal is to both achieve synergies between cash transfers' different programmes and to coordinate cash transfers with other measures of social protection such as healthcare or social insurance (ILO 2011:82; UNICEF 2012; World Bank 2009a:97; 2012). Notably, 'systemic' approaches are a relatively recent development in the field of cash transfers, having appeared in the late 2000s (see Section 3.3).

2.1.3   Effects

Five effects characterise cash transfers as a policy idea. Firstly, cash transfers are supposed to counteract poverty. This is usually regarded as the main, most important effect. However, policy actors remain vague on its exact nature and oscillate between *poverty reduction* and *poverty alleviation*. In other words, it is left unclear whether an actual reduction of the number of poor or merely a reduction of the poverty gap is the desired outcome (e.g., ILO 2009b; World Bank 2009a). Even though *poverty reduction* is often mentioned as a goal of development policy, closer analysis of many policy documents reveals a tendency towards *poverty alleviation* as a goal of cash transfers, especially of the most severe forms of poverty (DFID 2005:5, 2006b:iii, 2011:15; ILO 2009b:24, 2010a:6–10; World Bank 2009a:172–173). The goal of counteracting severe poverty is often narrowed down to securing an absolute minimum level of consumption for the poor, emphasising the existential minimum of nutrition (e.g., DFID 2011:2; GTZ 2005:3, 16–20; World Bank 2009a: 31).

   This is not to say that policy actors never mention poverty reduction. It is, however, notable that a reduction of the poverty headcount is rather seen as a long-term effect of cash transfers. Many proponents of cash transfers emphasise their potential to interrupt the intergenerational transmission of poverty from parents to children (DFID 2005:17, 2011:6; ILO 2009b:36, 2010a:97; UNICEF and ODI 2009:7; World Bank 2009a:1).

   Even a detailed analysis of policy documents does not give a definitive answer to the question whether policy actors prefer reduction or alleviation of poverty. Which goals are emphasised dependent on whether development in general or cash transfers in particular are being discussed and/or the intended time horizon of, that is, alleviation in the short term or reduction in the long term (e.g., ILO 2010b:6, 14).

   Secondly, cash transfers are expected to reduce social inequities through their redistributive nature as tax-financed benefits. This effect is closely related to poverty reduction, and most actors tend to limit it to increasing the income of the poorest (DFID 2005:1, 2011:17; ILO 2009b:6, 2010a:42; World Bank 2008:1, 2009a:1, 172–173). In addition, reducing the unequal treatment of women is often an intended effect of cash transfers (DFID 2005:16, 2011:6; HAI 2006b:4; ILO 2001:3; World Bank 2009a:9). Cash transfers are intended to improve the social inclusion and status of marginalised groups by providing them with resources which facilitate the use of economic and educational opportunities.

Crucially, a reduction of social inequities is also expected from other instruments of social protection and other social policies, cash-based or not (ILO 2010a; UNICEF 2012; World Bank 2012). The specific role of cash transfers in conjunction with other means of social protection is to raise the living standard of the poor, that is, cash transfers only deal with a certain form of social inequity. The living standard and social problems of higher income groups is perceived as a challenge for other instruments, such as social insurance (e.g., ILO 2010a:19).

Thirdly, cash transfers are meant to protect their beneficiaries from all sorts of 'risks', 'shocks' and 'crises', an idea that has been strongly influenced by 'social risk management' as advocated by the World Bank (DFID 2005:5, 17; ILO 2009b:7, 36, 2010a:16, 45, 105–108; World Bank 2001a; 2009a: xii, 123). Risks, shocks and crises are perceived to range from individual life events such as unemployment or illness to large-scale threats, like natural catastrophes, and constant conditions like climate change. The main idea is that such events will drastically impede the livelihoods of the general population, but the poor are nearly always described as particularly vulnerable due to their low resources. The regular transfer of cash is then expected to stabilise the earnings of the beneficiaries at an adequate level, to protect their well-being.

Again, a reduction of risk is also expected of other means of social protection. The mitigation of risk is regarded as a major goal of traditional social security measures, particularly social insurance (e.g., ILO 2010c:15). Again, cash transfers are perceived to focus on the most extreme effects of such risk: significant drops in living standard, which would push the victims below the poverty line or deepen poverty. This is described as a slight difference from social insurance: while insurances also protect against drops in living standard, they might maintain levels of welfare well above the poverty line. This is used as an argument to include cash transfers into a system of social protection in which different types of schemes protect different groups against specific risks. The ILO's 'global social floor' is a typical and relatively elaborate example of such thinking: cash transfers form the actual 'floor', which offers a baseline of protection against risk to the poor but should be complemented by a 'staircase' of advanced protection for higher income groups (ILO 2010a:18–20).

Fourthly, cash transfers are thought to have a positive economic impact on two levels. On the individual level, the regular availability of cash is supposed to cultivate the autonomous economic activity of the beneficiaries and enable them to make investments. Such investments include the human capital of beneficiaries and/or their children, which is believed to stimulate long-term economic growth. On the aggregate level, the mass influx of cash is assumed to invigorate 'local markets', as the recipients are deemed likely to spend much of their benefits on daily consumption. Taken together, both effects are thought to support economic growth as a whole (DFID 2005:7, 17; ILO 2009b:16, 20, 2010a:33, 104–105; OECD-DAC 2009: 44–45; UNICEF and ODI 2009:20; World Bank 2006:148, 2008:21–24).

Again, social protection in general is also seen as an economic stabiliser, which facilitates employment and supports consumer demands under adverse economic conditions (e.g., ILO 2011:16–22). If anything, policy actors assume cash transfers to be especially effective at achieving this, since the poor are perceived to lack the resources for economic activity. Even a small transfer of resources is supposedly used at once, for example, to fund job searching or to create a small business, and can therefore achieve economic effects by creating or invigorating demand for goods in local markets (e.g., DFID 2011:34–36).

Finally, many global organisations assume that cash transfers will strengthen 'social cohesion'. The assumption is that the poor are less likely to cooperate with each other due to a lack of resources and will be isolated because of their low social status. In addition, receiving a regular transfer of cash from the government is imagined to strengthen the bond between the recipients and the state – referring to the premise that many citizens in developing countries have little interaction with their supposedly weak governments. Besides, it is also argued that cash transfers will function to legitimise national and global policies, or even globalisation as a whole, by imparting a feeling of participation or compensation.

The promotion of social cohesion is also attributed to social protection in general. Cash transfers are not given specific role in strengthening social cohesion, except for the issue of legitimisation. Since cash transfers cater to the lowest strata of society, they can function as compensation for the losers of social change or economic reform. Other social protection measures, for example, social insurance, are also seen as stabilisers but rather through the stabilisation of higher income levels (DFID 2005:25; HAI 2004: 33–34; ILO 2009b:7, 35, 2010a:45, 108–110; OECD-DAC 2009:18; World Bank 2006: 155; 2008:431).

All five effects – poverty reduction, reduction of social inequities, protection from risk, promotion of growth and promotion of social cohesion – are perceived to apply to all variants of cash transfers equally and provide the basic legitimisation for each model. However, as the following analysis of four specific variants of cash transfers illustrates, different policy models may be further attributed with specific effects that legitimise the utility of that specific variant of cash transfer.

In addition, the analysis of the effects attributed to cash transfers allows a first look at the place that global actors give cash transfers in relation to other means of social protection. Unsurprisingly, cash transfers are usually intended to provide for the poorest, while groups with higher incomes are covered by other means. The analysis of policy models in the next sections also demonstrates that cash transfers are primarily intended for certain target groups – specifically, the working-age poor are generally intended to be covered by other means of basic social protection.

2.2   How to make a global model – four variants of cash transfers

As mentioned earlier, four variants of cash transfers are primarily advocated by global organisations: family allowances, conditional cash transfers, social pensions and general household assistance.

What is more, public employment programmes, near-cash transfers and universal basic income are commonly perceived as alternative models, albeit they play different roles in the global debate on cash transfers.

Table 2.2 sums up the most important characteristics of all models: target groups, effects attributed specifically to the model and advocacy organisations.

The following analysis provides four crucial observations on the career of cash transfers in global policy. Firstly, that the pathway to institutionalisation as a policy model was different in each of the four cases, resulting in different degrees of institutionalisation. The four policy models are not all similarly legitimate. Secondly, that these processes of construction were actively driven by global organisations – almost all policy models are primarily advocated by one specific organisation. Thirdly, that specific national examples are frequently used to construct the global models. Fourthly, that scientific evidence in the form of statistical comparisons is essential to the construction of a model.

2.2.1   Family allowances: the globalisation of a Northern model

Family allowances are generally defined as regular cash benefits to poor families with children. Actors justify the targeting of benefits with the

Table 2.2 Policy models: social cash transfers and alternative policies

Policy model	Target groups	Effects	Supporting organisations
Social cash transfers			
Family allowances	– Poor and vulnerable families with children – Poor and vulnerable children as individuals	– Alleviate the specific vulnerabilities of children – Human capital formation	– UNICEF – Save the Children – ILO (as part of the 'global social floor') – DFID
Conditional cash transfers	– Poor and vulnerable families who underinvest in the human capital of their children	– Human capital formation – Long-term poverty reduction – Economic growth	– The World Bank – The Inter-American Development Bank
Social pensions	– Poor and vulnerable older persons	– Alleviate the specific vulnerabilities of older persons – Improve the social status of beneficiaries – Alleviate general poverty via sharing in the family	– HelpAge International – ILO (as part of the 'global social floor') – DFID
General household assistance	– All poor and vulnerable households, including working-age poor		– ILO (as part of the 'global social floor') – DFID (as 'household benefits')
Alternative policy models			
Public employment programmes	– Working-age poor	– Build up infrastructure and generate income	– The World Bank – ILO (particularly the 'employment sector')
Near-cash transfers	– All categories of the poor and vulnerable	– Motivate use of social services (vouchers)	– DFID (vouchers in particular)
Universal basic income	– All individual citizens	– Promote self-fulfilment and autonomy of beneficiaries	– BIEN – BIG Coalition (Namibia)

specific vulnerability of children to poverty, based on their relatively limited mental and physical capacities and their low social status (e.g., UNICEF and ODI 2009:13). Besides general poverty reduction, family allowances are supposed to support the human capital development of children by facilitating school enrolment, better nutrition and better healthcare (ILO 2010a:20; UNICEF and ODI 2009:27–28).

While family allowances were known as a policy model in the Global North since the 1950s, their applicability in developing countries was constructed by UNICEF starting in the mid-2000s. Family allowances only emerged as a strong global model due to the advocacy of UNICEF. In this process the model in itself remained unchanged – only the perceptions of policy actors shifted.

Indeed, an analysis of relevant document demonstrates that global organisations have known a distinct model of family allowances for decades: a 'family benefit' is mentioned in the ILO's seminal Social Security (Minimum Standards) Convention No. 102 of 1952 (ILO 1952; Articles 39–45). The Convention explicitly allows both for contributory and tax-financed benefits (ibid.; Article 43; Article 71). Such ILO conventions set globally binding standards which member states are expected to implement (ILO 2014a). Thus, the inclusion of non-contributory family allowances into the ILO's Convention on minimal standards for social security indicates that they were already regarded as a policy model for member states of the ILO.

However, the degree of institutionalisation should be regarded as relatively low at this point because Convention No. 102 pertains to social security in general and treats family allowances as one specific component. What is more, the model remains vague: it is not determined whether such schemes should be contributory or tax-financed.

Nevertheless, the inclusion of family allowances into the ILO's social security standards seems to have had an impact on global policy: 'family assistance' or 'family allowances' were advocated by the World Bank under the umbrella of 'safety nets' during the 1990s. At this point, their utility was mostly constructed by referring to positive experiences in developed countries of the Global North and the transitional countries of Central Europe (Subbarao et al. 1997; Roddis and Tzannatos 1999). In so far, the origin of the policy model lies in the Global North, since these were the first national examples which were discussed by development organisations.

However, the construction of family allowances as a strong global model did not begin in earnest until the early 2000s: 'Child Poverty and Cash Transfers', published in 2004, for instance, is one of the earliest journal articles which emphasises the potential use of family allowances in the Global South (Barrientos and DeJong 2004). The text makes a case for the particular poverty risk of children and the use of cash transfers as a solution, referring to national examples from the Global South: the South African child grant, family benefits in Central and Eastern Europe and conditional cash transfers in Latin America. Crucially, non-contributory 'family allowances' to alleviate poverty are virtually taken for granted as a type of cash transfer, referring to the World Bank's work on safety nets in the 1990s (545–546). This supports the observation that such schemes were already policy models to a certain extent.

Advocacy for family allowances further intensified after 2004. At this time, UNICEF, as the major specialist IO for child policy, picked up the model and began to argue for its use in developing countries by publishing research studies and policy papers.

Since UNICEF specialises in child-centred policy, the late emergence of interest in family allowances seems puzzling. A general overview of UNICEF publications from the 1980s to the early 2000s, while showing a clear concern with child poverty and welfare, indicates that supporting children's rights and education were the preferred policy options (e.g., UNICEF 1997, 2000). An interview with a former senior staff member of UNICEF indicates that the organisation's interest in social cash transfers was motivated by the World Bank's activity on CCT in the early 2000s (Interview 3):

Q: When did you first become aware of social security as a subject of global debate?
A: I believe it was in 2005, in the context of a UNICEF conference in New York, a brainstorming session, where we reflected what the new issues were.
Q: In your opinion, what was the motivation at that time to include social security specifically?
A: Well, for that specific occasion it was that the World Bank had begun to systematically think about social transfers, and in their case I believe it was strongly motivated by the social transfers in Latin America.

In fact, UNICEF began to advocate social protection and cash transfers after 2005, by funding pertinent research, culminating in the development of an own social protection strategy in 2012. Beginning in 2005, family allowances was advocated as the model which best served the needs of children, but UNICEF also argued for the positive impact of cash transfers in general. The policy model of family allowances remained the same as in ILO Convention No. 102, but its applicability in developing countries was constructed using new arguments and statistical data. Two studies in particular serve as examples of this process.

Firstly, 'Making cash count', a study on social protection measures in Africa, published in cooperation by UNICEF, HelpAge International and Save the children (HAI et al. 2005). The publication centres on the new argument that not only family allowances but also social cash transfers in general will support poor children in developing countries even if they are not the primary beneficiaries because of the money shared in entire beneficiary household. In respect to family allowances, this new argument on the sharing of transfers was used to support the basic idea that cash transfers are good for poor children.

Secondly, 'Child poverty: a role for cash transfers?, a UNICEF study on cash transfers in West and Central Africa, carried out by the Overseas Development Institute (ODI), an eminent British think-tank (UNICEF and ODI 2009). The study illustrates how policy actors changed their perceptions regarding the applicability of family allowances in developing countries, without actually changing fundamental parameters of family allowances as a model. Indeed, the actual definition of family allowances presented in the study does not differ significantly from the ILO Convention No. 102 (see earlier and UNICEF and ODI 2009:17). Crucially, the feasibility of this policy model in developing countries is proven by detailed statistical simulations of its effects and costs for several countries in the Global South – in each case the results are positive, suggesting that cash transfers will reduce poverty (27–36).

Following the publication of these studies, UNICEF moved on to develop its own concept of 'child-sensitive social protection' which was endorsed by a broad coalition of actors, including DFID, StC, the ILO, the World Bank and the ODI, which had helped to produce the study mentioned earlier (UNICEF et al. 2009). The concept in itself is rather encompassing and, besides social insurances and social services, includes cash transfers and family allowances as a matter of course (3).

Finally this was followed by the publication of 'Integrated Social Protection System – Enhancing Equity for Children', which serves as UNICEF's (2012) first official policy strategy for social protection in general. Within the strategy, 'cash transfers', including family allowances, are regarded as an important tool to reduce poverty and vulnerability (32–36). In this context, family allowances are treated as a self-evident policy model for developing countries, referring to the 2009 study mentioned earlier (33).

Taken together, the treatment of family allowances as a self-evident model within the concept of child-sensitive social protection and the social protection strategy indicate that the institutionalisation of this policy model grew stronger through the activities of UNICEF. In a first step, the 2009 study constructed family allowances as a viable policy for developing countries. In a second step, UNICEF convinced a broad coalition of other policy actors to support the concept of family allowances in a joint publication (UNICEF et al. 2009). By endorsing child-sensitive social protection, the other policy actors imply that they take the utility of the policy model for granted. In a last step, the model became an unquestioned part of UNICEF official policy strategy, based on the initial statistical study. All in all, family allowances gradually gained a status of practically unquestioned legitimacy by the year 2009.

Currently, they are both part of the World Bank's policy advice and the ILO's global social floor and are recognised as useful by virtually all relevant policy organisations (Commission for Africa 2005:210; DFID 2005:10, 2011: 91; ILO 2010a:20, 39–42, 46; HAI et al. 2005:3; OECD-DAC 2009:20, 133; UNICEF and ODI 2009; World Bank 2006:150, 2008:257, 263, 321–322). In so far as family allowances are globally taken for granted as a model of development policy, I argue that they have achieved a relatively high degree of institutionalisation.

Three conclusions can be drawn from the construction of family allowances as a policy model. Firstly, the analysis supports the hypothesis that statistical comparison is an important discursive practice for constructing global models. Family allowances were already an established model in the global policy before the current discussion on cash transfers began, but they were perceived as a policy model for the developed nation states in the Global North. In debate on cash transfers, the actual content of this model – that is, design, target group and effects – did not alter significantly. Only perceptions regarding the applicability of the model in developing countries changed. This is the result of an active process of redefinition by global actors, starting in the early 2000s. The 2009 UNICEF/ODI study and its comparative statistical simulations seem to have played an essential role – family allowances only gained even wider recognition after its publication.

Secondly, that national examples play a significant role in the construction of global models. Studies on family allowances used examples from the Global North (Subbarao et al. 1997; Roddis and Tzannatos 1999) and the Global South (Barrientos and DeJong 2004) to argue for the utility of the model.

Thirdly, the analysis illustrates that the specific advocacy of a global organisations is crucial to the construction of a global model. Until circa 2005, family allowances lacked an advocate on the global level and was not widely recognised as a policy model. Then UNICEF discovered cash transfers and began to argue for the policy model that best fit its organisational mandate, that is, family allowances. UNICEF thereby entered an active process construction which culminated in the institutionalisation of family allowances within a broader concept of social protection, recognised by a many development organisations that do not necessarily specialise in children, for example, the World Bank and the ILO.

To conclude, the career of family allowances as a global model also raises one interesting question. The construction of family allowances as a global model has been surprisingly seamless – especially in comparison to the case of general household assistance. Evidently, there has been a certain amount of focused advocacy by UNICEF but less than in the cases of conditional cash transfers or social pensions. How can the ease of transition to the global level be explained? I posit that discursive factors can provide an explanation for the relatively seamless career of family allowances.

2.2.2   Conditional cash transfers: strategic uptake of innovative national models in the Global South

Conditional cash transfers are defined as regular cash benefits to poor households with children, paid on the condition that the children are sent to school and/or receive preventive healthcare. They specifically target families who do not invest optimally into the human capital of their children, either from the perspective of their individual assets or from the perspective of broad socio-economic interest (World Bank 2009a:22, 169–173). This often contains the implicit assumption that parents in the target families are unable or unwilling to make sufficiently rational decisions by themselves.

The behavioural conditions are mainly justified as promoting a long-term investment into the human capital of the children, meant to break intergenerational cycles of poverty and stimulate the economy. Even though redistribution in general, the short-term reduction of poverty and offering a 'safety net' against negative life events are also seen as viable goals, the World Bank clearly emphasises the utility of such transfers for long-term economic growth and thus long-term poverty reduction (World Bank 2009a:47).

Some actors, for example, the ILO, under-emphasise conditions as an instrument to achieve economic growth and treat the promotion of human capital as an inherently valuable goal, using the term 'human development' (e.g., ILO 2010a: 39–42; see Chapter 3 for a detailed analysis).

The career of CCT as a policy model began in Latin America. Starting with the construction of positive statistical data on several non-contributory transfers in Brazil and Mexico that used conditions, the World Bank further conceptualised an abstract model of CCT and attributed it with the long-term effects and policy goals specified earlier. This model finally became an unquestioned part of the Bank's official social protection policy but is criticised by other organisations, resulting in a medium degree of institutionalisation.

The two specific programmes from Latin America which attracted the World Bank's attention were Mexico's PROGRESA/Oportunidades, established in 1997, and Brazil's Bolsa Familia, started in 2003 (but with predecessor programmes going back as far as 1995). The PROGRESA became known globally because the Mexican government quickly produced publicly available programme evaluations, proving positive outcomes in poverty reduction (see Sugiyama 2011:253–255, 262, for a detailed account). The positive reaction of global organisations to these sets of data again indicates the importance of statistics to the construction of policy models – in the case of CCT, the evaluations seem to have been the first step in the construction of the policy model.

An interview with an experienced policy advisor and researcher in the field of cash transfers indicates that Bolsa Familia attracted the attention of the World Bank in a similar manner (Interview 2):

Q: Would you see the same thought processes with other participants of the discussion? Do they also take national examples?

A: Yes, if you look at the background to say Bolsa Familia, you can trace it back to about 1994, in several municipalities in Brazil, there was an acute economic crisis and municipalities, they had to address the consequences of the crisis. One of the municipalities was Campinas and they developed a program of this type. And so the government became interested around 1999, 5 years later, because by then, something like one third of the municipalities were experimenting with this kind of program. And so the government decided to introduce that at the national level. You see, the World Bank comes in probably about 2000.

Q: So your point is that they became very interested in this experience and adopted it for themselves, as I understood you.

A: Yes, and so then they began to think, well, this is a good thing, we could see how it can work elsewhere. There is a direct linking to one person, which is Francisco Ferreira, he works for the Bank and he was involved in Brazil in one of the attempts to develop a national policy and then he joined the Bank.

As the interviewee points out, the World Bank became increasingly aware of Bolsa Familia only after its national implementation in Brazil and spurred policy development by hiring local expertise. In fact, Francisco H.G. Ferreira was involved in a national discussion on cash transfers in Brazil in the early 2000s (e.g., Camargo and Ferreira 2001) and has held a number of senior positions in the World Bank since 2002 (IZA 2014). This coincides with an increase of publications on CCT, and Ferreira himself has directly contributed to a number of important policy documents (e.g., Bourguignon et al. 2002, 2003; World Bank 2009a).

However, neither PROGRESA nor Bolsa Familia were initially presented as 'conditional cash transfers' by their respective national governments. Early references to these cash transfers by global organisations – including the World Bank – often describe them only in vague terms or call them 'targeted human development programmes' (see the World Development Report 2001; World Bank 2001c:158). This indicates that conditional cash transfers did not exist as a specific policy model at this time.

Document analysis indicates that the specific process of construction proceeded incrementally from the early 2000s onwards, beginning after PROGRESA and Bolsa Familia had gained global attention. Starting in the early 2000s the World Bank adopted the term 'conditional cash transfers' and slowly became the leading organisation for CCT.

Indeed, one of the earliest usages of the actual term 'conditional cash transfers' can be traced back to an evaluation of the Bolsa Escola programme by the 'Latin America and the Caribbean Regional Office' of the World Bank (World Bank/LACRO 2001). While this evaluation was mostly positive, praising plans to expand the programme, the term is not specified in detail. What is more, even though the main objectives of poverty reduction and offering a safety net are mentioned, there is little elaboration relative to the more recent publications – the specific ideas behind CCT are already present but remain too vague to establish a clear policy model (compare World Bank 2009a). Nevertheless, the regional office remained active on CCT, including a 2002 workshop in Mexico, where World Bank staff and officials from countries with CCTs financed by the Bank exchanged information (predominantly Latin American countries, including Mexico and Brazil; see World Bank 2003a).

It is likely that the exchange of further information facilitated the construction of CCT as a model. The number of publications on conditional cash transfers slowly grew significantly between 2004 and 2006 – the World Bank itself and a number of closely related organisations dominated this trend (e.g., Skoufias and Parker 2001; Maluccio 2003; Dureya and Morrison 2004). For instance, the Inter-American Development Bank (IDB) apparently coined the term 'targeted human development programs', in 2001, to describe a number of cash transfers in Latin America, but quickly switched to calling them conditional cash transfers under the influence of the World Bank (compare IDB 2001 and Dureya and Morrison 2004).

Conditional cash transfers became increasingly clearer as a model within World Bank publications during this phase. After 2004, publications from the Bank's Social Protection Sector begin to delineate a consistent idea of CCT, elaborating on the effects on long-term economic growth (e.g., Rawlings 2004; Rawlings and de la Brière 2006). By 2006, the World Bank seemed to have gained a position of discursive dominance in the field of CCT: after this point, most other organisations refer to Bank publications when discussing CCT, be it positively or negatively (e.g., DFID 2011:49–51; Freeland 2007; ILO 2010a:39–42; Künnemann and Leonhard 2008). The process of construction culminated in two major World Bank publications, both of which drew heavily on the research since 2001. Firstly, 'For Protection and Promotion', a volume that updated the World Bank's safety net approach to include CCT, with a greater emphasis on the 'promotive' aspects of social protection such as human capital development and the long-term elimination of intergenerational 'poverty traps' (World Bank 2008; compare World Bank 2001a). Secondly, 'Conditional cash transfers – reducing present and future poverty', a sizeable study which systematically collects all evidence on CCT to date and provides an elaborate rationale for their implementation, including all of the effects described in the beginning of this section (World Bank 2009a).

This indicates that CCT were increasingly institutionalised between 2004 and 2009. The World Bank established a clear idea of what CCT should encompass, and other policy actors began to recognise it as a distinct type of policy which was useful in developing countries. This process continued in so far as CCT became part of a pillar of social protection policy in the Bank. The second Social Protection Sector Strategy (SPSS) of 2012 indicates that 'Promotion' of economic activity via human capital development has become a new core aspect of social protection in the World Bank policy, focusing on CCT and PEPs as policy models (World Bank 2012:1–3; 25–27). Comparable to family allowances in the UNICEF strategy, the use of CCT for certain purposes is treated as self-evident by the Bank.

While the Bank has thus developed into the strongest advocate of conditional cash transfers since the early 2000s, other participants of the debate have continuously questioned the effectiveness and moral appropriateness of the eponymous conditions, often referring to human rights. It is claimed that human rights establish an individual entitlement to unconditional benefits, and that beneficiaries would invest in human capital even if there were no conditions – making them an unnecessary form of paternalism (e.g., Freeland 2007; Künnemann and Leonhard 2008). Most relevant actors, however, still see CCT as one of several context-dependent options, with specific drawbacks and advantages, and have neither endorsed nor condemned them entirely (e.g., DFID 2011:49–51; ILO 2010a:39–42). In so far, it appears that conditional cash transfers are less strongly institutionalised than family allowances: their utility is only treated as self-evident by the World Bank and associated organisations, for example, the IDB. Other actors only accept them as useful depending on specific national conditions or reject them outright. Notably conditional cash transfers are the only policy model whose utility is questioned on such a fundamental level and is regarded as possessing a medium degree of institutionalisation – family allowances are legitimate to a higher degree, but general household assistance is less institutionalised.

Again, I would like to make three observations on the process from which conditional cash transfers emerged. Firstly, statistical data again played a crucial role in constructing the global model. Both PROGRESA and Bolsa Famila attracted the attention of the World Bank because of statistical programme evaluations which suggested a positive impact of the programmes. World Bank publications which later elaborated on CCT as a policy model also heavily rely on statistical comparisons between programmes in different countries (see especially World Bank 2009a).

Secondly, as in the case of family allowances, national examples are at the beginning of the process of construction. PROGRESA in Mexico and Bolsa Familia in Brazil motivated the World Bank to construct CCT as a policy model and are used as archetypes to this day.

Thirdly, the construction of conditional cash transfers as a policy model was mainly driven by the World Bank as a single organisation – the emergence of the model sped up significantly as soon as the Bank intensified research and publication on CCT in the early 2000s.

But why did the Bank choose two advocate CCT in the first place? Interviews with international experts suggest that there is constant pressure to discover innovative policies of poverty reduction in the field of development policy in general (Interview 3):

Q: In your opinion what is the origin of the debate on social security, on the level of donor organisations?

A: I have the impression that, at least in United Nation circles, it was strongly motivated by the experiences in Latin America, in particular that specific form of transfers with conditions, which was showing first success.

Q: In your opinion, what exactly was the point that made an impression with all these actors? Why was this perceived as such a success?

A: Well, you can interpret this malevolently or benevolently. Malevolently, one would say that the World Bank discovered a new area for loans, and benevolently, well, simply that, in development, policy, you are always looking for instruments which make sense for poverty reduction in particular, even if the improvement is marginal.

The interviewee suggests that development policy is marked by a tendency to seek innovative solutions for social problems like poverty, even if there is only a small advantage. This observation is interesting because this general pressure to innovate, stemming from the nature of the policy field, may coincide with specific pressures to innovate within single development organisations. HelpAge International is one such example of potential organisational pressures (see later).

To conclude, the career of CCT as a global model raises two problems. One, the analysis of CCT does not fully explain why the transfer programmes in Latin America *specifically* attracted the attention of the World Bank in contrast to others, for example, those which served to construct family allowances or social pensions. Two, it does not clarify why the World Bank attributed the model with the specific target group and effects found in the current policy model – only select aspects of PROGRESA and Bolsa Familia, especially the conditions regarding education and healthcare, were chosen as aspects of the policy model. As Sugiyama (2011:253–255) argues, existing differences in design and origin were omitted to portray both programmes as variations of the same basic idea; PROGRESA, for instance, was a project of the national government, while Bolsa Família emerged from municipal social programmes. Again, I propose that global discourses can further explain the salience of conditional cash transfers and the way the policy model was conceptualised by the World Bank (see Chapter 4).

2.2.3 Social pensions: creating a global model through focused advocacy

Social pensions are defined as regular cash benefits to older persons, usually those above an age threshold around 60. In addition, the disabled are frequently mentioned as a potential target group. As with family allowances, the rationale behind this model is the specific vulnerability of the elderly or disabled to poverty and other social problems due to lack of labour power and low social status (DFID 2005:16–17, 2011:32, 41; HAI 2006b:3–5; OECD-DAC 2009:134; UNICEF and ODI 2009:18; World Bank 2006:148, 2008:361).

Poverty reduction and increased welfare of the elderly are thus defined as primary effects of social pensions. However, these effects are expected to transcend the actual beneficiaries: by sharing of the pensions within the households and families of the pensioners, other people, especially their grandchildren, supposedly share the positive effects of the transfer. The payment of school fees by grandparents, that is, increased educational chances, improved nutrition and health status are frequently mentioned as outcomes of social pensions. What is more, social pensions diverge from other cash transfers in the social effects which are ascribed to them. Proponents of social pensions often define low social status due to low economic productivity as a particular problem of older people. Pensions, as a regular source of cash, are expected to boost the social prestige of beneficiaries considerably, since they are enabled to contribute to their families.

Global organisations first recognised 'non-contributory pensions' as a policy model in the mid-1990s. However, the model did not gain significant global attention until it was attributed with the effects described earlier, especially the indirect impact on children, and re-labelled as 'social pensions'. The construction of social pensions as a model was strongly driven by HelpAge International through research publications on specific national examples and the organisation of conferences.

Social pensions are the earliest variants of cash transfers to be advocated at the global level. The World Bank included a concept of 'non-contributory pensions' to alleviate poverty into its multi-pillar pension model in 1994 (see World Bank 1994:238–242). The Bank's initial approach to tax-financed pensions, however, only saw them as a residual safety net which complemented the contributory pillars. Even though there was research into 'non-contributory pensions' in developing countries in the late 1990s and early 2000s (e.g., Case 2001; Barrientos and Lloyd-Sherlock 2002), these studies did not designate such schemes as social pensions and did not mention any particularly useful effects.

The term 'social pensions' was first used in global policy documents around 2001. In particular, 'Social pensions in Namibia and South Africa', a paper published by Stephen Devereux at the Institute of Development Studies (IDS; an eminent British think tank in the field of development and social protection in the Global South) in 2001, helped spread a new perspective on non-contributory pensions. Devereux describes the history of social pensions in both countries in detail, referring to intra-national South African debates of the 1960s, and offers a general assessment of their impact. This includes a set of statistical data which are employed to prove a number of the effects in detail, particularly the sharing of pensions within the family or household – the benefits to grandchildren receive separate mention (Devereux 2001:41–49).

Global advocacy for social pensions, however, did not significantly increase until 2003, when HelpAge International began a coordinated campaign for social pensions. Between 2003 and 2007 HAI produced a number of widely quoted publications on social pensions and organised several workshops and conferences. It is noticeable that, during this time, HelpAge frequently cooperated with several important global organisations, often including the World Bank, the ILO and DFID.

Among the publications of HelpAge are several empirical studies which attempt to prove the beneficial effects of social pensions first claimed around 2001.

The 2003 study 'Non-contributory pensions and poverty prevention – A comparative study of Brazil and South Africa' is a notable example (HAI and IDPM 2003). On the one hand, the document mostly applies the older World Bank terminology of 'non-contributory pensions' and only employs the term 'social pension' in describing South Africa. On the other hand, comparing the two countries, both quantitative and qualitative data are used to prove four separate beneficial effects of social pensions in detail. HelpAge publications before 2003 also mention the beneficial effects of non-contributory pensions on the beneficiaries' households and families but do so only in passing, with comparatively sparse statistical data for single countries (e.g., HAI 2002:15; this example contains only a single table for older people's expenses in South Africa).

'Making cash count – lessons from cash transfer schemes in east and southern Africa for supporting the most vulnerable children and households', a 2005 HelpAge study, is also of interest. As the name suggests, it mainly revolves around the welfare of children but goes on to mention social pensions as a specific option for their support, arguing with the effects of sharing within the family (HAI et al. 2005:47). In fact, the document is the product of a UNICEF-financed study on social protection, executed in cooperation by HAI, the IDS and the child-centred NGO Save the Children. The introduction to the document explicitly underlines the similarities between the goals and conceptual frameworks of HelpAge and Save the Children (iii). Furthermore, the study categorises basic pensions in other countries than South Africa as 'social pensions' and uses the term in a more general manner.

As in the cases of family allowances and conditional cash transfers, it is notable that the creation of social pensions as a policy model began with the production of statistical data on their beneficial effects in several countries. I posit that the availability of detailed statistics and the utilisation of country comparison gave the debate on non-contributory pensions a significant boost by enabling the construction of the mentioned policy effects as global phenomena – thus making global diffusion of social pensions a viable idea.

The empirical studies organised by HelpAge were complemented by a number of declaratory policy documents which combined their results with a strong human rights argument for social pensions (HAI 2004, 2006b). 'Age and security' (HAI 2004) is a particularly important example: this flagship publication is the first document to state a human rights case for the global implementation of social pensions and to compile numerous empirical studies (including HAI and IPDM 2003) to prove their affordability and effectiveness. Furthermore, the document establishes a link between social protection as a human right and the rights of older people, describing social pensions as a 'key element' of a human rights approach to development (23–24). Notably, the document makes a strong case for universal social pensions, that is, benefits paid to all older people without preconditions.

In addition, HelpAge spread global awareness for social pensions by organising conferences and workshops on social protection and cash transfers. It is evident that HelpAge used such events to gain the attention of the most significant actors in development policy. Take, for instance, the workshop on 'Breaking the poverty cycle: securing rights to cash benefits for older people and children through national commitments and community action (October 2006), which was organised as a side event to the EU/ILO World Conference on Social Protection and Exclusion (HAI 2006a). The workshop, which brought together representatives from the ILO, from several other global organisations and from countries with social pension systems served to emphasise the common commitment to the expansion of cash transfers in general. It is, however, notable that the discussion of practical examples focused on social pensions.

The focused campaign initiated by HelpAge was successful. Since the mid-2000s, social pensions are treated as self-evidently useful by all relevant global organisations: both the ILO and the World Bank have integrated them into their respective social protection frameworks, and UNICEF is advocating their positive effects on children. Current publications often cite the early studies and declaratory documents by HelpAge and generally employ the same arguments (e.g., DFID 2005:13, 39; ILO 2009b:7; World Bank 2008:361).

In sum, it can be argued that the established but weakly advocated model of non-contributory pensions, which was regarded as a residual instrument of social protection, gained increased recognition around 2005 after having been attributed with new effects during the early 2000s. The process resulted in a high degree of institutionalisation, comparable to family allowances. Virtually all relevant policy actors treat the utility of social pensions as self-evident (e.g., DFID 2005:13, 39; HAI 2004; ILO 2009b:7; OECD-DAC 2009:24–26, 28–29, 44–45; World Bank 2008:361).

The three conclusions drawn in the cases of family allowances and conditional cash transfers also apply to social pensions.

Firstly, the process which led to the re-labelling of non-contributory pensions as 'social pensions' was initialised by the provision statistical data and country comparisons in several studies, which constructed new effects for the model. Secondly, national examples also played a significant role: the social pension of South Africa has been consistently used as a positive example of the newly constructed effects since the early 2000s. Thirdly, social pensions were also constructed as a model due to the efforts of a single specialised organisation, HelpAge International, which led a focused advocacy campaign. This campaign is notable because HAI managed to form cross-cutting alliances to child-centred organisations like Save the Children and UNICEF.

It should, however, be asked why HAI began to promote social pensions as a policy model. I posit that a primary interest in promoting social pensions was drawing attention to the general organisational mandate, that is, older people's rights and needs. HelpAge staff claim that the situation of older people has traditionally played only a marginal role in development policy (Interview 4). By entering the new field of social cash transfers with its own policy model, HAI has managed to strengthen global concern for older people, who became a preferred target group for cash transfers (Interview 3; see Chapter 4).

In addition, there is some evidence that HAI operates under significant pressure to provide innovative policy advice, stemming from its organisational structure. HelpAge International is chronically lacking funds and is mostly dependent on external financing for its operations, which is often tied to specific projects (Leutelt 2012:8–9). Interviews with HelpAge staff indicate that this is a strong motivation to constantly provide new and innovative projects in order to secure external funding (ibid.).

To conclude, the career of social pensions as a global model raises problems for further analysis. One, HAI entering the field of cash transfers with its own model to draw attention to its mandate only makes sense if social cash transfers already had a recognisable potential to become highly legitimate policy at this point, that is, in the early to mid-2000s. Why cash transfers in general had already increased in legitimacy by this point cannot be explained by the efforts of HelpAge. I will shortly return to this question in the chapter conclusion, where I argue that shifts in global discourses can explain why cash transfers in general gained the potential to become policy models.

2.2.4   General household assistance: from archetype of SCT to weak policy model

I use 'general household assistance' to designate regular cash benefits to any household which can be identified as poor, using a means test or a comparable method.

Benefits are paid irrespective of household composition. That is to say, this model targets all age groups and categorical groups, as long as they are members of a poor household. Evidently this includes the target groups which are covered by the other three policy models mentioned earlier: families with children for family allowances or conditional cash transfers and older people for social pensions. Crucially, the target group of 'general household assistance' is also perceived to include able-bodied working-age poor, that is, those who are in the economically active phase of the life cycle between childhood and old age and are not impeded by a disability – as long as they are part of a poor household, they would theoretically receive benefits.

The perception of working-age poor as a primary target group of general household assistance, significantly affects the position of policy actors regarding this model. To be precise, participants of the debate on cash transfers strongly differentiate between two major sets of target groups: older people, the disabled and children on the one hand, and working-age poor on the other. The first three groups are generally thought to be non-working members of society, due to their lack of labour power – this makes them deserving of support, since they are thought unable to earn their own living (DFID 2005:16–17, 2011:32, 41; HAI 2006b:3–5; OECD-DAC 2009:134; UNICEF and ODI 2009:13, 18; UNICEF et al. 2005; World Bank 2001b, 2006:148, 2008:361). In contrast, working-age poor are primarily expected to support themselves via employment – according to most organisations the availability of labour power makes them less deserving of support because they are expected to contribute to society (ILO 2010a:20, 2011:17; World Bank 2008:137–145, 297–323).

As a result, most global organisations are sceptical of cash transfers which target working-age poor, including general household assistance. Indeed, general household assistance is the only model of cash transfers which is confronted with a strong alternative model in the form of public employment programmes (see later). The existence of alternatives to general household assistance – PEPs for working age poor and the three targeted cash transfers analysed earlier for children and older persons – is compounded by the vague and indistinct character of general household assistance as a policy model which is illustrated by three observations.

Firstly, there is considerable terminological confusion regarding general household assistance. A fixed term for assistance to poor households, comparable to 'conditional cash transfers' or 'social pensions', cannot be found in the global debate. 'Social assistance' is often used interchangeably, both to designate public support to the poor as a general idea and support to poor households as a specific model (e.g., DFID 2005:6; ILO 2010a:20–21; UNICEF and ODI 2009:13–14:231, 233; World Bank 2009a:1, 6). The term 'social assistance' is thus problematic, since it may encompass all of the policy models mentioned in this chapter, as well as the provision of social services such as education and healthcare. Because of this, I designate this policy model with my own term of 'general household assistance', which describes the essential idea behind the policy model, that is, assistance to poor households in general, irrespective of the presence of specific categorical groups.

Secondly, general household assistance is rarely given a precise defini-tion by global policy actors and is only treated sparingly and briefly in most policy documents on cash transfers, even though definitions of cash transfers as a general model are strictly speaking open to all forms of tax-financed benefits and should logically include general household assistance.

Take, for instance, DFID's (2005:5) definition of 'social transfers' from the seminal 'practice paper' of 2005: 'Social transfers are regular and predictable grants – usually in the form of cash – that are provided to vulnerable households or individuals. They are a form of social protec-tion, in other words, part of a system of public actions put in place to protect and transform the livelihoods of citizens, including the vulner-able and chronically poor'.

This definition could well include general household assistance which also covers working-age poor. The same document specifically states 'pensions and child and household benefits' as examples of social cash transfers on the first page (DFID 2005:1). Due to the terminology, it can be assumed that 'household benefits' are synonymous with general household assistance, but the rest of the paper spends much more time on elaborating pensions and family allowances and does not give a detailed description of 'household benefits' (9–12).

General household assistance is also part of the 'global social floor', as conceptualised by the ILO. The policy advice which is given, however, is similar to DFID's definition of 'social transfers' (ILO 2010a:20):

> With regard to income security, the suggested social security guar-antees consist of providing income security to those who cannot or should not work: in particular to children [...], to pregnant women, to older people and to people with disabilities. At the same time, income support should be combined with employment guarantees and/or other labour market policies for those able and willing to work, but who are excluded from access to employment that would provide sufficient income.

Even though the 'floor' would thus also be open to general household assistance, in the form of 'income support for those able and willing to work', the commitment remains vague and is only mentioned as a second priority after benefits to specific categorical groups. Indeed, the passage goes on to explicitly mention 'the possibility of sequen-tial implementation' of the various benefits, financial support to work-ing-age poor being last in line (see also ILO 2006a:33, which advises to focus first on 'benefits with a strong investment character', i.e., family allowances).

Thirdly, although general household assistance is also attributed with the positive effects which are attributed to cash transfers as a general model, such as reducing poverty, it is not perceived to have a positive effect which is *specific* to the model (see references earlier and DFID 2005:5; GTZ 2005:8; ILO 2001:66; World Bank 2008:247). This is a difference to the other three variants of cash transfer: each one is perceived to alleviate the particular vulnerabilities of its target group in an especially effective manner or is perceived to produce other beneficial outcomes, such as the promotion of growth in the case of conditional cash transfers.

All in all, general household assistance occupies a strange position in the debate on cash transfers. While this variant is implicitly recognised by many organisations, family allowances, conditional cash transfers and social pensions are widely preferred as forms of basic social protection. With this in mind, an analysis of the career of general household assistance needs to examine why this variant of cash transfer did not emerge as a strong policy model comparable to the other three.

Interestingly, general household assistance was the first type of cash transfer to be discussed on the global level in the late 1980s but failed to emerge as a global model at this time. In the early 2000s a general household assistance scheme in Kalomo, Zambia, was among the first pilot projects which drew global attention to cash transfers. Once again, this did not result in the emergence of general household assistance as a strong policy model, most likely because no global organisation specifically advocated for this type of transfer.

The earlier debate on social cash transfers in the 1980s was initiated by Bernd Schubert, an eminent German development consultant and scholar. In 1985, Schubert (1985, 1987) published an article in the German weekly *Die ZEIT*, later reproduced in English in the international journal *Food Policy*. In these articles, Schubert criticised classic instruments of development aid for neglecting the poorest of the poor, whom he defined as incapable of helping themselves out of poverty due to lack of labour power. Therefore, he asserted that the poorest could not benefit from classic development aid which relied on the capacity of its recipients to help themselves, and were in need of different instruments. Defining hunger as the most pressing problem for his target group, Schubert argued for direct transfers of cash to the poorest because cash would enable the recipients to immediately satisfy their basic needs in local markets, which would also stimulate local production of food, that is, have a developmental effect.

Schubert's advocacy for cash transfers was met with a mixed reception. On the one hand, he connected his ideas to wider debates on the 'poorest of the poor' and the growth of hunger in developing countries, partially driven by the World Bank (1988). On the other hand, other development experts were still sceptical regarding the applicability of cash transfers in developing countries, referring to political context, inadequate local infrastructure and concerns of causing dependency (e.g., Reutlinger 1988).

Despite such criticism, Schubert managed to find support for cash transfers at the German Technical Cooperation (Deutsche Gesellschaft für technische Zusammenarbeit, GTZ; now renamed Deutsche Gesellschaft für internationale Zusammenarbeit, GIZ), the semi-public development agency of the German government (Interview 6). The GTZ organised a workshop on cash transfers in 1989, which resulted in the publication of GTZ-funded study on cash transfers by Bernd Schubert in 1990 (GTZ 1989; Schubert and Balzer 1990). Receptions remained mixed: most participants of the workshop voiced concerns, for example, lack of administrative and fiscal capacity in developing countries and lack of proof for developmental effects of cash transfers. Nevertheless, Schubert used the study on cash transfers in 1990 to develop a tentative policy model which included both general household assistance and benefits to categorical groups but emphasised the former (Schubert and Balzer 1990:7, 33–34). Schubert further specified the target group as those households who were both below the existential caloric minimum of food consumption and lacked available labour power to earn their own living (8–10, 15–20); in short, those whose survival is threatened in the long term.

Criticism by other scholars aside, the GTZ remained supportive of Schubert's ideas and motivated the government of Mozambique to implement a cash transfer programme (Interview 6). Bernd Schubert was hired as a consultant and technical advisor from 1990 to 1992 and wrote two reports on the programme (Schubert 1990; Schubert and Antezana 1991), which was labelled as a 'food subsidy scheme' but actually consisted of direct cash payments to the 15 per cent poorest households in Maputo, the capital of Mozambique (Schubert 1990:1). Schubert's consultancy for the 'food subsidy scheme" ended with a change of staff at the GTZ. The newly responsible officers did not support cash transfers and withdrew funding, even though the programme has continued and had grown to reach 372,000 households by December 2013, with plans for a further extension in 2014 (Bernd Schubert, personal communication, October 2014). Notably, the food subsidy scheme did not receive further attention by the global policy community and is virtually unknown today. To a certain extent, this may have been caused by an initial perception of poor programme performance, reflected in Schubert's reports.

Even after the loss of support for the Maputo programme, Schubert remained an advocate of social cash transfers but found no support with global policy actors. However, in 2003, the GTZ again changed its position on cash transfers and offered to fund a pilot project in Kalomo, Zambia, which Schubert was hired to support until 2006 (Interview 6). An analysis of relevant GTZ documents points out two potential reasons for the renewed interest in cash transfers. Firstly, the GTZ was involved in poverty research in Zambia in early 2003 which indicated a large number of 'incapacitated poor' in Zambia, that is, extremely poor households without labour power – Schubert's original target group. This research criticised the inadequate performance of existing 'safety nets' for the 'incapacitated poor' and argued for more permanent and generous social protection measures (MCDSS and GTZ 2004:2–7; see also GTZ 2005:18–19). Secondly, the first official GTZ publication on the Kalomo pilot project repeatedly mentions the Millennium Development Goals (MDGs), especially poverty reduction, as a motivation for introducing cash transfers (GTZ 2005:3, 8). It can be assumed that the MDGs, due to their significant global prominence, motivated development organisations to follow specific policy goals – for example, goal of reducing extreme poverty.

The Kalomo pilot project itself basically implemented Schubert's model of cash transfers: the scheme was explicitly targeted on 'labour-constrained', 'critically poor' households, that is, those that are in danger of starvation and have few or no members who are able to work (GTZ 2005:20). It is, however, notable that the targeted households were assumed to have an unusually high share of certain categorical groups among their members, particularly older people and children (ibid.). In so far, the Kalomo project was factually portrayed as a policy which mainly benefited these categorical groups, even though the actual target group of poor households implied that all imaginable target groups, including working-age poor, were potential beneficiaries.

In contrast to the 'food subsidy scheme' in Mozambique, the Kalomo pilot project received significant attention from global development organisations. Schubert himself reports of being invited to talk about Kalomo numerous times (Interview 6). It was also a centrepiece of the 2006 'Livingstone Conference' in Zambia, organised by DFID, HelpAge

International and the African Union (HAI 2006a, 2006b). The conference brought together representatives of 13 African governments to discuss new approaches to poverty discussion and resulted in a 'Livingstone Call for Action' which declared the intent to promote social protection, especially cash transfers, in Africa (HAI 2006a:4, 30–31). The second day of the conference consisted entirely of a field trip to Kalomo, meant to demonstrate the 'successes and challenges' of such a scheme (9).

The Livingstone Conference demonstrates that a scheme which followed a model of general household assistance was instrumental in establishing cash transfers as a general policy model. In fact, various global policy documents from 2004 onwards refer to the Kalomo project and statistical evaluations of the scheme, when arguing for the general use of cash transfers, and use it as a positive example (e.g., DFID 2005:16, 18; HAI 2004:28, 32; ILO 2006a:33; 2010a:88–89, 98; UNICEF and ODI 2009:20; World Bank 2008:18, 141, 264).

The point is that the Kalomo scheme is consistently used to argue for the use of cash transfers *in general*, not for the use of general household assistance as specific model – some organisations, such as HelpAge International, even employ Kalomo to argue for a different model like social pensions (see HAI 2004). In conclusion, the model of general household assistance was used as an 'archetype' in establishing the overall legitimacy and feasibility of social cash transfers but was quickly eclipsed by the more specific categorical benefits analysed earlier. Thus, general household assistance was a leading model of cash transfer in the earliest phases of the policy shift towards basic social protection, only to be neglected as soon as other variants had been constructed.

Regarding the degree of institutionalisation, it can be argued that general household assistance is only weakly institutionalised. On the one hand, this model has been used as a general archetype to initialise the debate on cash transfers, and it is at least implicitly part of the policy advice of many organisations. This suggests that its utility is basically recognised by these organisations. On the other hand, there is significant scepticism regarding the effects of general household assistance on working age poor. Therefore, the utility of general household assistance is not perceived as self-evident by most organisations. What is more, the model as a comparatively vague and indistinct, even lacking a widely shared terminology.

This situation is especially surprising because Schubert has successfully continued to advocate the Kalomo model of cash transfers and has personally participated in spreading similar pilot projects to ten further African countries besides Zambia since 2003, for example, a

2006 UNICEF pilot in Malawi (Interview 6; UNICEF 2006). In spite of its low legitimacy in global discourses, general household assistance is evidently fairly widespread in development practice, as evidenced by the continued existence of the Maputo food subsidy scheme, in spite of a lack of global attention and the virtual non-existence of global research or policy documents on such schemes.

The three observations made in the cases of family allowances, conditional cash transfers and social pensions also apply to general household assistance but to a lesser extent. In fact, the comparative absence of the three factors identified in case of the other policy models – statistical data, national examples and advocacy – serves to explain why general household assistance was not strongly institutionalised as a policy model.

Firstly, even though some statistical data on general household assistance was available to policy actors, there is a lack of extensive comparative studies as in the cases of the other models. As mentioned, policy actors do refer to evaluations of the Kalomo project when arguing for the use of cash transfers (especially GTZ 2005), but even if comparative studies on general household assistance exist, none are quoted or discussed by global development organisations.

Secondly, as in other cases, Kalomo as a national example of general household assistance which was perceived as successful played a significant role. However, Kalomo was merely a pilot project with limited scope, in contrast to nation-wide schemes like PROGRESA in Mexico or the social pension in South Africa.

Thirdly, there is no organisation which lobbies for the utility of general household assistance in global development policy. In contrast, the family allowances, conditional cash transfers and social pension are strongly advocated by certain organisations, for example, UNICEF, the World Bank or HelpAge International. Notably, this seems to be related to the target group of the given policy model. Each model which is advocated by a specific organisation is linked to one of two target groups which is perceived as especially deserving of support, that is, children or older persons, and organisations like UNICEF and HelpAge portray themselves as advocates in the name of these groups. Crucially, general household assistance is often perceived as a transfer to working-age poor – and there is no global organisation which represents the interests of this group.

But why is there no such specialised organisation which might have driven the career of general household assistance? It could be argued that the spread of Schubert's model of general household assistance in Africa had the potential to be framed as a success story – such pilot projects are often used to argue for the utility of other types of cash transfers. I propose that the reluctance of global organisations to endorse this policy model can be explained by the characteristics of global discourses.

Previous research into the career of cash transfers in general suggests that they were traditionally rejected by the dominant political ideologies or 'ideological discourses', both on the national and the global level, because they were perceived to cause dependency and/or stigmatise beneficiaries (Leisering 2008:77–78). Leisering argues that an increase in universalism in all of these ideologies pre-meditated the success of cash transfers as a policy model – universalism meaning that all target groups should be treated the same and receive the same support. In fact, many policy actors have adopted human-rights-based universalism into their policy and claim that human rights give everybody an equal right to social protection, both basic and advanced (e.g., DFID 2006b:73; ILO 2009b:36; HAI 2004:23).

Evidently, the reluctance of a majority of global organisations from diverse ideological backgrounds to advocate general household assistance does not quite match the observation that universalism has legitimised cash transfers. If universalism had really spread in global discourses, all target groups, including working-age poor, should be perceived as being equally deserving of basic social protection in situations of need. This would make general household assistance a feasible policy model because it offers support to any person who is part of a poor household.

Therefore, a reference to political ideologies and spreading universalism cannot sufficiently explain why some variants of cash transfer are strongly institutionalised while general household assistance is barely recognised by global organisations. An analysis of abstract global discourses which cut across ideologies will clarify why this specific policy model and cash transfers to working-age poor are mostly rejected in global development policy (see Chapter 4).

2.3   Alternative models of basic social protection

The global debate on basic social protection is not limited to policy models that can be described as cash transfers in a strict sense. Several other models are considered as alternatives: public employment programmes (PEPs), near-cash transfers and universal basic income. In the following, I will briefly discuss each alternative model.

2.3.1 Public employment programmes

Public employment programmes are generally conceptualised as fixed-term programmes for the construction of public infrastructure through low-wage labour. Policy actors assume that the poor will self-select participation in these programs if the wage is set so low that participation is no longer profitable for the non-poor (e.g., Del Ninno et al. 2009; Devereux and Solomon 2006; Subbarao et al. 1997; World Bank 2008:297–302). The PEPs are generally legitimised by a mixture of policy goals: on the one hand, they are expected to foster development because they build up infrastructure and offer employment; on the other hand, they are intended to reduce poverty and mitigate shocks because they are targeted at the poor (Del Ninno et al. 2009:1, 4–6; Lieuw-Kie-Song and Phillip 2010:8–10, 13). Currently, public employment programmes are widely conceptualised as part of a long-term strategy of social protection that tackles poverty and other social problems and includes cash transfers, social insurances and social services, as exemplified by the global social floor (ILO 2010a; Lieuw-Kie-Song and Phillip 2010; World Bank 2008, 2012). Notably, this is the result of a slight change in the way that policy actors perceive PEPs since the 1980s (see later).

As mentioned earlier, public employment programmes are consistently defined as a good alternative to non-contributory cash transfers for working-age poor, who are expected to take up the available work in PEPs to support themselves. For instance, both the World Bank and the ILO clearly state that they prefer PEPs over cash transfers which target working-age poor. In 'For protection and promotion', the World Bank's (2008:137–145) most recent major publication on safety nets and cash transfers, 'labor disincentives' are defined as a fundamental issue of cash transfers to working-age poor. That is, such transfers are perceived to cause dependency and keep beneficiaries out of employment. Demanding a work input in return for transfers, as in the case of PEPs, is mentioned as a good instrument to avoid disincentives (142, 143).

The ILO exhibits a similar, if less distinct, preference for PEPs: the ILO has advocated the global implementation of a set of basic cash transfers and social services in the form of a 'global social floor' since the mid-2000s (ILO 2004b:5, 66, 110, 2006a:22–23, 32, 2010a). Significantly, in 'Extending Social Security to All', the ILO's major publication on the floor, clearly advocates family allowances for children and social pensions for the elderly under any condition (ILO 2010a:20–21). In contrast, working-age poor are only intended to receive support if they cannot find employment – and even then it is left open whether this is to be achieved via general household assistance or employment schemes. Furthermore, later ILO publications on the 'global social floor' explicitly name 'a decent job' as the best form of social security for working-age poor and PEPs are pointed out as a preferable alternative to cash transfers (ILO 2011:17).

In sum, the utility of PEPs for supporting working-age poor is practically unquestioned, also due to the relative weakness of general household assistance as a policy model. The common perception that working-age poor can and should work to support themselves naturally gives a stronger legitimisation to schemes with a work input than to purely non-contributory cash transfers.

Regarding the career of PEPs in the global debate on basic social protection, I assert that the basic design features of the model have remained the same since the 1970s, while the associated goals have increasingly shifted from purely developmental construction of infrastructure towards reduction of poverty and social protection, in conjunction with the broader discursive shifts during the 1980s and 1990s (see Chapters 3 and 4).

When public employment programmes were first advocated and implemented by development organisations in the Global South during the mid-1970s and 1980s, they were mostly conceptualised as a short-term instrument to offer employment and jump-start economic development by building up infrastructure during times of economic crisis or in other emergency situations – the design of such programmes was already the same as today, that is, public construction programs with low wages to motivate self-selection of the poor (Garnier 1982; Gaude et al. 1987). Redistribution of income to the poor is also mentioned in early documents on PEPs but is given less emphasis than the long-term effects of new infrastructure on development (e.g., Gaude et al. 1987:424).

During the 1990s, policy actors still emphasised the potential of public employment to construct useful infrastructure but also increasingly mentioned that PEPs strongly benefited the poor by providing additional income that helped to mitigate poverty and stabilise livelihoods, a position strongly advocated by the World Bank in the context of its 'safety net' approach (Ravallion 1991; Subbarao et al. 1997:69–83; World Bank 1990:97). Indeed, by the early 2000s, policy actors began to define the reduction of poverty as a primary function of public employment programmes, on par with the promotion of development (Devereux and Solomon 2006). This parallels the construction of cash transfers as instruments against poverty and matches with the increasing focus on poverty in global policy that emerged during the 1990s – I propose that the legitimisation of cash transfers and the re-interpretation of PEPs can be both regarded as an outcome of the emerging focus on poverty reduction in development policy (see Chapter 3).

In addition global development organisations became interested in India's 'National Rural Employment Guarantee Act' (NREGA), a public employment programme that guarantees eligible beneficiaries 100 days of paid labour per annum and pays an unconditional cash benefit in case no work is available (Ministry of Law 2005). The ILO in particular emphasises that such employment guarantees can turn PEPs into an instrument of long-term social protection and development with a strong impact on poverty reduction because of the regular cash benefit that they provide (Lieuw-Kie-Song and Phillip 2010:8–10, 21–22) – explicitly in combination with cash transfers in terms of a global social floor that provides support to non-working poor (18, 19–21). In general, PEPs are now regarded as one option in a long-term approach to development that not only builds up infrastructure, but also mitigates shocks and reduces poverty (Del Ninno et al. 2009; Lal et al. 2010). In so far, public employment programmes have been integrated into the systemic approaches to social protection that have also shaped the career of cash transfers as policy models and are advocated as one target group-specific instrument of basic social protection – a significant shift in comparison to their initial conceptualisation as short-term crisis response.

2.3.2 Near-cash transfers

Another type of basic social protection policies also relies on regular transfers but exchanges the cash component for something else, such as vouchers for food or social services, or a transfer in kind. Such transfers are often called 'near-cash transfers', because policy actors perceive the transferred vouchers or goods to be similarly flexible to cash, if not quite as freely usable by the beneficiaries (DFID 2005:9; World Bank 2008:255–256). In the case of vouchers, for instance, the degree of flexibility depends on the associated goals: They may be bound to specific distributors of goods but leave the type of goods open. However, some policy suggestions tie them to the use of specific services such as education or health (e.g., ILO 2010a:36). In short, beneficiaries are not meant to have complete choice concerning the needs or wants that are served by the transfer. This links to a further difference to cash transfers: vouchers, at least, are not always meant to alleviate poverty in general, but are focused on specific needs. In kind benefits are also limited, since they often narrow down to some form of food aid and do not cater to other needs.

Various global organisations in the field of basic social protection discuss the advantages and disadvantages of near-cash transfers in central publications (ILO 2010a:36; World Bank 2008:256–283). While vouchers or in kind benefits are not usually perceived as a better alternative to cash transfers, they are discussed as context- or goal-dependent alternatives which may be able to replace cash transfers certain situations. Neither vouchers nor in kind benefits are attributed with specifically useful effects.

Notably, cash transfers are now even regarded as an adequate policy solution in humanitarian emergencies, based on criticism of in-kind benefits, which were long regarded as the best option for emergency aid (e.g., ODI and World Vision 2008; World Bank 2008:266). This serves to illustrate the high legitimacy of cash transfers as a policy model. Payments in cash have been attributed with many advantages, for example, flexibility and regularity. Since near-cash transfers are perceived as weakly equipped with these characteristics, cash transfers are even regarded as an alternative in emergencies, where in kind transfers were traditionally the instrument of choice (ODI and World Vision 2008).

2.3.3   Universal basic income and social cash transfers

An analysis of basic social protection would be incomplete without referring to the idea of 'universal basic income', 'unconditional basic income' or 'basic income' in short, that is, a regular minimum income, individually paid to all citizens of a nation state without further preconditions or means-testing of any kind (Van Parijs 2000). The potential connection to the debate on cash transfers is obvious at first glance: basic income could be seen as an especially generous type of social cash transfer, in so far that it is conceptualised as regular monetary transfer which is intended to support general living expenses. In recent years, a vibrant public and academic debate on the effects and feasibility of a basic income has developed, both in many nation states of the Global North and South, as well as on the global level. National and global organisations which specialise in advocating this idea have sprung up, for example, the Basic Income Earth Network (BIEN 2014), which functions as a global network for advocates of global income and regularly organises international workshops and conferences.

The debate on social cash transfers, however, is conspicuously silent on basic income. With very few exceptions (e.g., ILO 2004a; Künnemann and Leonhard 2008), flagship publications by global organisations on basic social protection and cash transfers do not consider basic income as an option. This does not mean that universal benefits in general are ignored. They are, however, limited to certain categorical groups, that is, children and the elderly. As mentioned earlier, UNICEF and HelpAge advocate universal variants of family allowances and social pensions, respectively. Interestingly, advocates of 'universal basic income' often see such categorical benefits as first steps of a development towards their model, but policy literature on cash transfers does not present them as such.

This seems puzzling in the face of the continuing public debate in some nation states (e.g., Standing and Samson 2003 on a 'basic income grant' for South Africa). A long-standing problem for proponents of basic income was the lack of empirical examples: no scheme was in existence, and discussions were limited to the hypothetical level. This changed in between 2008 and 2011, when pilot projects on basic income were set up in Namibia and India.

The Namibian pilot project was started by a coalition of local civil society organisations in the small village of Ocivero and began paying a modest 'basic income grant' to all residents in 2008 (BIG coalition 2009). The organising 'BIG coalition' attributes basic income with many of the positive effects also associated with cash transfers and has published an evaluation which supports these claims (ibid.). The project gained some attention amongst German development organisations because it was supported by German development organisations and churches (Interview 1) but has not yet entered the global debate on cash transfers in any significant way, potentially due to the fact that the pilot project in Ocivero does not have the support of the Namibian government (Interview 1).

The Indian pilot project, set up by the Indian 'Self Employed Women's Association' (SEWA) and BIEN, is much more complex. In 2011, after securing partial funding from UNICEF and the UNDP, SEWA began to pay out a basic income grant to households in an urban district of Delhi and several rural villages in the district of Madhya Pradesh (BIEN 2012). In order to produce convincing evidence, the organisers of the project follow an elaborate methodological and experimental design, including control groups and multiple comparative surveys over time.

However, the organisers of these pilot projects have deliberately kept publicity at a low level, due to strong political resistance from political groups within India which claimed that the introduction of a basic income would impede other social policies, such as food subsidies. Therefore, the results of the three surveys were not made available immediately, even though the organisers of the pilot project claim that they prove positive effects of poverty reduction, increased economic activity and increased educational participation (participant observation, BIEN world congress, September 2012; Standing 2013). In how far the announced publication of a detailed report on the effects of the pilot project in India will influence global policy actors cannot be predicted – although the fact that the evaluation report on the Namibian pilot was virtually ignored in the official publications of global development organisations makes it seem unlikely that new information will radically change their position.

These observations, however, do not sufficiently answer the question why global organisations do not consider basic income as a policy option in spite of the continuing popularity of social protection and seemingly ignore relevant pilot projects – especially since UNICEF and UNDP have supported the Indian pilot project. Again, I propose that the nature of global discourses that shape and inform the debate on basic social protection can offer an explanation. All in all, global discourses should explain why certain alternatives to cash transfers such as PEPs are highly regarded, while others like in kind benefits and basic income are marginalised or entirely excluded.

In conclusion, the analysis of global policy models has illustrated that four variants of cash transfers are institutionalised to different degrees, resulting from heterogeneous processes of institutionalisation. Differences between the four models aside, three factors have emerged as crucial for the construction of a global model in general: the advocacy of a global organisation, the availability of one or several national examples from which the model is initially fashioned and finally, the usage of statistical data and country comparisons to construct the model as globally applicable. However, while these factors sufficiently explain *how* a model is successfully fashioned, they do not clarify *why* specific national examples attract the attention of global actors and *why* global models are attributed with specific design features and effects.

I argue that global discourses can provide such an explanation by showing how shifts in fundamental ideas change the perceptions of policy actors and lead them to recognise specific national schemes as useful policy. In other words, I formulate the hypothesis that shifts in global discourses open a discursive window of opportunity which policy actors can then exploit to construct new global models which fit with changed global discourses. In Chapter 3, I will attempt to illustrate how such a process took place in the case of cash transfers, when social protection emerged as a new policy paradigm in development policy during the 1990s.

3
Social Protection as a Paradigm of Development Policy (1990–2000)

In the following, I move further into the discursive background that legitimised the four variants of cash transfers analysed in Chapter 2. Following my analytical framework, I analyse whether the legitimisation of cash transfers was facilitated by the emergence of a new policy paradigm on the global level.

However, before proceeding with the analysis, it should be clarified in how far the concept of a policy paradigm can be applied on the global level. I propose that Peter Hall's original definition of a paradigm based on an analysis of national polities is not applicable to global policy, but that his approach is easily adaptable to the global level, given the openness of the original concept.

3.1 Conceptual prelude: paradigms on the global level

Peter Hall (1993:279, 291) developed the concept of policy paradigms in reference to national polities and specified one property of paradigms which can apply on the national level, but not on the global. Hall states that a national policy paradigm is a highly coherent system of ideas that prescribes which policies actors recognise as feasible and appropriate. Such a system of ideas fundamentally shapes the policy of a national government by becoming institutionalised in the form of bureaucratic procedures. Following the lead of the government, all policy actors are then influenced by the same paradigm, that is, tend to hold the same ideas and advocate the same policies. In short, a policy paradigm shapes policy because it has become institutionalised in the national government as the fixed centre of power.

This is problematic regarding global policy because there is no fixed centre of power comparable to a national government. Global policy is rather characterised by the interaction of a large number of non-state actors. Therefore, it seems unlikely that a policy paradigm on the global level is comparable to a national paradigm – it cannot become institutionalised in a similar manner, and should have less impact on policy actors. In consequence, one would expect more variation between different actors regarding their ideas and the policies they advocate.

Indeed, the analysis of policy models in Chapter 2 indicates that the positions of policy actors on cash transfers show some variation. Global development organisations agree on a basic idea of cash transfers, but specific variants of cash transfers are supported in varying degrees by different organisations. In addition, conditional cash transfers are subject to conflict between different actors: while the World Bank supports them strongly, other actors reject them entirely.

If a fixed and coherent set of ideas were to exist in the field of basic social protection, a variation in support for different policy models would be unlikely. In consequence, I assert that Hall's original definition of a policy paradigm cannot apply to this specific case of global policy. Nevertheless, Chapter 2 has demonstrated that there is a shared general idea of cash transfers. In so far, there is some evidence that global policy actors do share a set of ideas, but one that is flexible enough to allow for variation regarding policy.

Hall's original article on policy paradigms actually provides a concept which circumscribes such flexible sets of ideas: He observes that the example of national 'macroeconomic policy-making' upon which his analysis is based is quite specific, due to the 'technicality' of the subject matter which is connected to economics as a highly specialised body of knowledge and the long tenures of responsible government officials. He acknowledges that policy paradigms in fields with different structural characteristics may be of a different nature. He states that, in such a case, 'the web of ideas affecting the direction of policy will be looser and subject to more frequent variations' (Hall 1993:291).

The structural characteristics which he mentions are indeed different in the case of cash transfers: they are not associated with a specialised body of knowledge comparable to economics, and there is no world government with officials whose tenure may affect policy-making.

Therefore, I posit that the policy field of social cash transfers does indeed have a type of paradigm, but one that should not be described as a fixed and coherent set of ideas, but as a loose and variable 'web of ideas'. Hall gives no further specification of how such a loose web of ideas may be structured. In the specific case of cash transfers analysis suggests the following structure: all policy actors share an essential set of ideas but interpret these basic ideas differently and sometimes use different terminology to accentuate their specific version of a common idea. In short, the web of ideas is characterised by a tension between a baseline consensus and surrounding ideational variation.

In the following, I analyse both the baseline consensus and the ideational variation in detail and attempt to demonstrate where differences between policy actors occur and have an impact on cash transfers. In the first part of this chapter, I analyse the web of ideas in its current state, focussing on two types of ideas that characterise the paradigm which legitimises cash transfers: problem definitions and frames. I also examine in how far the tension between the baseline consensus and ideational variation is reflected in the relationships between different policy actors by asking if there is a fixed policy community that supports cash transfers. In the second part of this chapter, I trace the emergence of the web of ideas historically and attempt to show how and when the discursive window of opportunity opened and how policy actors used it to legitimise cash transfers.

3.2 The web of ideas in its current state – problem definitions, frames and policy community

I conceptualise the web of ideas as a set of loosely interrelated ideas which shape the perceptions of policy actors regarding basic social protection as a field of policy. In the case of cash transfers, two types of ideas in particular shape the perceptions of global development organisations. First, problem definitions, that is, ideas on the types of shared problems that policy needs to solve. Crucially, the way in which problems are defined has an impact on the type of solution that is perceived as useful – the design of the four policy models analysed earlier is shaped by the way problems have been defined by policy actors.

Second, frames, that is, established ideas that policy actors use to portray policy models positively, by putting them in the context of shared values or commonly recognised goals. However, frames have a mostly legitimating function in the case of cash transfers and do not influence the design of policy models in a significant way.

3.2.1 Problem definitions

The web of ideas contains definitions of four social problems which cash transfers are expected to mitigate: poverty, social inequities, social disintegration and structural problems of social security. Regarding problem definitions, the baseline consensus is that virtually all policy actors perceive these four phenomena as problems in need of solution.

The ideational variation is based upon different perceptions of *why* the indicated problems are problematic at all: each problem definition has several facets which construct the problem differently (see Table 3.1). Poverty, for instance, is perceived as problematic because it clashes with moral values, because it inhibits economic growth and because it is a violation of human rights. Similar patterns can be found for each of the three other problem definitions. Crucially, different policy actors put emphasis on different facets of the same problem, leading them to focus on different effects of cash transfers.

3.2.1.1   Poverty

One of the most fundamental and unquestioned assumptions in global development policy is that poverty, especially in its most severe forms, is the most pressing global problems and in urgent need of a solution (e.g., DFID 2005:5, 2011:6; ILO 2010a:13). As indicated earlier, there is ideational variation around the baseline consensus that poverty is a pressing problem, stemming from the fact that different actors have different positions on why poverty is a problem. It is possible to distinguish three facets of poverty as a social problem: a moral facet, an economic facet and a human rights facet. Most policy actors tend to emphasise one specific facet when speaking about poverty, leading to variations in their policy.

Table 3.1   Problem definitions

Problem definition	Main idea	Facets
Poverty	The material and social deprivation of a large share of the global population	– Moral problem – Economic problem – Human rights problem
Social inequities	Unequal distribution of resources and opportunities between different social groups	– Moral problem – Economic problem
Social disintegration	The destruction of social trust and social networks that make societies cohesive and stable	– Economic problem – Security problem
Structural problems of social security	Inadequate administration and funding of social security systems	– Human rights problem – Security problem

The moral facet of poverty constructs this problem as an infringement of globally applicable norms and values. Global policy documents, for instance, describe poverty as a violation of 'common decency' and argue for action on the grounds of 'our common humanity' (Commission for Africa 2005:29, 66). Sometimes a generalised moral duty to help 'those less well off then ourselves' is identified (DFID 1997:5). It should be noted that this is a traditional and well-established definition of poverty as a problem, which can be traced back for several decades (see, e.g., the eminent UNICEF publication 'Adjustment with a Human Face' in Cornia et al. 1987:141). In fact, most, if not all, actors in the field of social protection refer to poverty as a moral problem in some way, even though they may differ in the values that they use to frame this idea. DFID in particular has been employing a simple moral problem definition of poverty since the late 1990s, calling global poverty a 'scandal' or a 'shame' and evoking the general duty to help the poor mentioned earlier (DFID 1997:5, 2006b:iii, 2009:16–17). References to specific values such as 'social justice' and 'social solidarity' can also be found (e.g., ILO 2008:6; UNICEF 2012:8), but the concept of 'equity' is much more common, usually indicating equality of opportunities. 'Equity' is mentioned by virtually all organisations and also functions to define other problems and goals besides poverty, as explained later (DFID 2011:6; HAI 2006c:6; ILO 2006a:11, 2010a:45; UNICEF 2012:4; World Bank 2006:2, 2009a:20, 2012:i).

The economic facet of poverty is contested, in contrast to the widely shared moral facet. The nature of poverty as an economic problem is emphasised by the World Bank, which identifies a lack of resources in the lower strata of society as an obstacle to optimal economic efficiency. This is conceptualised as a 'market failure' which leads to needlessly low or even false investments, since the poor are unable to make use of economic opportunities due to lack of human capital and resources (World Bank 2006:2, 93, 2009a:49, 56). Therefore, the optimum of potential investments is not achieved and the situation is detrimental to aggregate economic growth.

Other organisations also define poverty as economically problematic because they perceive the poor as having unused productive and human potential – few organisations beside the World Bank, however, emphasise this strongly, and a connection to aggregate growth is usually a secondary concern (DFID 2005:5, 7, 21, 2011:3, 15; ILO 2001:7, 2009b:36, 2010a:33). Nevertheless, cash transfers are expected to have positive effects on the local economy. It is expected that the poor will immediately use most of the transfer to satisfy their basic needs, leading to an increased demand on local markets. In that sense, many actors see poverty as an economic problem from a different perspective – the lack of consumption by the poor deprives others of economic opportunities, as general purchasing power is low (e.g., DFID 2005:17, 2011:22, 35; HAI 2004:31; ILO 2010a:103; OECD-DAC 2009:45; UNICEF and ODI 2009:20).

The human rights facet of poverty has become widespread in global policy since the early 2000s but is selectively ignored by the World Bank. The basic idea is simple, referring to global human rights treaties, particularly the Universal Declaration of Human Rights and the International Covenant on Economic, Social and Cultural Rights. Policy actors identify poverty as a violation of rights and entitlements specified therein (DFID 2005:6–7; HAI 2004:10, 23; ILO 2009b:9, 38).

Even though neither of the two treaties contains an explicit right to be free from poverty, policy actors interpret articles 22, 23 and 25 of the Universal Declaration and articles 9 and 11 of the International Covenant on Economic, Social and Cultural Rights (ICESCR) – the right to social security and the right to an adequate standard of living – as containing an individual right not to be poor. This is seen to entail a duty of state parties to the ICESCR to prevent and reduce poverty (e.g., DFID 2005:6, 25; ILO 2009b:38).

The human rights perspective on poverty is part of a recent movement towards 'rights-based approaches' in development policy. Non-governmental organisations such as HelpAge International have been working with rights-based arguments for poverty reduction since the early 2000s and have taken up cash transfers as an option to fulfil human rights (e.g., HAI 2000:4–5, 2004:23–24). The ILO also works with a rights-based approach to social protection in general but with a focus on the human right to social security (see later).

Crucially, the World Bank does not define poverty as a human rights violation and does not frame cash transfers as a fulfilment of human rights. This is a source of conflict with other policy actors. Conditional cash transfers are frequently regarded as being at odds with human rights and therefore are rejected by certain policy actors. Since the World Bank tends to under-emphasise human rights in general and does not mention them in the context of cash transfers, it does not share this assessment.

In sum, the definition of poverty as a social problem is complex and multi-faceted. Naturally, the distinction between the different facets is analytical – empirically they are closely entwined. A simple moral condemnation of poverty is the undercurrent of most policy documents.

Actors who also construct poverty as a human rights problem can easily combine these two facets, by referring both to the moral repugnance of poverty and a global obligation to reduce poverty embodied in international human rights treaties (e.g., DFID 2005). A moral argument against poverty is also often closely combined with economic definitions, resulting in a description of the problem which gives both normative and utilitarian reasons for poverty reduction (e.g., ILO 2010a).

In spite of the frequency of such combinations, policy actors do differ in the relative emphasis which they put on certain aspects. The World Bank's leading argument is clearly that poverty is detrimental to general economic development, a position which the other development banks share, while the ILO, DFID and the GIZ, for instance, combine it with moral and human rights facets. Conversely, many NGOs like HelpAge International and UN organisations like UNICEF construct poverty as a human rights problem and barely refer to the economic facet.

In consequence, different global organisations emphasise different effects of cash transfers: the World Bank consistently perceives social cash transfers as a tool to facilitate economic growth (e.g., World Bank 2006:2, 93, 2009a:49, 56). The ILO, UNICEF and DFID also expect cash transfers to foster economic growth but add that cash transfers are also morally right because poverty is generally repugnant and a violation of human rights (DFID 2005:5–7, 21, 25, 2011:3, 15; ILO 2001:7, 2009b:36–38, 2010a:10, 33; UNICEF 2012:4; UNICEF and ODI 2009:20). HelpAge, in turn, rarely advocates cash transfers as an instrument of economic growth but rather as a fulfilment of human rights (HAI 2004:23–24).

3.2.1.2 Social inequities

Virtually all policy actors define three variants of social inequality as a problem, which can be analytically subsumed under the overarching category of 'inequities'. First, there is a concern that socio-economic inequality, that is, unequal distribution of income or wealth, could be a problem (DFID 2005:5, 7, 13, 18; HAI 2004:2, 2006c:4; ILO 2008:5–6; World Bank 2008:1, 12, 2011:1). This does not usually translate into strongly redistributive policy, since the problem definition is connected to the theme of severe poverty. Policy actors are concerned with the position of the poor relative to the rest of society but seldom care about income distribution above the poverty line. Second, many policy actors talk about an inequality of opportunities, not income (e.g., DFID 2006b:57, 2009:71; OECD-DAC 2001:44; World Bank 2006:xi, 2009a:20). Third, the unequal treatment of specific categorical groups is treated as problematic, particularly the unequal treatment of women and girls. The unequal access of women to education is a particularly salient issue, both morally and economically (ILO 2001:3; OECD-DAC 2001:40; UNICEF and ODI 2009:14; World Bank 2006:2).

Even though there is thus a baseline consensus, that social inequities are a problem, there is also ideational variation, again stemming from different positions on *why* social inequities are problematic. The problem definition of social inequities has two facets, a moral facet and an economic facet. There is less variation regarding these facets than in the case of poverty – significantly, there is a strong consensus on the economic facet.

The moral facet of social inequities constructs the problem as a violation of globally applicable values like 'social justice', 'fairness' and 'equity'. Virtually all policy actors agree that social inequities clash with commonly held values but there is some variation in the values which social inequities are perceived to violate.

Empirically, the moral facet of social inequities is usually closely intertwined with moral facet of poverty, and the two are hard to separate analytically (e.g., ILO 2004b:x, 8). There are, however, differences between the different types of social inequality subsumed under social inequities. In the case of economic inequality, the construction of the problem is basically congruent with poverty as a moral problem, since policy actors focus on the poverty side of inequality in any case. This entails an emphasis of values which are less demanding than a strict concept of equality – ideas such as 'fairness' and 'equity' essentially refer to an equality of opportunities, not outcomes.

The moral condemnation of the unequal treatment of women, however, is different because it refers to stronger, more demanding values. In the case of women there is a strong reference to the equality of genders as an inherently valuable goal which goes further than mere reduction of poverty – it is frequently pointed out that paying cash benefits to the female members of households or the mothers of targeted children will increase their social status in the family and their personal autonomy from patriarchal structures. Thus, the definition of gender disparities as a moral problem also has wider implications towards the role of women and the distribution of power in society (DFID 2005:16, 2011:6, 60; ILO 2001: 69).

While the majority of actors define social inequities as a moral problem, there are differences in the values which are employed. While 'equity' has certainly become the most widely shared value in social protection policy, it is mainly championed by the World Bank (2012) – consider the second social protection sector strategy, named 'Resilience, Equity and Opportunity', which clearly evokes values of 'fairness' and equality of opportunities. Other organisations, notably the ILO and UNICEF (2012:8), also consistently employ 'equity' to define social inequities as a problem but also refer to 'social justice'. The ILO in particular champions 'social justice', which implies an interest in economic outcomes, not just opportunities. The ILO (2008:1) declaration on 'Social Justice for a Fair Globalisation', for instance, demands 'improved and fair outcomes for all' and names the 'promoting of social justice' as an original organisational mandate (see also ILO 2010a). Conversely, HelpAge International tends to focus purely on 'social justice' and rarely emphasises 'equity' (e.g., HAI 2004:11).

The economic facet of social inequities constructs the different types of social inequalities as problematic because they are perceived to inhibit economic activity and economic growth (e.g., World Bank 2001c:57, 2009a:49).

The basic issue, which virtually all policy actors perceive in a similar manner, is a lack of economic activity by the poor, caused by a lack of resources and human capital (DFID 2006b:1; World Bank 2006:2, 7, 20–23). Many policy actors argue that sustainable economic growth at an optimal level is impossible without at least basic measure of redistribution, since a society as a whole cannot reach its full potential without giving equal opportunities to all citizens. Both the World Bank and the ILO have prominently taken up this position, the former with the World development report 2006, titled 'Equity', the latter by declaring 'Growing with equity' as a primary goal of policy (World Bank 2006; ILO 2009b:35, 2010a:45).

Other organisations like DFID and UNICEF also share the economic facet of social inequities, but do not formulate it as elaborately or explicitly as the two large IOs (HAI 2006a:7) – in fact, DFID quotes the World Development Report 2006 in regards to this issue (e.g., DFID 2005:7; see also HAI 2004:11 for a comparable reference to the ILO research).

In sum, the problem definition of social inequities is less faceted than the problem definition of poverty. There is also less variation between policy actors in the emphasis which is put on different facets. In consequence, policy actors expect only slightly different effects from cash transfers because virtually all organisations see cash transfers as a tool of redistribution to mitigate inequities. For example, while the World Bank aims to equalise opportunities and offer better life chances to the poor, the ILO additionally advocates a reduction of income inequality, that is, an equality of outcomes (e.g., Holzmann and Jorgensen 2000:20; ILO 2008:1; World Bank 2012).

3.2.1.3   Social disintegration

The majority of policy actors also perceive the disintegration of social structures, 'social peace' or 'social cohesion', that is, mutual trust and cooperation in society, as a significant problem that basic social protection can solve. Social disintegration is generally seen as a result of poverty and social inequities and of the impact of risks, shocks and crises (as defined in the social risk management approach of the World Bank, seen previously). The impact of these various social problems and hazards is expected to increase in crime, to destabilise families and civil society, via lack of mutual trust, and to deteriorate relations between the government and its citizens, due to the perceived incompetence of the state in solving social problems (DFID 2009:15, 71; ILO 2009b:1, 2010a:42, 108; OECD-DAC 2009:25; World Bank 2008:431). The latter effect in particular is deemed crucial: low government legitimacy is expected to further decrease the capacity for appropriate policy response or political reform. This is strongly connected to the idea that social protection can help in the task of 'nation building' by building up trust in government and a feeling of security and stability (DFID 2011:16, 42; Holzmann and Jorgensen 2000:23; HAI 2006a:31; ILO 2010a:108, 110, 2010b:31).

All in all, there is a baseline consensus that poverty, social inequities, risk, crises and shocks are a threat to the stability of societies, but different policy actors once again assume different positions on *why* social disintegration is problematic, leading to ideational variation. The problem definition of social disintegration has two facets: social disintegration as an economic problem and social disintegration as a security problem.

The economic facet of social disintegration concerns the background conditions of economic activity. Social disintegration is widely perceived to inhibit economic activity and thus economic growth. The argument is that social disintegration is synonymous with a social environment lacking in trust, stability and security, which inhibits economic activity on three levels: (1) local economic actors will not feel secure enough to undertake risky, but profitable investments; (2) foreign investors are perceived to avoid countries with such unstable conditions, leading to a shortage of capital; and (3) social cleavages may distort the distribution of public spending in an economically inefficient manner. As a result, the economy will not function efficiently, lacking sufficient social foundation (DFID 2009:15; 2011:44; ILO 2001:42; 2006a:27; 2009b:35;

OECD-DAC 2009:18; World Bank 2001c:127). Furthermore, policy actors assume that a non-integrated society, for example, in 'fragile' or 'failed states', will tend to refuse political reforms which would be economically useful, since government is too weak to legitimise initial economic or social costs (DFID 2005:25; ILO 2009b:7; World Bank2008:3). As an ultimate result, 'social disintegration' is believed to lower the overall economic strength and growth rate, unless governments take stabilising countermeasures, for example, social protection.

The security facet of social disintegration mostly remains implicit in policy documents. Some policy actors see social disintegration in itself as a problem of security in the sense of public safety, since the idea of disintegration is at least partially synonymous with an increase of crime. As such, social disintegration is simply perceived as a threat to the livelihoods of the people in developing countries (e.g., UN 2011:5, 47–50; World Bank/Poverty Group 1999:18).

A smaller subset of actors, however, goes further and constructs the security issue as a problem with global implications. Unsafe or unstable social conditions in nation states are perceived to spread insecurity to neighbouring states and even the rest of the world, including the Global North. The DFID, for instance, warns that social disintegration may make countries 'hotbeds' for the regional spread of armed conflicts and the growth of international terrorist cells which may target the Global North (Commission for Africa 2005:23, 38, 84, 159; DFID 1997:67, 2005:8, 2009:17). Similarly, the UN Department of Economic and Social Affairs warns of the long-term consequences of the global economic crisis since 2008, including a global increase in violence, civic unrest and mental illness (UN 2011:57–59).

In summary, there is some ideational variation around the baseline consensus in the case of social disintegration, but not as much as in the case of poverty. Most relevant policy actors agree that social disintegration is an economic problem, including DFID, the World Bank and the ILO. The World Bank and the ILO can be identified as the two strongest proponents of the economic facet of social disintegration. There is little difference between the position of these two organisations on the economic facet, except in terminology. While the World Bank usually speaks of lacking 'social cohesion' or sometimes lack of 'social capital', the ILO often points out that cash transfers can facilitate 'social peace'.

3.2.1.4 *Structural problems of social security*

Finally, many policy actors perceive that social protection systems function inadequately because of bad administration and lack of political support and do not deliver their expected outcomes, for example, poverty reduction. Essentially, this problem definition circumscribes structural problems of social security as a general idea, but analytically, it is easier to distinguish two sub-problems that specify the perceived issue: a coverage gap and a fragmentation gap.

The first sub-problem is generally called the 'coverage gap' by many global organisations that regularly point out that a majority of the world population, usually estimated at 80 per cent, is not covered by any system of social security, be it contributory or non-contributory (HelpAge and IDPM 2003:7; HAI 2004: 24; ILO 2009b:1, 24, 2010c:7; World Bank 2009b, 2012:22–24). The problem definition of a 'coverage gap' was originally an outcome of a debate on social insurance and the informal sector in developing countries in the 1990s which was led by the ILO (e.g., ILO 1999) – it was redefined to encompass non-contributory benefits in the early 2000s (see Section 3.3). Nevertheless, the idea of a 'coverage gap' still implies that not only cash transfers, but also contributory insurance systems should be extended globally. As such, it is connected to an agenda which transcends the issue of basic social protection, spearheaded by the ILO, which uses the 'global social floor' to advocate the extension of cash transfers and, in the long-term, of social insurance.

The second sub-problem, the 'fragmentation gap' (compare World Bank 2012), does not refer to the extension of social security, but rather to its administration, which is regarded as uncoordinated and fragmented. Most policy actors currently define the state of social security administration and policy in the Global South as problematic since it does not follow a 'systemic approach' (ILO 2011:130; UNICEF 2012:17–19, 42–46; World Bank 2009a:99, 2012:15). That is to say, while single social security programmes may be well planned and implemented, coordination between them is lacking, leading to adverse effects and unnecessary costs.

In sum, there is a strong baseline consensus among policy actors that lack of political commitment and inadequate administration cause social security to function inefficiently. The extension and quality of social security benefits is not perceived as optimal due to structural reasons. However, there is again ideational variation on *why* structural problems of social security are problematic. The problem definition of structural problems of social security has two facets: a security facet and a human rights facet. These facets do not apply to both sub-problems: the 'coverage gap' is perceived as a security and a human rights problem, while the fragmentation of social security administration is only regarded as a security problem.

The security facet of the coverage gap and the fragmentation gap deals with psychological effects of social security. The ILO perceives the need for security, that is, stable and predictable living conditions, as a human constant. It is claimed that people need institutions that offer them stable and secure conditions. Otherwise the threat of risks and crises is assumed to drive people to safeguard their resources, preventing economic investments and sharing of resources. That is, economic activity and the development of social ties and social trust are inhibited. Since this is seen to affect economic activity and the stability of societies in general, the ILO perceives structural problems of social security as a cause of social disintegration (ILO 2004b:4, 2006a:9, 2009a:87, 2010a:5). The ILO deems social insurance and cash transfers to be the best instruments to foster a sense of stability which fulfils the human need for security. Only few other actors seem to perceive structural problems of security as a security problem similar to the ILO (see e.g., World Bank/ Poverty Group 1999:7, 18).

The human rights facet of the coverage gap frames the global lack of coverage as a violation of rights enshrined in international human rights treaties, that is, the Universal Declaration of Human Rights (UDHR) and the ICESCR. The main point of reference is the right to social security, usually deduced from article 22 UDHR and article 9 ICESCR (e.g., DFID 2005:7; ILO 2010a:10–13). From this perspective, all citizens of state parties to the treaties have an individual entitlement, both to non-contributory transfers and social insurance. As in the case of poverty as a human rights problem, the treaties are seen as the legally binding embodiment of a global consensus. The ILO, having originally coined the term 'coverage gap', plays a special role in advocating the human rights facet. In addition to an official rights-based approach to development, the ILO also emphasises its own conventions and standards on social security, especially convention number 102 on 'Minimum Standards of Social Security' (ILO 1952) and the recent Social Protection Floors Recommendation (ILO 2014b). This is used to strengthen the pressure exerted by human rights alone. Nation states who have ratified the ILO conventions on social security are perceived as having further confirmed the rights of their citizens to social security, so that a lack of coverage is even more problematic (e.g., ILO 2010a:10–13).

In summary, the position of different policy actors on the different sub-problems and facets of structural problems of social security is fairly complex. The ILO is clearly the strongest promoter of the entire problem definition, including both sub-problems and facets. Notably, the ILO originally developed and popularised the idea of a 'coverage gap'. With the development of the 'global social protection floor' as a guiding concept, the ILO also began to talk about the fragmentation of social security as a problem because the floor essentially consists of a coordinated set of social cash transfers across the life cycle and is thus a systemic approach to social security.

Conversely, the World Bank long ignored the idea of a coverage gap and chose to focus on administrative problems of social security systems (e.g., World Bank 2009a:7–8). However, in 2009 the World Bank published an anthology on social pensions titled 'Closing the Coverage Gap', which also contained contributions by the ILO staff (World Bank 2009b). What is more, the second Social Protection Sector Strategy of the World Bank also defines the coverage gap as a problem but further mentions two other gaps: a 'flexibility gap' and an 'opportunity gap', both constructed as an outcome of bad administration (World Bank 2012:22–27).

3.2.2   Frames

While the four problem definitions mentioned here have substantial roles in the construction of policy models, there are three more concepts that function as *frames*. That is to say, while these frames are used to legitimise cash transfers, their content is mostly peripheral to the design of policy, and they are rarely discussed in detail. Policy models are put into the context of frames in order to increase their legitimacy as globally applicable instruments. The web of ideas in the field of basic social protection contains three such frames: human rights, the Millennium Development Goals and the idea of globalisation (see Table 3.2).

Virtually all policy actors use these frames in a similar manner. In so far, they are part of the baseline consensus. The frame of human rights is the sole exception. Here there is ideational variation to the extent that the World Bank selectively ignores this frame and legitimises

Table 3.2   Frames

Frame	Framing social cash transfers as:
Human rights	morally appropriate on a global scale.
Millennium Development Goals	rational means to globally agreed and quantifiable ends.
Globalisation	tools to modify an inevitable process of social change.

conditional cash transfers with other ideas, while different organisations use human rights to de-legitimise CCT.

3.2.2.1 *Human rights*

The importance of human rights in the career of cash transfers is evident, as two of the major social problems described earlier have a human rights facet and as important global organisations like the ILO now follow a rights-based approach. Nevertheless, policy actors do not normally discuss fundamental questions of human rights in connection with cash transfers. As mentioned earlier, select articles of the Universal Declaration of Human Rights and the International Covenant on Economic, Social and Cultural Rights are frequently quoted as justifications for the introduction of social cash transfers and serve to construct social problems.

Such references, numerous as they may be, remain limited to the context of policy. That is to say that human rights in question have little influence on the actual structure of the policy models – human rights are a *frame* in the sense that they merely support the basic argument for social cash transfers without significantly affecting the content of policy. This is not to say that human rights are in any way less important than problem definitions like poverty, but rather that they serve a qualitatively different function. The contextualisation of social protection and specific models of social cash transfers with human rights is an important source of legitimacy since a connection to human rights supports the claim that such policies are universally adequate and necessary (DFID 2005:6–7; HAI 2004:10; ILO 2001:56–57, 2009b:1, 2011:10–15, 22).

However, it should be noted that this is an active interpretation of the existing human rights treaties in the case of cash transfers. While both the UDHR and the ICESCR do contain a general right to social security and a right to an adequate standard of living, they do not specify a right to basic social security. The first official policy document which indicates such an entitlement is the ILO's Social Protection Floors Recommendation, which is not a binding obligation (ILO 2012b). Furthermore, the original idea of a recommendation on a global social floor was changed to specific 'national social protection floors' during ILO negotiations, weakening the claim that a single set of policies may be universally desirable (see ILO 2012a).

Nevertheless, policy actors have been referring to the original human rights treaties and associated documents, for example, ILO standards to justify cash transfers from at least 2005 onwards and assume that existing rights provide a sufficient basis. Policy documents often begin

with a short paragraph that references a variety of human rights documents, and specific sections dealing with a rights-based justification for
cash transfers are equally common.

The sole exception to this rule is conditional cash transfers. The
conditions which are an inherent part of the model have always been
contested from a human rights perspective. In fact, as indicated, the
World Bank, the biggest promoter of conditional cash transfers, does
not usually frame its own social protection policy in terms of human
rights. Other organisations, however, evidently employ human rights
to frame CCT negatively. Conditions are portrayed as a violation of an
entitlement to cash transfers, which supposedly follows from international human rights treaties.

3.2.2.2   *Millennium Development Goals*

A second idea which is consistently used to frame cash transfers positively are the Millennium Development Goals. At first glance, this may
be surprising since the MDGs themselves do not contain any reference
to social protection, let alone social cash transfers. However, the first
MDG, to halve global poverty by 2015 (UN 2012a), seems to have facilitated the global agenda of poverty reduction which prepared the ground
for cash transfers.

Indeed, most policy actors have used the Millennium Development
Goals to frame social cash transfers since the early 2000s because they
perceive the MDGs as the embodiment of a global consensus to reduce
poverty. As in the case of human rights, the MDGs merely serve to
support arguments for the general need of basic social protection and
are rarely used to construct specific features of policy models. The
frame in itself, however, often dramatises the situation, as policy actors
frequently point out the danger of failing to achieve the MDGs in light
of current statistical data on global poverty, child mortality and health
(DFID 2005:5; HAI 2004:10–11; HAI and IDPM 2003:22; ILO 2009b:3,
2010a:13–14; UNICEF and ODI 2009:18–19; World Bank 2003b). Social
protection and cash transfers are then constructed as the best method
to facilitate fulfilment of the MDGs due to their ability to reduce
poverty.

In contrast to the moral rationale of human rights, the MDGs therefore rather function as benchmarks for the outcomes of global development policy and furnish proponents of cash transfers with a technocratic
rationale. That is to say, while human rights frame social cash transfers
as morally and legally appropriate, the MDGs serve to frame them as
rationally feasible and useful since they are perceived as the best means

to reach a quantifiable end (e.g., DFID 2005:18, 33; GTZ 2005; ILO and WHO 2009a:1–4, 11; UNICEF 2012:1).

I assert that the new post-2015 development goals which are currently being discussed by the global community will continue to provide such a technocratic rationale to social protection. The first suggestions for new development goals give a prominent role to social protection in reducing global poverty (UN 2014).

3.2.2.3 Globalisation

Last but not least, the idea of globalisation is also used to frame social protection and social cash transfers as necessary policies. In general, policy actors follow the common understanding of the term 'globalisation as a process in which international connections multiply and become more intense, causing social and economic change at an accelerating pace (DFID 2009:6; ILO 2009b:27; OECD-DAC 2009:132; World Bank 2001a:1, 2012:1). On the one hand, this is seen as a primary cause behind the various social problems described earlier. Globalisation is seen to threaten national economies and local livelihoods, causing poverty as well as exacerbating inequities and social disintegration. Notably, the increased global interconnectivity is also perceived to facilitate the spread and transmission of risks, crises and shocks, for example, in the case of economic downturns 'travelling' from one nation state to others (e.g., DFID 2011:8; UN 2011:19).

On the other hand, globalisation is also described as an opportunity for stronger economic growth, which may ultimately help to solve social problems and lessen risk (e.g., Holzmann and Jorgensen 2000:5; ILO 2008:5). In general, the process of globalisation is described as inevitable, and possible causes are not discussed. Due to its ambiguous nature, policy actors do not suggest to stop globalisation, but rather to shape its consequences and to legitimise its outcomes via appropriate policies – take, for instance, the ILO's concept of a 'fair globalisation' (ILO 2001:46, 2009a:87; ILO 2004b).

Because of their assumed effects on social problems and their redistributive nature, social cash transfers are seen as ideal policy models to mitigate and legitimise globalisation. The rationale is that nation states need to be economically and socially open to their environment in order to be able to compete and succeed in the process of globalisation. However, this will also expose them to the negative sides of globalisation, producing 'losers', who suffer from social problems, exposure to risk and feelings of insecurity. In such a situation, social protection measures are expected to mitigate the consequences of globalisation, provide a feeling of security and placate the losers' by redistributing some of the gains. In so far, cash transfers are generally seen as necessary policies to balance out the effects of globalisation – an assessment shared by many policy actors but formulated most explicitly by the ILO and the World Bank (e.g., ILO 2004b:vii; World Bank 2003b:20).

In sum, globalisation serves as a frame by tying the problem definitions to a common cause, whose own definition is vague and thus compatible with the different political positions of global organisations. Not least, 'globalisation' as an underlying process behind all social problems offers the web of ideas a useful background narrative which illustrates why and how striving for certain policy goals with certain policy models makes sense. Social cash transfers become part of a larger process of social change in which the inevitable progress of globalisation is moulded according to values of equity, resulting in increased welfare for all. While this background narrative is certainly important to legitimise social protection as a whole, it does not influence the details of policy models, which are rather based upon the definitions of specific social problems.

This concludes the analysis of the web of ideas in its current state. In sum, the baseline consensus on social protection embodied in the global policy paradigm can be described as 'growth through redistribution'. The baseline consensus is based on the widely shared assumption that poverty, social inequities and social disintegration are economic problems because they inhibit the economic activity of the poor. It is further assumed by most policy actors that the transfer of resources to the poor will mitigate the three mentioned social problems sufficiently to activate the dormant economic potential of the poor, thus facilitating aggregate economic growth. Virtually all policy actors agree that social cash transfers are the appropriate means to redistribute resources to the poor in this manner. More generally, social protection has thus become a paradigm in the field of development policy.

The positive effect of cash transfers on the poor and economic growth is perceived to result from two mechanisms. Firstly, the transfers are expected to foster the individual economic potential of the poor, which is generally conceptualised as human capital (e.g., DFID 2006a, 2011:5; ILO 2010a:16; UNICEF and ODI 2009:7; World Bank 2009a:1). The increased human capital of the poor is then expected to have a positive impact on aggregate economic growth (e.g., Commission for Africa 2005:27; DFID 2011:3; ILO 2004b:62, 2009a:124–125, 2011:16–18; World Bank 2001c: 57; 2008:14–16, 431). As illustrated in Chapter 2, cash transfers are expected to promote the human capital of beneficiaries.

Secondly, cash transfers are perceived as offering security to benefici-aries – see the security facets in the problem definitions of social disin-tegration and structural problems of social security. To reiterate, the regularity of transfers is widely perceived as a core characteristic of cash transfers – the regular receipt of cash is expected to give beneficiaries a sense of stability by protecting them from risks and crises and moti-vate them to undertake more risky economic investments (e.g., DFID 2011:6–9; ILO 2009a:86; World Bank 2009a:26, 197).

These two mechanisms in the baseline consensus indicate which global discourses and more general schemes of interpretation have aided in constructing the web of ideas and the four policy models. Apparently, policy actors see the poor as potential contributors to economic growth, as long as their individual potential – that is, human capital – is fostered and they are protected from ubiquitous harmful events – that is, risks and crises. This indicates that global discourses on poverty and on risks and crises may play a role in the case of cash transfers. This utilitarian rationale for cash transfers which portrays them as an instrument of economic growth is widely complemented by a reference to human rights, which give a strong moral rationale for cash transfers – they are perceived as the fulfilment of essential entitlements of each indi-vidual human being. This is illustrated by the human rights facets in the problem definitions of poverty and structural problems of social security. In so far, it seems likely that human rights generally played an essential role in the legitimisation of social cash transfers, indicating that a human rights discourse may also be important.

3.2.3 Policy community

The preceding analysis suggests that policy actors in the field of basic social protection share a policy paradigm that helps to construct social cash transfers as policy models. In so far, the legitimacy of cash transfers is evidently based on structures on the level of ideas – but in how far is the policy paradigm mirrored by social structures, that is, relation-ships between policy actors? As indicated in Chapter 1, I specifically ask whether there is a stable policy community in the field of social protec-tion, which may give specific organisations that belong to an inner circle institutionalised power in the field of cash transfers.

An examination of the relationships between different global organi-sations that participate in the debate on social protection shows that networks of actors do exist in the case of cash transfers but that they are not institutionalised to an extent of a policy community in the narrow sense of the term.

To be true, certain organisations have communicated regularly about cash transfers since the early 2000s. Especially a number of British organisations stand out in this respect: DFID, based on the new initiatives of the Blair government, drew on research by the ODI and the IDS to develop a position on social protection and facilitated an exchange of ideas with the ILO and the World Bank in the early 2000s. DFID also gave funding to HelpAge International, which was employed to advocate social pensions and other cash transfers. The Livingstone Conference in 2006 (see Chapter 2), which also involved the GTZ and the ILO, is a good example of the cooperative activities that facilitated the career of cash transfers.

However, as mentioned earlier, there is no encompassing consensus on cash transfers, and different organisations tend to advocate the policy model that best fits their preferred target group. No single organisation or set of organisations can be identified as an inner circle that prescribes policy to other actors. Instead, I propose that policy actors in the field of basic social protection are organised into different, overlapping issue communities that coordinate internally to represent the interests of specific target groups or specific policy goals and therefore advocate certain variants of cash transfers. Four issue communities can be differentiated, each of which primarily advocates one model of cash transfers.

The first issue community, led by UNICEF, is concerned with children's rights and the welfare of children. This issue community emphasises the vulnerabilities of children affected by AIDS, either as sufferers of the disease or as orphans of HIV-positive parents. Besides UNICEF, World Bank staff in the 'Human Development Network' have advocated more support to children affected by HIV/AIDS (e.g., Levine 2001; UNICEF 2007). The UNICEF has reinforced the connection between social protection and children by cooperating with Save the Children United Kingdom, HelpAge International and the IDS – considering the seminal, UNICEF funded study 'Making Cash Count' which emphasises the beneficial effects of cash transfers, especially social pensions, on children (HAI et al. 2005). The major focus of this community, however, is the widely accepted UNICEF concept of 'child-sensitive social protection' which has been co-signed by HelpAge, Save the Children United Kingdom, DFID, the IDS, the ODI, the ILO and the World Bank, amongst others (UNICEF et al. 2009). These actors all advocate family allowances in some form, even though only UNICEF has expressed support for universal, non-means-tested benefits (see UNICEF and ODI 2009).

The second issue community, led by the World Bank, focuses on the promotion of economic growth and market-based solutions to poverty. Besides the World Bank, regional development banks such as the Inter-American Development Bank and the Asian Development Bank (e.g., ADB 2008; Bouillon and Tejerina 2006), as well as several think tanks like the International Food Policy Research Institute (IFPRI; see Maluccio 2003; Skoufias and Parker 2001). This set of actors mainly advocates conditional cash transfers as a tool for the promotion of human capital, that is, the development of national economies – the World Bank's flagship publications on safety nets and CCT synthesise the relevant body of knowledge (World Bank 2008, 2009a) and claim that there is an 'International CCT Community of Practice', referring to a number of international conferences (World Bank 2009a:97). However, as pointed out earlier, many global organisations who engage conditional cash transfers as a concept are highly critical of this policy model. Some, such as DFID, do still regard it as a viable option under certain circumstances and can be regarded as participants in this issue community (e.g., DFID 2011:49–51)

The third issue community, led by HelpAge International, is concerned with older persons' rights and the welfare of older persons. A varied set of actors, including Save the Children United Kingdom, UNICEF and DFID, strongly cooperated with HAI in the early 2000s, as explained earlier – this issue community is strongly connected to the one concerned with children. Indeed, a senior staff member of HelpAge International reports that she easily transitioned from working for child-centred organisations to advocating the rights of older people when she was hired by HelpAge in 1999, since a similar model of thinking is employed in both fields (Interview 5). After all both issue communities advocate the rights of life-cycle groups. Contact with former employers in child-centred organisations enabled HelpAge staff to form strategic alliances with child-centred organisations in the early 2000s (ibid.), involving new initiatives like the 'Grow up free from poverty coalition', founded by Gordon Brown of the British Labour Party in 2000 (GFP 2012). This coalition mostly involved British NGOs, but also UNICEF, United Kingdom. The further work of HelpAge also drew in the ILO and the World Bank. As such, this issue community is relatively well established, even though HAI staff claim that it is still relatively difficult to advocate for older persons' rights in wider development policy (Interview 4; Interview 5).

The fourth issue community, led by the ILO, advocates basic social protection as a human right and is focused in promoting the concept of a 'global social floor'. Because the 'floor' encompasses a complementary set of cash transfers and other instruments of social protection, this issue community essentially advocates all variants of cash transfers equally (e.g., ILO 2010; UNICEF 2012). The issue community is evidently centred on the ILO, but UNICEF has officially endorsed the 'floor' and taken it up as part of its own social protection strategy and can thus be regarded as a member of the community. Many other global organisations have also publicly expressed support for the 'global social floor' as part of official UN policy, for example, the WHO (ILO and WHO 2009a, 2009b), and thus participate in this community. What is more, the UN Chief Executives Board officially adopted the 'floor' as an initiative to counteract the global financial crisis in 2009, giving strong support to the ILO in establishing a community of organisations that advocate basic social protection (UN-CEB 2009).

Even though these four issue communities can be separated analytically, global organisations are naturally not limited to participation in one single community. In fact, several global organisations are notable for their participation in several communities and may in fact function as brokers between the different networks of policy actors. Firstly, DFID: starting in the early 2000s this organisation began to support many activities in different issue communities either with funding or research. It is notable that DFID occupies a middle ground in the debate on cash transfers, that is, remains very close to the baseline consensus and supports all policy models to a certain extent.

Secondly, the IDS and the ODI: both of these research institutes are notable because they have produced research for a wide variety of the other policy actors in the field of cash transfers, covering various issues and policy models. Since both are primarily research facilities, neither organisation has taken a particularly strong stance regarding any single policy model. They have, however, been important in supplying more narrowly interested organisations with data and, ultimately, arguments for their respective agendas (e.g., Devereux 2001; HAI et al. 2005; ODI and GTZ 2005; UNICEF and ODI 2009).

Thirdly, both the ILO and the World Bank play specific roles as large IOs with global mandates and significant research capacity. In between 2001 and 2012, only these organisations had official strategies of social protection with a claim to global applicability. Since both of the initial strategies of the ILO and the World Bank covered social protection in general, including all types of basic social protection, the ILO and the World Bank connected to most issue communities and published papers on a wide range of issues in social protection. Such publications are often used by more issue-specific organisations to argue for their own position.

In sum, an 'inner circle' of specific policy actors who dominate basic social protection is absent. Social cash transfers are equally influenced by a large number of organisations which hold different variations of the same basic ideas. These organisations have formed a set of fluid and over-lapping issue communities. Those organisations who have more general mandates and goals (e.g., ILO, World Bank, DFID) or who specialise in research (e.g., ODI, IDS) tend to function as nodes which connect the various communities. Because channels of communication are not fixed and tend to change according to current challenges, I assert that the relational structures in the field of social cash transfers approach the character of a policy community without reaching the necessary level of institutionalisation.

3.3 The historical emergence of the web of ideas

Keeping in mind that development organisations long rejected cash transfers, how did the current global paradigm of basic social protection emerge? I propose that the current web of ideas emerged in between 1990 and the late 2000s, in three distinct phases of development.

The first phase was a gradual *socialisation of global policy* between circa 1990 and 2000, during which the basic concepts of the web of ideas were constructed and became interconnected. In this phase, global organisations developed an interest in social protection in general. The second phase, between circa 2000 and 2009, can be described as *policy development*, during which policy actors constructed cash transfers as policy models. In this phase, global organisations developed an interest in basic social protection and cash transfers. The third phase is marked by the creation of *global consensus*, starting around 2009. In this phase, global recognition of cash transfers was further strengthened by official agreements and declarations that constructed cash transfers as part of global policy strategies to counteract widely perceived crises and problems.

The following analysis of the three phases also illustrates how a discursive window of opportunity emerged from changes in global ideas and how it was used to construct new policy models. I argue that the window of opportunity essentially opened during the *socialisation of global policy* and was used to construct new models during the phase of *policy development*. In the phase of *global consensus*, the construction of the new models can be regarded as complete and the window of opportunity as closed.

3.3.1   The socialisation of global policy (1990–2000)

The first phase, here designated as the *socialisation of global policy*, is marked by a general trend towards social issues in global development policy, even though cash transfers did not yet become a focus of global debate. More precisely, several debates which focused on social policy, poverty and related issues can be readily identified during the 1990s Firstly, a global debate on 'social development' and 'human development' took place in the mid-1990s. Secondly, the World Bank sparked a debate on pension reforms which led into a wider debate on social protection in the 2000s. Thirdly, global policy actors developed an increasingly differentiated perspective on poverty. Taken together, these seemingly heterogeneous debates prepared the ground for intensive coordination between different policy actors in the early 2000s, ultimately resulting in the baseline consensus which legitimises cash transfers.

The first debate during the *socialisation of global policy* dealt with the status of social policies within development policy and revolved around the highly similar concepts of 'human development' and 'social development'.

The UNDP (1990) created the term 'human development' in 1990 with the publication of the first 'Human Development Report' (HDR) and further elaborated this perspective in regular iterations of the report. The authors of the first report explicitly point out the need for a new concept of development in the face of an accelerating pace of global social change and propose that directly investing in human capabilities is the best strategy (iii, 9–11). That is to say, the UNDP suggested that the agency and self-fulfilment of the poor should be fostered by improving their standard of living and meeting their basic needs. On the level policy, this translated into an emphasis on improving education, healthcare and nutrition via social policies and infrastructural policies (42). Interestingly, 'income support schemes' to 'households in extreme poverty' are also mentioned in the first HDR, if only as a secondary priority after infrastructural policies due to a perceived lack of financial and administrative capacity in developing countries (62–63). The second HDR, however, no longer mentions any form of cash transfers, instead focuses on the expansion of social services and policies which facilitate the usage of economic opportunities, such as 'credit schemes for the poor' (UNDP 1994:38–40).

A further outcome of the global debate on human development was the United Nations 'World Summit on Social Development', which convened in Copenhagen in March 1995. The main idea behind social development was that social policies were equally important as economic policies and indeed necessary to secure economic growth and to reduce social problems in developing countries (Midgley 1995).

The summit had a wide range of participants, including not only national government delegates, but also representatives of NGOs and specialised UN agencies, such as the ILO and the World Bank. It resulted in an official declaration and a common 'Programme of Action' to combat poverty and inequality, foster employment and facilitate the 'social integration' of societies (UN 1995). However, the 'Programme of Action' emphasises the creation of a favourable economic environment and enabling the poor to exploit economic opportunities through legal reforms, structural policies and social services rather than direct income transfers. The Programme does shortly refer to social protection measures under the objective of 'eradicating poverty' but remains ambivalent in its suggestions (52–56).

On the one hand, the 'strengthening and expanding [of] programmes targeted to those in need, programmes providing universal basic protection' is demanded, as well as special attentions to the needs of children and the elderly. These categories could potentially include cash transfers, for example, social pension or family allowances, but such transfers are not mentioned in the programme. In addition, 'a strategy for a gradual expansion of social protection programmes that provide social security for all' is to be developed, at least 'where necessary' – foreshadowing the ILO's global campaign for the extension of social security by 6 years. On the other hand, promoting the 'self-sufficiency' of the poor is a stated goal. Therefore, short-term 'safety nets' aimed at helping people into 'productive employment' are pointed out as a good policy option.

In sum, the debate on social development and human development in the 1990s fundamentally opened a window of opportunity to construct cash transfers as policy models. Social policies in general were discovered as a central element of development policy, especially those aimed at the poor. Poverty and inequality were identified as social problems by the United Nations.

Furthermore, the concept of human development introduced the idea that direct investment into the human capabilities of the poor is a feasible goal of policy. Even though cash transfers were not presented as the instrument of choice, the idea of investing in human capabilities in general opened a window for policies that transferred resources to the poor.

However, there were still strong ideas which stood against cash transfers: social protection, particularly basic social protection, did not play a significant role in this debate. Generally, the fiscal and administrative cost was perceived as too high for developing countries. In addition, policy actors had not yet constructed the positive effects of social cash transfers on human capital and economic growth.

Social protection did not become more important until the mid- to late 1990s, when the second debate in the *socialisation of global policy* was initiated. In the mid-1990s the World Bank began to advocate pension reforms on a global scale, provoking reactions by other global organisations (Maier-Rigaud 2009; Orenstein 2008). For the purpose of this book, the details of the Bank's pension reforms are only partially significant. The World Bank's seminal study 'Averting the Old Age Crisis' (World Bank 1994) already contained non-contributory pensions as an element of the Bank's multi-pillar model. The focus of the debate, however, was more on the multi-pillar model and its strong drive towards privatisation, that is, on pension systems and contributory transfers.

Even though the Bank's work thus predominantly concerned pensions as a sub-type of social protection, it opened up development policy to social protection in general. It can be argued that the ILO had to react to the World Bank's encroachment on its traditional territory of social protection but remained in a mostly defensive position during the 1990s, finally taking up parts of the World Bank approach (Maier-Rigaud 2009:173–176, 179–182).

Nevertheless, the ILO also began intensive research work to strengthen its position on social protection in general, resulting in a 'developmental approach to social security' which included the idea of 'protection floors' for countries at different levels of development (Maier-Rigaud 2009:173–176, 179–182). An important part of these research efforts in the late 1990s concerned the 'informal sector', that is, workers who do not have a formal contract and are thus not covered by conventional social protection systems (e.g., ILO 1999; van Ginneken 1999). These efforts led directly to the construction of the 'coverage gap' as a global problem, as the ILO noticed a near complete lack of social protection coverage in the informal sector and began to adapt its approach to perceived conditions on developing countries (ibid.). Interestingly, it was also proposed to include 'widows, orphans and older people' under the concept of the informal sector because it was assumed that these categorical groups lacked sources of regular income. As this indicates an inability to pay insurance contributions, it strongly implies that the ILO staff were advocating the introduction of non-contributory benefits for this segment of the population (see van Ginneken 1999:51–52).

Initially, the ILO's work on the informal sector did not translate into unequivocal support for cash transfers. Some ILO representatives rather argued for the extension of social insurance (e.g., Beattie 2000). Other ILO staff, however, began to advocate a departure from traditional definitions of social protection in the ILO. While the established ILO conventions emphasised social insurance and named tax-financed benefits as a secondary option, it was now proposed to more strongly include publicly financed benefits 'to protect against low or declining living standards arising from a number of basic risks and needs' into ILO conventions (van Ginneken 1999:50–51). This definition was explicitly meant to be wider than the traditional ILO conventions, in order to accommodate conditions in developing countries. The important point is that such a wide definition was a first step in dismantling the long-standing priority of social insurance in ILO policy in favour of non-contributory benefits. Not least, it was also emphasised that social protection should be seen as a right and an individual entitlement – evidently human rights were already seeing first use as a frame in the late 1990s.

In sum, the debate on social protection in the 1990s is significant because it motivated significant global organisations like the ILO and the World Bank to dedicate attention to different instruments of social protection, leading to the construction of new social problems and target groups. In fact, the construction of the informal sector and the coverage gap, as well as the associated goal of extending social protection globally brought a number of important conceptual changes into the debate, which further opened the window of opportunity for cash transfers. The definition of social protection shifted to include non-contributory benefits and global development organisations first began to show elevated interest in human rights. In so far, common definitions of social protection were now opening up to non-contributory benefits like social cash transfers, and the crucial frame of human rights began to emerge in development policy. In addition, as interest in the informal sector grew, the poorest of the poor and vulnerable categorical groups like children and older people gained increased attention as targets of social protection – further opening a window of opportunity for policies aimed at these groups, such as cash transfers.

The third debate in the *socialisation of global policy*, which revolves around poverty as a social problem, is strongly entwined with the first two. Poverty was increasingly recognised as a pressing social problem during the 1990s. Both the debate on human development and the new research on social protection in the mid- to late 1990s recognised poverty and social inequities in general as a major issue.

At first glance, this may seem trivial, but, as Noël (2006:305–306) points out, poverty was mostly a residual issue to policy-makers in between circa 1970 and 2000, both in national governments and global development organisations. But in time, the debates on human development and social protection led to a 'global anti-poverty consensus' in the late 1990s, as actors on all levels of global society now agreed that poverty was the most pressing social problem (ibid.). The perceived failure of the development and economic policies deployed in the 1980s was now complemented by economic crises in Latin America and Asia and the election of left-wing or 'third way' governments in several nation states (e.g., 'New Labour' in the United Kingdom or the German coalition government under Gerhard Schröder; Noël 2006:311–321). As a result, the reduction of poverty became a major poverty goal by the late 1990s, both for national governments and global organisations, irrespective of political ideology and policy mandate. New Labour, for instance, immediately declared the elimination of global poverty to be a major goal of DFID, then the newly created development agency of the United Kingdom (DFID 1997), albeit without reference to basic social protection.

While cash transfers were thus mostly insignificant in the growing debate on poverty during the 1990s, developments within that debate prepared the ground for the eventual construction of policy models. A crucial process in the debate on poverty was the increasing differentiation between different groups among the poor that later became the target groups for different types of cash transfers.

The first attempt to establish social cash transfers as development policy in the late 1980s is an early example of how different types of poor people were constructed as target groups. As explained earlier, Schubert tried to justify social cash transfers by identifying the 'poorest of the poor' as a target group, using a term originally established by the World Bank. In Schubert's 1989 study, this target group is defined as the lowest 30 per cent of the 'absolutely poor' and deemed unreachable by conventional development policies (GTZ 1989:17). During the debate on Schubert's proposal, 'labour constraint' crystallised itself as the main trait of this group, that is, insufficient ability to earn the minimum income necessary to survive (37–39; Schubert and Balzer 1990:7–11). While other participants of the contemporary debate agreed with Schubert's definition of the poorest, they did not necessarily agree that cash transfers were the best policy, or even feasible, in developing countries (GTZ 1989).

Even as the first attempt to establish cash transfers failed, the attention of global development organisations continued to focus on particularly poverty-stricken groups because common policies seemed to have consistently failed at eradicating poverty (Noël 2006). The World Bank's early work on this topic, to which Schubert referred, had already defined the 'poorest of the poor' or the 'ultra-poor' as the lowest 10 per cent of the income distribution and emphasised incisive qualitative differences to the less poor (World Bank 1988). Similar to Schubert, World Bank staff assumed that the 'ultra-poor' were marked by the inability to procure sufficient nutrition due to lack of labour power and therefore were unable to respond to conventional poverty reduction policies. The World Development Report 1990, simply entitled 'Poverty', went further in measuring and classifying poverty (World Bank 1990:24–38). The poor in general were identified as a heterogeneous group and differentiated according to household composition, social and economic context as well as duration and depth of poverty, that is, distance to the poverty line, or 'poverty gap' – perceived as indicators for 'access to income-earning opportunities and the capacity to respond' (38).

The Human Development Report 1990 contains similar arguments, emphasising that 'the poor are not a homogeneous group' and differentiating between 'chronic', 'borderline' and 'newly poor'. The 'chronic poor' are described as 'constantly suffering from extreme deprivation' – which is essentially compatible with the World Bank's definition of 'ultra-poor' (UNDP 1990:22). The growing interest in human development in general was connected to a growing concern with poverty as a social problem and the specialisation of different policies for different groups of the poor, even though this did not always mean a focus on the poorest. The final report of the World Summit for Social Development, for instance, does not mention any such group, besides vague references to 'poverty in its various forms' and 'absolute poverty' (UN 1995:41). Nevertheless, women, children and older people are identified as being in special need of support, foreshadowing the elevated status these groups currently have in basic social protection (52–56).

Similarly, the ILO's work on the informal sector in the late 1990s does not mention the poorest but defines widows, orphans and older people as groups in need of special support, as they lack income from labour or informal family support (van Ginneken 1999:51–52).

To conclude the three interrelated debates – on human development, poverty and social protection – which characterised the *socialisation of global policy* opened up a discursive window of opportunity that was highly favourable to cash transfers. Following the debate on human development, policy actors explicitly advocated social policies that directly invested into the human capabilities of the poor. Therefore, targeted policies of redistribution like cash transfers became more interesting to policy actors.

The accelerating debate on social protection resulted in a redefinition of the concept which ended the traditional emphasis on social insurance. Even though non-contributory benefits had not yet been identified as the most promising option for developing countries, their potential utility was now recognised and some organisations began to examine cash transfers from a human rights perspective.

Finally, the debate on poverty led to a consensus that poverty needed to be eliminated and that policy should start with the poorest, giving legitimacy to any policy that could be constructed as counteracting poverty (HAI 2000; ILO 2001; World Bank 2001c). In addition, the identification of older persons and children as preferred target groups facilitated the construction of policies that promised to support their specific needs and rights. The table for the construction of cash transfers as legitimate policy models was set.

3.3.2 Policy development (2000–2008)

Based on the three debates during the *socialisation of global policy*, basic social protection finally became a focus of global policy in the early 2000s, as several important IOs published relevant declarations or frameworks. This marks the beginning of the second phase in the emergence of the web of ideas, here designated as *policy development*.

The most significant organisations to publish new strategies were the World Bank and the ILO (ILO 2001; World Bank 2001a). This signifies that social protection in general had become accepted as appropriate development policy – but this was not an automatic process but the result of active communication, partly organised by British development organisations.

For instance, before ILO and the World Bank published their new strategies, DFID tasked the ODI with the organisation of an 'inter-agency workshop' in March 2000, in order to improve the communication on social protection policies between global development organisations, which resulted in a comprehensive report (Conway et al. 2000). The inter-agency workshop is crucial because it demonstrates how the three debates that characterised the *socialisation of global policy* came together to form a more coherent debate on basic social protection as development policy.

Besides DFID and the ODI, this workshop included representatives from the ILO, the World Bank, the IDS, the UNDP and UNICEF (Conway et al. 2000:4). Minor arguments aside, the report documents an emerging agreement on basic social protection, foreshadowing the baseline consensus in the current web of ideas. Not least, 'social assistance', that is, social cash transfers, were advocated by participants of the workshop.

The DFID, as the organising agency, perceived a focus on 'risk and vulnerability' and 'support to the poorest' as the major outcome of the meeting (Conway et al. 2000:1). Indeed, all three major organisations emphasised these aspects in the draft papers that they presented, and the authors indicate that the other participants of the workshop received these ideas positively – that is to say, the perception that risks and crises are a ubiquitous threat to the poor which can be counteracted by social security seems to have taken root around this time (65–77).

Based on a literature review, the report sums up the common goal as promoting 'dynamic, cohesive stable societies through increased equity and security'. This indicates that both social disintegration and social inequities were also defined as social problems in conjunction with poverty (Conway et al. 2000:7). Furthermore, the workshop participants emphasised the 'heterogeneity of the poor', pointing out that different groups of the poor are in need of special policies and criticising a 'bias towards the conventional instruments of social protection as developed in industrialised countries', that is, social insurance (77).

Interestingly, the policy actors which were present at the workshop did not perceive the emergence of the baseline consensus on basic social protection, even though non-contributory benefits to the poor gained wide recognition among the participants. While the 'lessons learnt' of the workshop bemoan the lack of an adequate 'common understanding' of social protection (Conway et al. 2000:78), the continuing debate on categories of the poor evidently helped to further establish cash transfers as a feasible policy option. In his contribution to the meeting, the ILO representative at the workshop openly advocated the implementation of cash transfers to the poor, especially 'old-age pensioners, widows, orphans and disabled people' since they have 'left the labour market' (39). This seems to have been picked up by the other workshop participants: a table in the workshop summary that maps possible roles for different actors in social protection points out 'social assistance' as a responsibility of the state to the 'persistently poor' (80).

In sum, the inter-agency workshop illustrates that policy actors were indeed beginning to exploit the window of opportunity which had opened up during the *socialisation of global policy*. The discovery of the poorest as a new target group and the widened definition of social protection were employed to think about new and useful policies. The only element still lacking was a set of new policy models with proven global applicability.

Significantly, the early 2000s also marked the start of a phase of intensified research into national policies of basic social protection which led to the construction of the four policy models analysed in Chapter 2. Looking at the careers of the four major policy models, a pattern in the timing and content of publications becomes apparent, which suggests that the global policy paradigm that legitimises cash transfers had mostly stabilised by 2005.

Starting around 2001, the first papers dealing specifically with social pensions and conditional cash transfers were published by the IDS, the IDB and the World Bank (e.g., Devereux 2001; IDB 2001; World Bank/LACRO 2001). However, the number of such papers remains relatively small until 2003, when the frequency of publications on social cash transfers and social protection in general begins to increase and remains high until circa 2007. Significant comparative studies on social pensions and family allowances were completed between 2003 and 2005, while the World Bank produced a large number of papers on CCT between 2004 and 2007 (e.g., HAI and IDPM 2003; HAI et al. 2005).

In addition, the year 2003 marks the start of the Kalomo pilot project, which immediately received significant global attention, ultimately leading to the Livingstone conference in 2006, which established cash transfers as part of a development agenda for Africa (e.g., HAI 2006a). The publication of DFID's (2005) 2005 practice paper on social transfers in 2005 signifies a breaking point in the debate – it is the first document to include all four policy models and to advocate for their implementation under a common label. It seems reasonable to assume that all policy models were clearly defined and widely known by that point.

Therefore, I propose that the 'web of ideas' passed a critical threshold of coherence in between 2004 and 2005. The content of publications indicates that the connections between the different elements of the web were stable enough to establish a baseline consensus by circa 2005.

I argue that the basic building blocks to construct the new policy paradigm and the new policy models, problem definitions and frames, were already available from the *socialisation of global policy*. The studies and policy paper mentioned earlier merely used statistical data in the form of impact studies, programme evaluations and impact simulations, often in international comparison, to construct fitting policy models by making a reduction of poverty and inequities via the redistributive effects of cash transfers plausible.

After 2006 the frequency of flagship publications and seminal studies on social cash transfers lowers significantly. Even current papers on cash transfers often refer to the publications in between 2000 and 2006 to establish their arguments (e.g., ILO 2010a; UNICEF 2012; World Bank 2012). That is to say, the construction of policy models seems to have been finished by that time, concurrently resulting in a web of ideas with sufficient stability to legitimise cash transfers as an instrument of development policy. All four policy models analysed in Chapter 2 were now widely recognised.

Besides the development of new policy models, which can be regarded as mostly complete around 2005, one further innovation in social protection also took place during the phase of *policy development*: the creation of the 'global social floor' by the ILO.

The development of the global social floor began in earnest with 'A Fair Globalization', the final report of the ILO's (2004a) 'World Commission on the Social Dimension of Globalization'. To be true, the concept of a 'global social floor' was first mentioned in official ILO documents in 2001 but mostly referred to core labour standards identified at the "World Summit for Social Development" in 1995' (ILO 2001:97). The election of Juan Somavia to Director-General of the ILO in 1999 (ILO 2014c) and the subsequent adoption of 'decent work' as a guiding concept of ILO first opened up space for further development of the 'global social floor' (Interview 7).

In 2005, the ILO (2006:22–23) began to advocate the implementation of a 'global socio-economic floor' as a guideline for future policy. This included both the definition of social security as a human right and the assertion that such measures should not be seen as a cost, but an investment into economic growth (5–6, 27–28). While the social floor had little impact at this time, it became a centrepiece of global policy by 2008, as the ILO expanded the concept and incorporated cash transfers as part of the floor.

In conclusion, policy actors began to exploit the discursive window of opportunity which had opened during the 1990s in the early 2000s. The new problem definitions, frames and target groups which had emerged were perceived as a challenge to develop new and better policies. By

2005, intense research and advocacy by many global organisations had led to the construction of cash transfers as the best option to face this challenge.

3.3.3   Global consensus (2008–today)

Even though the global policy paradigm and the new policy models have stabilised in the late 2000s, basic social protection policy developed further in the following years. The events of the global financial crisis in 2008 led to the next phase, here designated as *global consensus*.

The economic and social upheaval in the wake of the near-collapse of the global financial system led global development organisations to look for specific solutions. The United Nations, specifically the high level 'Chief Executives Board' (CEB), composed of the leaders of 28 UN sub-organisations, declared a number of official policy initiatives to counteract the crisis (UN-CEB 2009). The CEB is and describes itself as the 'the prime instrument for supporting and reinforcing the coordinating role of United Nations intergovernmental bodies', that is, the principal coordinating body for global policy (UN-CEB 2012a).

Notably, Juan Somavia, then Director General of the ILO and a driving force behind 'decent work' and 'Global Extension of Social Security' as policy campaigns (Interview 7), was Chair of the CEB's 'High-level Committee on Programmes' in 2009, which is 'the principle mechanism for system-wide coordination in the programme area in the UN system' (UN-CEB 2012b). It seems plausible that Somavia has had a strong influence on the policy suggestions of the CEB at that time. Indeed, social protection was recognised as an 'urgent need' in times of crisis, while 'direct income support' was identified as a primary instrument to combat poverty (19). What is more, the implementation of a 'social protection floor' was declared as one of seven official policy initiatives to counteract the crisis, under the nominal leadership of the ILO and the WHO (20; ILO and WHO 2009b). The UN system thus officially adopted the ILO's concept of a 'global social protection floor' as a guiding principle of worldwide policy – 17 other UN organisations, including the World Bank, are listed as participants of this initiative. This should be qualified to a certain extent. According to policy experts, none of the listed organisations, UNICEF excluded, has officially recognised the 'social protection floor' as a guiding concept of policy in their own publications (Interview 7).

Nevertheless, the adoption of the 'floor' by such a high-level body of global policy has significant symbolical value, reinforcing the ILO's claim that its mandate includes the global extension of social protection (e.g., ILO 2010a:18–19). Indeed, the International Labour Office further developed its approach into a 'social security staircase policy paradigm' which merely sees the extension of a 'global social floor', that is, basic social protection, as a first step leading to the implementation of statutory and voluntary social insurance mechanisms and social services which also cover the non-poor – resulting in a coherent and well-coordinated system of social security (18–20). Crucially, the newly elaborated concept of a global social floor now explicitly included a set of cash transfer to children, older persons and the disabled, in conjunction with work-based forms of basic social protection such as PEPs for the working-age poor (ILO 2010a). With the official recognition of the social floor, the United Nations thus also gave increased legitimacy to cash transfers.

In addition, the recognition of the social floor also marks the beginning of the general movement towards systemic approaches around 2008. Both the World Bank and UNICEF also published new frameworks on social protection policy in 2012. The UNICEF (2012:5, 23) in particular, not only emphasised human rights in its new framework, but also explicitly named its approach of 'integrated social protection systems' as a contribution to a 'Social Protection Floor', as specified by the CEB initiative. The World Bank (2012:25–27, 29–30), in contrast, while also strongly emphasising systemic approaches, focused on the 'promotive' aspect of basic social protection, that is, building human capital and creating economic opportunities. That is to say, of the various elements of the ILO's social floor, only the focus on building coordinated systems of social protection became part of the global baseline consensus. Further elements, especially the goal of scaling up such systems by including social insurance, are not as widely recognised.

In spite of this mixed reaction to the ideas of a social floor, with each organisation filtering the concept in terms of its own mandate, the drive towards comprehensive systems of basic social protection remained strong. In June 2010, the ILO adopted a new Recommendation which on social protection floors that advised all member states to implement a social floor consisting of different instruments of basic social protection, including cash transfers – even though the idea of one single model constituting a *global* social floor was qualified (ILO Recommendation No. 202; ILO 2012a). ILO negotiations prior to the adoption of Recommendation No. 202 led to a rethinking of the social floor approach to the extent that the implementation of different national social floors is now advised, in order to adapt to specific national circumstances (ibid.).

Finally, the phase of global consensus also encompasses a certain saturation of the debate on social cash transfers. While the fundamental agreement on relevant social problems as well as policy goals and the effects of social cash transfers is well established, some actors are beginning to review the evidence built up through pilot projects, evaluations and studies since the early 2000s. Especially DFID (2011) is at the forefront of the global discourses, as illustrated by the 'Cash Transfers Evidence Paper' of 2011. On the one hand, this paper reaffirms the basic consensus on cash transfers: that they are a good instrument to reduce poverty by developing the human capabilities of the poor and including them in processes of economic growth. On the other hand, the authors admit that empirical evidence for many of the effects attributed to cash transfers is lacking (17–49). Only the effects of poverty reduction and human development are regarded as having sufficient support by empirical evidence. Further outcomes of cash transfers, for example, increased social cohesion, the promotion of economic growth and better adaptation of the poor to climate change are only seen to have a 'strong logic', that is, inherent plausibility but insufficient proof. Ultimately, any potential effects are seen as strongly dependent on the specific local context and design of a transfer programme. While no other organisation has published a similarly exhaustive synthesis of available scientific data on cash transfers, this implies a process of change behind the established global consensus on the implementation of basic social security (see also ILO 2010a:108).

Social cash transfers are still de facto recognised as a legitimate and useful instrument of development policy. But now that this basic consensus is stable and almost a decade worth of data on social cash transfers exists, policy actors are beginning to take a closer look at the actual impact of pilot projects and cash transfer programmes – for instance, even the World Bank (2009a:141–154) has admitted that CCT will often increase school enrolment of poor children but not necessarily result in better grades, that is, school outcomes. In fact, systemic approaches are often seen as a way to improve the outcomes of cash transfers by embedding them in a wider context of other financial benefits and social services. The point is that cash transfers, even though they are still seen as globally applicable policy models, have lost their idealised character to a certain extent, due to difficulties of implementation – policy actors are beginning to emphasise that these relatively abstract models will have to locally adapted.

This does not indicate that social cash transfers will lose their legitimacy in development policy. When questioned as to the future importance of cash transfers in development, policy experts mostly answered that they expected cash transfers to remain a central instrument in the coming years. However, some also implied that they expect basic social protection to become one instrument amongst others, that is, one specific option of many, chosen according to local circumstances, policy goals and available resources (Interview 3). This seems likely; eminent scholars, for example, Gustav Ranis (2005:127–131), have criticised development policy for following certain fashions and declaring the newest policy option as a 'silver bullet' that can solve all social problems at once. The phase of global consensus seems to indicate that cash transfers are starting to loose their status as a 'silver bullet'. However, the official recognition of a social floor by both the UN-CEB and the ILO does increase the likelihood that social protection will remain a significant part of development policy – after all systemic approaches have been added to the web of ideas as a new element on which the majority of actors agree, even if the social floor is still contested.

In sum, the phase of *global consensus* has hitherto involved little change to the web of ideas. The baseline consensus has not been modified in recent years, barring the addition of systemic approaches and the symbolically important social floor. Therefore, it can be argued that the discursive window of opportunity was filled by the construction of cash transfers. After all, the developments during the phase of *global consensus* mostly affected the symbolic recognition of cash transfers and did not involve changes in basic ideas or the introduction of more policy models.

4
Global Discourses: The Ideas behind Cash Transfers

The analysis of the policy paradigm behind cash transfers in the previous chapter demonstrates that different ideas emerged and combined from the early 1990s onwards to form a web of ideas that legitimises non-contributory benefits to the poor as development policy. I assume that the emergence of a new paradigm is the result of prior shifts in global discourses that fundamentally changed the ideas of policy actors (see Chapter 1).

In the following, I analyse four global discourses that have in fact enabled the legitimisation of cash transfers. The guiding questions of this chapter are in what way shifts in these four discourses facilitated the emergence of a new paradigm and in how far the nature of global discourses has influenced the way cash transfers were designed.

The four global discourses and their most significant shifts are as follows:

1. A discourse on poverty which shifted specified target groups and began to emphasise the agency of the poor.
2. A discourse on development which shifted to construct the poor as potential drivers of social progress.
3. A newly emerging discourse on risks and crises which gave a rationale for social protection as an economic and social stabiliser.
4. A human rights discourse which gradually shifted to emphasise social rights and provided a moral rationale for social protection and cash transfers.

The analysis of each discourse proceeds in two steps. Firstly, I attempt to delineate a *phenomenon structure*, consisting of the basic categories which construct the subject matter of a discourse (Keller 2008:248–252).

Secondly, I analyse each discourse historically and attempt to trace the discursive shifts which have enabled the construction of cash transfers as policy models.

4.1 Poverty: the construction of agency

I begin my analysis with the global discourse on poverty as a social problem in the Global South. The discourse on poverty had pivotal impact on the legitimacy of cash transfers because it changed the way global policy actors perceived the poor. In development policy, poor people were long perceived as mostly passive beneficiaries of development and economic growth. During the 1980s and 1990s this position was qualified, as the poor were gradually attributed with more and more agency. Ultimately, policy actors began to perceive the poor as potential drivers of economic growth, at least if given appropriate support. In consequence, cash transfers gained legitimacy because they could be constructed as an instrument that directly strengthened the agency of the poor and allowed them to participate in markets – giving a strongly economic rationale for basic social protection.

In the following, I first analyse the complex *phenomenon structure* of poverty discourse with six categories (see Table 4.1), in order to illustrate how shared ideas currently legitimise cash transfers. I then conclude the chapter by analysing the discourse on poverty historically and demonstrate how exactly the discourse shifted to portray the poor as agents of development.

4.1.1 Problem definition

The first category circumscribes definitions of poverty as a multi-dimensional social problem. This is nearly common sense in global policy and influences the other categories of poverty discourse (Eberlei 2012:726–727; see also the Human Development Reports, e.g., UNDP 2010). Indeed, policy actors in the field of cash transfers distinguish between three dimensions of poverty: an economic dimension which emphasises human capital, the dimension of 'vulnerability' and the severity of poverty (DFID 2011: 3; HAI 2000:5; OECD-DAC 2001:38, 2009:20–21; UNICEF and ODI 2009:12; World Bank 1990:79, 2001a:19, 2008:453–455).

The economic dimension of poverty is perceived to consist of three sub-dimensions: lack of income, human capital and/or economic assets. Crucially, lack of human capital is regarded as an essential dimension, since it affects the ability of the poor to participate, both socially and

Table 4.1   Phenomenon structure of poverty discourse

Category	Content
Problem definition	Poverty is perceived as a multi-dimensional social problem. Policy actors define four major dimensions: • an economic dimension, consisting of income poverty and lack of human capital, with an emphasis on human capital; • vulnerability to risks, crises and shocks; • severity of poverty, that is, both depth of poverty or how far the poor are below the poverty line; and • duration of poverty.
Causes	Poverty is attributed to a number of causes. They seem strongly conflated with the dimensions of poverty: • shocks and crises; • lack of resources, especially human capital; • structural conditions in economy and society.
Consequences	Poverty is expected to have multiple negative consequences, both for society in general and for the poor specifically: • a vicious cycle of poverty, as certain groups are unable to help themselves and transmit poverty to their children; • lower economic growth, since the poor cannot exploit available economic opportunities; • social disintegration, since the poor do not participate fully in society.
Victims	Because poverty is defined as multi-dimensional, the poor are seen as a heterogeneous group: • the focus clearly lies on severe poverty; • certain categorical groups are defined as 'deserving poor', since they are deemed especially vulnerable and deprived; • policy actors clearly prefer the poor to lift themselves out of poverty. An admitted problem is that some groups do not have the necessary agency. The SCT are expected to lift the target groups up to a threshold of sufficient agency.
Solutions	Poverty is usually conceptualised as a solvable problem, focussing on market-based solutions: • public support to the poor is generally limited to enabling participation in economic activity or markets in general; • 'pro-poor growth' is often perceived as the major tool of poverty reduction; • through 'trickle up', 'pro-poor growth' is also perceived to benefit society as a whole.
Social responsibility	The alleviation of poverty is seen as a public responsibility, especially due to human rights: • this public responsibility has limits. Most actors only intend to lift the poor up to the critical threshold of sufficient agency.

economically (DFID 2005:5, 13; GTZ 2005:10; ILO 2009b:20, 2010a:42; OECD-DAC 2009:44–45; UNICEF 2012:10).

Human capital is generally defined as a set of useful skills and abilities bound to individual persons, based on the availability of three basic necessities: education, health and nutrition (e.g., DFID 2006a, 2011:5; ILO 2010a:16; UNICEF and ODI 2009:7; World Bank 2009a:1). While virtually all policy actors agree on usefulness of human capital and perceive a lack of education, health and nutrition as a dimension of poverty, they differ in perceptions on why human capital is important.

One group of policy actors, most notably the World Bank, but also DFID and the ILO, prefers to use the term 'human capital' and emphasises that investing in human capabilities is a means to achieve economic growth. Here, human abilities are regarded as a productive factor (Commission for Africa 2005:27; DFID 2011:3; ILO 2004b:62, 2009a:124–125, 2011:16–18; World Bank 2001c:57, 2008:14–16, 431). Another group of policy actors, including the UNDP and many NGOs, prefers to talk about 'human capabilities' and argues that promoting such human abilities is an inherently valuable aspect of self-fulfilment. This position on human capital was mainly created by the UNDP's work on human development in the 1990s (e.g., DFID 2006b:iv; ILO 2004b:13; Künnemann and Leonhard 2008:16; UNDP 1990:10, 1994:14–19).

All in all, both proponents of 'human capital' and of 'human capabilities' agree that human abilities and skills are a crucial dimension of poverty and affect economic and social participation. Thus, the actual difference between the two variants amounts to a slight variation in policy goals, that is, economic growth versus self-fulfilment. Indeed, both positions human capital help construct cash transfers as useful policy models. The majority of policy actors see social cash transfers as an investment because it is expected that the beneficiaries will use the money to build human capital (DFID 2005:11; HAI 2004:32; OECD-DAC 2009:22; UNICEF and ODI 2009:19; World Bank 2008:13–14). Crucially, the concept of human capital also focuses policy on children as a target group. It is widely assumed that the foundations for human capital development during the life course have to be laid during childhood. Insufficient education, healthcare or nutrition is thought to cause significant loss of individual potential in later life (e.g., DFID 2005:17). Thus, when policy actors speak of cash transfers as an investment, they usually mean the effects of transfers on the development of children.

The third dimension of poverty can be described as 'vulnerability', that is, the susceptibility to risks, shock or crises. The poor are often marked as being especially 'vulnerable' due to their material and social deprivation – it is assumed that resources, human capital and social networks are necessary to cushion the impact of manifested risk (e.g., Holzmann and Jorgensen 2000:9; ILO 2010a:5; Kannan 2004:31). As mentioned earlier, this dimension of poverty was mainly established by the World Bank in the early 2000s, via the widely received social risk management approach (Holzmann and Jorgensen 2000; World Bank 2001). Crucially, the World Bank employed the concept of vulnerability to give an economic rationale for social protection. The damage to livelihoods done by manifested risks is expected to impede the economic activity of the poor, damaging economic growth in general (ibid.). In so far, cash transfers are legitimised by a strong economic rationale because they have been attributed with the ability to mitigate vulnerability (DFID 2011:83, 85; HAI and IDPM 2003:8; ILO 2010a:105, 115; ODI and GTZ 2005:5; OECD-DAC 2009: 17; World Bank 2006:148, 2009:xiii).

The final dimension, concerning the severity of poverty, consists of two specific variables: the 'depth' of poverty, that is, the distance of the poor to the poverty line, and the duration of poverty. These two traits enable policy actors to rank the poor according to the severity of their poverty. Poverty is regarded as more severe if the distance to the poverty line is large and the duration of poverty is long. The poor who are farthest below the poverty line and have endured poverty for the longest time are identified as most deserving of support – this is often circumscribed as 'deep poverty' for poor who are far below the poverty line and 'chronic poverty' for those who have been poor for a long time (e.g., Devereux and Sabates-Wheeler 2004:7; DFID 2005, 2011:3, 7; Holzmann and Jorgensen 2000:6; ILO 2009b:7, 2010a:1, 23; van Ginneken 2009:229; World Bank 2008:416, 2012:14). The deep poor and the chronic poor are seen as being the most needy for moral reasons, and from an economic perspective it is sometimes argued that even small investments will have significant impact on the livelihoods of the poorest (e.g., DFID 2011: 35).

I emphasise two points in particular that cut across the dimensions of poverty and have shaped the construction of cash transfers as policy models. Firstly, a lack of agency is implied as a crucial characteristic of poverty through these dimensions, especially in the case of the poorest. The analysis of the category of victims, found later, illustrates that the attribution of different groups of the poor with different degrees of agency has had a direct impact on the construction of cash transfers, to the extent that children and the elderly have become preferred target groups because they are perceived to have comparatively little agency.

Secondly, this set of dimensions is unusual in one respect. A deprivation of 'basic needs', which was long regarded as a defining characteristic of poverty in social and development policy, is not the major dimension (Munro 2010:34–37). This is somewhat surprising because a 'basic needs approach' dominated development policy in the 1970s and may have had significant influence on the MDGs (ibid.). Instead 'vulnerability' has moved into the foreground, specifically influencing anti-poverty policies. Policy models, including cash transfers, are not tailored to specific needs, but are targeted at the groups which are constructed as having the highest vulnerability.

This is not to say that basic needs do not play a role in the field of cash transfers, only that they remain implicit in global discourses. For instance, low human capital as a dimension of poverty is interpreted as lacking fulfilment of three basic needs: nutrition, healthcare and education. Still, the major categorical groups seem to be mostly defined in terms of their vulnerability, for example, the age-specific vulnerability of children to many risks.

Crucially, I argue that 'risk' and 'vulnerability' imply a different legitimisation for social cash transfers than 'needs'. The fulfilment of 'need' means that rectifying a current discrepancy to a predefined standard of living is the goal of policy. In contrast, lowering 'vulnerability' means that preventing contingent drops in welfare in the future is the intention. In short, the two concepts operate with different time horizons: unfulfilled needs are manifest problems in the present, while vulnerability signifies potential problems in the future. It is difficult to tell whether a stronger discourse on 'needs' would have resulted in different policy models. Indeed, as Munro (2010:39–40) argues, both schools of thought emphasise that social protection can be seen as an investment with tangible economic returns. However, the 'basic needs approach' also had an essential moral dimension, claiming that 'continuing to allow current levels of unsatisfied basic needs when they can be satisfied is morally repugnant' (35). 'Risk' and 'vulnerability', in turn, rather give a strong economic rationale for social protection as mentioned earlier (28–30).

4.1.2 Causes

Having established poverty as a major social problem, it should be asked which causes the discourse sets at its root. Even though policy documents seldom go into much detail concerning the causes of poverty, three causes do appear frequently: (1) lack of economic assets and human capital; (2) the effects of shocks and crises; and (3) structural features

of economy and society, including low economic growth and ineffec-
tive or corrupt governance (Commission for Africa 2005:101–102; ILO
2001:102; OECD-DAC 2001:43; UNICEF and ODI 2009:17; World Bank
2001a:ix).

It is notable that the three causes – lack of assets and human capital,
shocks and crises and social structures – are strongly conflated with the
three dimensions of poverty. Lack of assets and human capital in particular comes to mind here. Equally, being more susceptible to shocks
and crises is a dimension of poverty in terms of 'vulnerability'. Policy
actors do not seem to explore this conflation of the dimensions and the
causes in any way. Only the structural reasons for poverty and inequities
are truly external to the problem but are mentioned much less often.
Usually, policy actors merely indicate pre-existing inequalities in the
economy, such as unequal distribution of assets and economic opportunities (e.g., World Bank 2006:xi).

All in all, it appears that global discourses construct the problem of
poverty in a manner which gives such strong moral and utilitarian
rationales to mitigate poverty that the actual causes of the problem
appear secondary. Indeed, the pervasiveness of poverty in developing
countries in spite of economic progress is virtually taken for granted
by many actors without reference to causes (e.g., OECD-DAC 2001:9).
I argue that the lack of elaboration on causes of poverty has served to
stabilise the consensus on social protection, even though it seems to
be an emergent property of discourse rather than a strategy of policy
actors.

4.1.3   Consequences

The assumed consequences of poverty are a further important category.
Again, the actual content is strongly conflated with other categories.
A major outcome of poverty is expected to be further poverty. This is
usually designated as the 'poverty trap' or a 'vicious cycle' of poverty,
meaning that the poor are not able to overcome poverty by themselves
and will thus pass it on to their children (BIG Coalition 2009:53; DFID
2006a:1; ILO 2010a:97; UNICEF and ODI 2009:7; World Bank 2009a:1).
This assumption is based on two perceived effects of poverty. Firstly,
widespread poverty is thought to lower economic growth due to socially
inefficient exploitation of economic opportunities. Naturally, this
is also assumed to perpetuate poverty, since low economic growth is
constructed as a root cause of the problem. Secondly, poverty is seen
to cause social disintegration, which inhibits economic growth and
weakens social networks, further exacerbating poverty.

In the end, the significant overlap between the dimensions of poverty, its causes and its consequences can be regarded a discursive structure which serves to strengthen the image of poverty as the most significant global social problem. Not only is poverty at the root of other problems like social disintegration, but it also appears as self-perpetuating since causes, consequences and dimensions of poverty are at least partially identical and feed into each other. In consequence, cash transfers seem especially legitimate – this is further reinforced by the construction of the poor as victims of poverty.

4.1.4 Victims

The poor as victims of poverty are an important social category, which is constructed within the global discourse on poverty. The poor are generally perceived as a heterogeneous group because of the ranking of different sub-groups according to 'depth' of poverty, duration of poverty and vulnerability. Policy actors regularly differentiate between the poor in general and the poorest of the poor and further distinguish particularly vulnerable groups like children and older people. However, all categories of the poor are consistently attributed with agency, that is, the ability to contribute actively to the economy and society in general (e.g., DFID 2005:9,17, 2006a:3; Künnemann and Leonhard 2008:27; ILO 2009b:20, 2010a:33, 41; World Bank 2009a:171).

Significantly, the basic attribution of agency is differentiated according to life cycle categories that mirror the traditional distinction between 'deserving' and 'undeserving poor' (see Schäfer 2012:265–267). Policy actors attribute children and older people on the one hand and working-age poor on the other with different degrees of agency – which impacts the choice of target groups for cash transfers.

Firstly, children and older persons: policy actors do not usually define these groups as full participants in the labour market or economic growth because of limited agency (ILO 2010a:9–10; Künnemann and Leonhard 2008:14; World Bank 2009a:114; Interview 1). Due to their perceived lack of labour power, they are not expected to be able to exercise full economic agency and develop economic potential. In combination with the definition of these groups as especially vulnerable and group-specific human rights, this strongly legitimises cash transfers to children and older people.

Secondly, working-age poor: these are inherently perceived as full participants of the labour market and drivers of economic growth because they are attributed with full labour power and thus economic agency (e.g., ILO 2001:39). Therefore, cash transfers to working-age poor are less legitimate, as analysed in Chapter 2. Policy actors tend to prefer other forms of basic social protection that require some form of reciprocal input, like public employment programmes, and emphasise the need to create jobs in order to provide security through productive employment (DFID 2004:4, 2005:12; World Bank 2006:152, 2008:297–309).

The differentiation between target groups aside, the attribution of the poor with agency has had a significant impact on their expected role in development policy. Because they are attributed with agency, the poor are perceived as potential agents of economic growth and development (e.g., DFID 1997:12, 2011:1, 35–37; HAI 2000:4, 6, 2004:30–31; HAI and IDPM 2003:8; UNDP 1997:61; World Bank/Poverty Group 1999:1; World Bank 2008:25). The idea is that the poor, given sufficient resources, will realise their untapped economic and social potential and will strengthen society as a whole. This provides a strong legitimisation for cash transfers, which have been constructed as an instrument to transfers resources to the poor directly and are perceived to strengthen the agency of the poor by promoting human capital, by protecting from risk and by fostering social cohesion (seen earlier). However, the exact mechanisms through which cash transfers are expected to support the agency of the poor may be constructed indirect or long-term. Take, for instance, the supposed sharing of social pensions within the family that is expected to strengthen the whole social group or the idea that conditional cash transfers will build up the human capital of children and enable them to be more productive adults in the future (see Chapter 2). That the poor are attributed with agency to such an extent is a relatively recent shift in global discourses that has also had an impact on the discourse on development, analysed later. The process which led to the attribution of the poor with agency is analysed in greater detail later in this chapter.

4.1.5   Solutions

The attribution of agency to the poor also affects the solutions that policy actors suggest for poverty. The preferred way is that the poor free themselves from poverty, that is, to use their agency to help themselves, while cash transfers lend basic support. Both concerns of creating 'dependency' and 'paternalistic' policies which assume that the poor are unaware of their own best interest lead policy actors to look reject policies which would offer more extensive support than cash transfers (e.g., DFID 2005:9; Künnemann and Leonhard 2008; World Bank 2009a:47).

Generally economic growth and markets are identified as the major solutions for poverty, the idea being that a general increase in wealth will provide the poor with sufficient economic opportunities – naturally this requires sufficient economic agency to take up these opportunities.

However, policy actors only regard *specific types of economic growth* as appropriate solutions to poverty. Many global organisations emphasise that growth needs to be 'pro-poor' and assume that benefits to the poor will 'trickle up' to the rest of society by strengthening aggregate economic growth.

Originally, it was assumed that development policy merely needed to foster economic growth and that the general increase in wealth would automatically benefit the poor, eventually lifting them out of poverty – this expectation is usually designated with the term 'trickle-down', in the sense that aggregate economic gains are supposed to filter down to the lowest end of the income distribution (e.g., Commission for Africa 2005:223). Beginning in the 1980s, this idea was slowly discredited, when the traditionally strong focus on economic growth in development policy was perceived to have no effect on poverty or was identified as the cause for a deepening of poverty in developing countries (e.g., Cornia et al. 1987).

During the 1990s alternative ideas about growth and poverty were developed. Proponents of 'pro-poor growth' argued that economic growth does not automatically benefit the poor and needs to be flanked by social policies that ensure their adequate participation by enabling them to exploit economic opportunities. Such social policies include social services like education or healthcare, but since the mid-2000s, cash transfers are also recognised as a tool to achieve 'pro-poor growth' (Devereux and Sabates-Wheeler 2004:2; DFID 2005:16–17, 2006a:57, 2009:21, 2011:33–35; GTZ 2005:20; HAI 2006c:5; ILO 2009a:51, 80, 96, 126, 129, 144, 2010a:24; UNICEF and ODI 2009:39; World Bank 2006:2, 2009a:8).

But the shift in concepts went even further as the poor were increasingly attributed with sufficient agency to contribute economically. Policy actors began to perceive a virtuous cycle between economic growth and redistributive policies benefiting the poor. It is currently assumed that 'pro-poor growth' is not only good for the poor, but that it will also be stronger than 'normal' growth by unleashing the economic potential of the poor – in a reversion of 'trickle-down', this is sometimes known as 'trickle-up' (e.g., ILO 2004b:341). The unused economic potential of the poor is normally circumscribed in terms of under-investment in human capital, low economic demand and low economic investments by the poor. Social cash transfers are perceived as adequate means to remove such obstacles because they provide the necessary minimum of resources required to participate in the economy and promote human capital (DFID 2005:5, 13; GTZ 2005:10; ILO 2009b:20, 2010a:42; OECD-DAC 2009:44–45; UNICEF 2012:10). As DFID's (2005:22) seminal practice paper on cash transfers states: 'Regular, predictable cash transfers provide the potential for developing a market-based solution to chronic poverty, which is not possible with the current humanitarian approach'.

4.1.6 Social responsibility

Both the attribution of the poor with agency and the construction of economic growth as the primary solution influence the content of the final discursive category of social responsibility that circumscribes which actors are perceived as being responsible for finding solutions to poverty.

In general, action against poverty is seen as a public responsibility. Often arguing with human rights, nation states are identified as having obligations towards their citizens. The Universal Declaration of Human Rights (UDHR) and the ICESCR are perceived to embody a global consensus on the minimum standard of living which nation states owe to their population (e.g., van Ginneken 2009:236).

However, the public obligation to alleviate poverty is shaped by the idea that the poor should ideally help themselves. Analysis reveals that cash transfers are intended to lift people to the threshold of agency at which they can autonomously participate in the economy but provide no support past this point – other means of social protection, basic or advanced, are constructed as appropriate instruments to those who can independently earn their living.

Those poor who are perceived as having agency, for example, working-age poor, should only receive aid if employment is unavailable, and even then, conditions are usually attached. Consider the following quotation: 'Everyone of working age has a responsibility to contribute to the social and economic progress of the community or country he or she lives in and should be given the opportunity to do so' (ILO 2001:39). The strength of this discursive position explains the low legitimacy of general household assistance because this policy model may provide aid to working-age poor even when employment is available.

Aid to vulnerable groups like children and older persons, however, is still considered legitimate from a perspective of social responsibility. The fact that the state is meant to take responsibility for these groups implies that their agency is perceived as so far below the threshold of independence that direct support is appropriate. Due to their lack of labour power, children and older persons are deemed unlikely to remain above the threshold out of their own power. In the case of children, the emphasis on long-term promotion of human capital can also be seen as a further variant of fulfilling social responsibility: the investment into children appears as a pre-emptive intervention to ensure sufficient agency in later stages of the life cycle (e.g., DFID 2005:17). Indeed, a major goal of conditional cash transfers and family benefits is enabling children to free themselves from poverty in the future.

These fundamental ideas on social responsibility might also explain why basic income is marginalised in the debate on cash transfers. As explained earlier, concepts of basic income do not aim at enabling the poor to become economically independent, but rather point to the 'self-fulfilment' of beneficiaries as a major goal. Even though increased agency, for example, economic activity, is also an expected effect, ideas of transforming personal lives and societies are strongly associated with this policy model (e.g., BIG Coalition 2009:84). I assert that basic income is connected to a different idea of social responsibility, which is a marginalised discursive position. Proponents of basic income expect the state to provide all citizens with constant support, in order to aid the development of their capabilities, whether they contribute to the economy or not. The features of the four dominant policy models indicate that such a concept of social responsibility is not shared by a majority of policy actors, making the rejection of basic income a matter of common sense.

All in all, the discursive category of social responsibility in conjunction with the perceived agency of the poor thus functions to define a social minimum, below which no one should fall. However, it is notable that this minimum threshold remains vaguely defined: there is no commonly accepted quantity of resources or income that is necessary to facilitate agency. The idea of a social minimum within poverty discourse thus retains a rather symbolic character. Poverty is not to be tolerated, at least to the extent that it inhibits individual agency, but the social minimum which is presented as a solution can accommodate a wide range of policies, not all of which necessarily eliminate or significantly reduce poverty. For instance, level of benefits which was planned for the Kalomo project essentially amounted to a second meal per day per beneficiary household (GTZ 2005). Significantly, a similarly vague idea of a social minimum can be found in human rights discourse – see later.

4.1.7 Historical analysis

Having analysed the basic categories of the discourse on poverty, I now trace the essential history of poverty discourse on the global level since the late 1970s. The most important process for the career of cash transfers that took place in this timespan was the gradual attribution of the poor with agency. To reiterate shortly, the poor were originally perceived as rather passive beneficiaries of development and their agency was rarely talked about in global policy.

This changed in the 1980s, as perceptions of rising poverty in the Global South motivated policy actors to devote attention and research capacity to the poor. As more and more data on poverty and the impact of development policy was produced, the poor were gradually attributed with agency. Studies into the way the poor used development aid played a central role in this process, as did the emergence of human development and the concept of human capabilities. Ultimately, the construction of cash transfers as development policy strongly interacted with these prior shifts in discourse. While the initial window of opportunity for the construction of cash transfers depended on the perception that the poor had agency, the emergence of cash transfers as policy models further reinforced this perception to the point that the poor were attributed with the ability to contribute to development.

Be that as it may, early policy documents from the 1970s and 1980s do not categorise the poor according to their agency: it is merely pointed out that the poor do not automatically benefit from economic growth and need to be supported with special policies (Chenery et al. 1975; World Bank 1980). In this period, the poor were mostly categorised by employment status and geographic location, that is, rural or urban. It was claimed that the poor are simply excluded from markets and just need better access to appropriate resources and services for full participation. That is to say, the poor were not perceived as potential contributors to growth, but rather as a group that needed to be included with special means but had little impact on the economy.

In the early 1980s, specific target groups like children, older people or the disabled were occasionally mentioned as 'dependent poor' but without further elaboration (World Bank 1980:41). I assert that the classification as 'dependent' is actually based upon the traditional identification as 'deserving poor', since it implies the inability to survive without support or a lack of agency. However, the classification as dependent was not taken as an explicit reason to focus policy on these groups because the non-dependent poor were perceived as primary beneficiaries of growth and development processes (Chenery et al. 1975:xiv–xv). The assumption was that dependent poor' would automatically profit from aid to the non-dependent poor.

This begins to change with UNICEF's seminal study 'Adjustment with a human face', published in 1987 (Cornia et al. 1987). Here, children are singled out as especially vulnerable victims of economic reform in the developing world. According to the authors, this makes specifically targeted policies necessary because children embody the future 'economic potential' of a country (vii, 132–133). Two ideas are especially important here: firstly, it is no longer assumed that 'dependent poor' will invariably profit from general policies of economic growth and poverty reduction. Secondly, poor children are identified as future contributors to growth via the concept of 'economic potential', attributing them with agency.

Aside from children, other publications also began to construct more general target groups. Namely, the World Bank identified 'ultra-poor' as a problem of policy (World Bank 1988). Here, the 'lowest quintile' of the income distribution was constructed as a group with very specific characteristics that make it 'discontinuously' more vulnerable than the poor in general (1–2, 4–5). This discontinuity from 'poor' to 'ultra poor' is mainly attributed to lack of nutrition, which is seen as a result of low income and 'non-income characteristic', such as 'young age'. However, the main consequence of under-nutrition is again perceived to be a lack of labour power. Therefore, it is assumed that the 'ultra poor' will not benefit from policies of economic growth in comparison to the poor in higher 'income quintiles'. This illustrates how a lack of labour power, or agency, emerged as the main trait of a new target group consisting of the poorest people, which was mostly characterised by its lack of susceptibility to well-established policies of economic growth.

The debate on the poorest as a target group led directly to the first debate on cash transfers initiated by Bernd Schubert in the late 1980s. Notably, Schubert essentially not only repeated the World Bank's arguments on the 'ultra poor', but also extended them. Cash transfers were constructed as a policy intervention for the poor who were outside the reach of traditional development policy because they completely lacked agency (GTZ 1989:10–12, 17). This was narrowed down to older people and disabled, as well as widows and children, because it was expected that financial transfers would cause idleness and the deterioration of agency with other groups (ibid.). At this point, the traditional distinction between 'deserving' and 'undeserving' poor emerges quite clearly. On the other hand, some participants of the debate also saw the debate on cash transfers as a break from the general idea that 'the poor cannot be trusted with money' (25–26).

Indeed, the emerging perception that the poor could benefit from and productively use cash transfers, that is, had the potential for economic agency, seems to have spread in global policy around 1990. Take, for instance, the World Development Report 1990, simply titled 'Poverty'. The poverty reduction strategy suggested in the report focuses on the creation of economic opportunities and the facilitation of their use in order to extend the benefits of development to the poor (World Bank 1990:iii). In so far, it is a traditional strategy of development. However, the authors of the report also recognised that targeted interventions are necessary for those poor who cannot exploit economic opportunities on their own power. Even though these interventions were considered a residual part of the strategy, it demonstrates that poor who are 'unable to work' were increasingly recognised as a target group in its own right, not just 'dependent poor' (100–101). I argue that this was a first, tentative step in constructing the poor as a target of policies that facilitate agency – a process that would ultimately lead to a perception of the poor as agents of development, as the degree of agency which policy actors perceived slowly grew.

The World Development Report 1990 also contains an early example of a discursive practice which was instrumental in attributing the poor with agency: the use of short story lines or narratives on the lives of individual poor and the impact of policies (World Bank 1990: 99). Following a general pattern that can be observed in later examples, the narrative follows specific, named individuals, explaining how a certain policy impacts their lives. In the case discussed here, it is explained how a poor family in rural India uses a public employment programme to supplement income from other sources. Single family members and their activities are mentioned in detail and the course of a typical working year is described. This story focuses on the wife in the small family, illustrating how the PEP gives her opportunity for relatively well-paid labour, while still allowing her to take care of her children. What is more, the story finishes by saying that the family uses her wages to buy 'shoes, clothing and fuel as well as extra food' (ibid.), that is, it is emphasised that the extra income is used actively and in a productive manner. While the family is clearly presented as being capable of agency – the husband being an agricultural worker – this emphasis on the rational use of benefits is worth noting. It seems plausible to assume that the use of story lines in this manner strengthened the argument that the poor had agency.

The World Development Report 1990 is not an isolated example, but stands at the beginning of a long discursive shift. The basic idea that even the extremely poor had agency but needed support to be economically active established itself as common sense during the 1990s. The goal of lifting the poor to a threshold of agency via public intervention began to emerge in the debate on human development.

For example, the UN (1995:43) report on the World Summit for Social Development in 1995 proposes policies of economic growth which build upon the 'self-help organizations of people living in poverty' and thus respond 'to their actual needs'. Here, the concept of rational poor who have the agency to improve their own lives is clearly present. Furthermore, social protection programmes are identified as an instrument 'to help people become self-sufficient as fully and quickly as possible' and 'to reintegrate people excluded from economic activity' (53). This clearly expresses the principle of social responsibility analysed earlier. Social protection is offered to the poor up to the point of self-sufficient economic agency – state and market work together to reduce poverty.

Other documents from the late 1990s contain similar statements on the agency of the poor. For instance, one of the earliest publications of the newly formed DFID (1997:12) in 1997 states the following: 'Given the necessary support, the poor can be the means as well as the beneficiaries of sustainable development. Where poor people have rights and choices, they are able to make good use of them'. This accords relatively high agency to the poor, since they are named not only as potential participants, but also as drivers of development. The position that the poor are rational and will make good use of opportunities is stated clearly and unambiguously, in contrast to documents from the 1980s and the early 1990s.

The Human Development Report 1997 provides a further, if slightly different example (UNDP 1997:61): 'The poorest stay in poverty throughout the year, over the year, for a lifetime and pass poverty to the next generations [...] The challenge of poverty eradication is to strengthen people's ability to cope with these adversities-to build resistance and resilience, to seize opportunities for escape'. Here the poor are not constructed as potential drivers of development, but it is explicitly stated that even the 'poorest' can be lifted to a threshold of agency.

Newly emerging perceptions of agency also had influence on the World Bank, leading to new research initiatives. In preparation for the World Development Report 2000, the Bank's 'Poverty Group' undertook a global opinion survey of the poor. These 'Consultations with the Poor' were presented as an authentic overview of poverty in the

Global South, involving 20,000 respondents in 23 countries (World Bank/Poverty Group 1999:1). The publication of the results is introduced by the statement that 'the poor are the true poverty experts' and have changed the researcher's opinion on 'development' or 'good social change'. Even though this research is only shortly mentioned in the World Development Report (e.g., World Bank 2001c:16), the examples demonstrate that the agency of the poor had come to be perceived as facts by development experts.

However, at this point in time, policy models to lift the poor to the threshold of economic agency were still lacking – policy actors generally suggested the improvement of social services and good economic governance (e.g., UNDP 1997). Cash transfers were already being discussed but mostly in the form of residual 'safety nets', which were not seen to improve the agency of the poor (e.g., Subbarao et al. 1997). This changed only slowly and within the process of construction that resulted in the legitimisation of cash transfers as development policy.

Consider the case of HelpAge: 'The mark of a noble society', an early policy document, strongly emphasises older people's potential to make 'economic and social contributions' but only suggests the fulfilment of their group-specific human rights (HAI 2000:4, 6). Both the inability to work or generate other income and the unavailability of social security are mentioned as problems of poverty in old age; nevertheless, cash transfers are not discussed anywhere in the text.

In contrast, 'Non-contributory pensions and poverty prevention', the 2003 study which was an important step in constructing social pensions as a policy model, makes a clear connection between cash transfers and agency (HAI and IDPM 2003:8): 'The main hypothesis of the study is that the implementation of well designed and sustainable non-contributory pension programmes in developing countries can reduce poverty and vulnerability among older people and their households and facilitate their contribution to the development process'. While the hypothesis is explicitly left open (21), this marks one of the first points in the global debate where a positive influence of financial transfers to the poor on agency is claimed, in contrast to more traditional concerns of causing dependency.

HelpAge International's seminal publication 'Age and security' of 2004 finally introduces the argument in full and specifies the connection between social pensions, older people's agency and development. It is stated that social pensions not only motivate the beneficiaries 'to invest even small cash transfers in income generation and acquisition of productive assets' (HAI 2004:31), but also facilitate employment of younger people in their households, for example, by supporting migration (30). In so far, cash transfers are perceived to directly augment the agency of different categories of the poor. Referring to the ILO, it is further claimed that these effects have a direct and positive impact on local markets and wider 'economic progress', introducing the idea that economic growth is an instrument against poverty.

Again, brief narratives play a crucial role in supporting these ideas. In the first part of 'Age and Security', the increased incidence and severity of poverty for older people is mostly illustrated through statistics (HAI 2004:16, 18, 20), even though some short stories telling of individual elderly people suffering from poverty do appear here (19–20, 23). In the second part, the impact of social pensions is demonstrated mostly by narratives – statistics on the use of pensions are only given on a single page (28). The narratives in the question follow the established format: short stories on the lives of individual beneficiaries and the way they use their benefits (26–27, 29, 33–34, 36). The narratives presented here do not contain an example of a pension being used to finance economic activity in the sense indicated earlier. However, they all emphasise how the beneficiaries use them to cover necessary living expenses for themselves and their families, and some contain explicit statements that the transfer promotes the independence of older people from external support. That is to say, the narratives transport an image of poor with economic agency and imply that concerns about creating dependency through cash transfers are unfounded – indeed, an obverse effect is made plausible.

In the case of the World Bank, a similar shift from recognising the basic agency of the poor to seeing them as potential contributors to development took place.

The World Development Report 2000 defines poverty as a lack of capabilities to participate in markets and social or political institutions, pointing to material deprivation, 'voicelessness and powerlessness' and exposure to risk (World Bank 2001c15–16). At the same time, the restoration of these 'capabilities' via 'empowerment' and 'social risk management' is suggested (39, 135, 146). Similarly, the first Social Protection Sector Strategy defines social protection as a 'springboard' to 'provide poor people with the capacity to climb out of poverty' (World Bank 2001a:9). In short, World Bank publications in this phase imply the restoration of the ability to earn income and manage risk as a crucial aspect of poverty reduction and thus recognise that the poor can develop agency. Cash transfers, however, are still criticised for creating dependency, although this is perceived as a context-dependent result, not a certainty (World Bank 2001c:57).

The World Development Report 2006 shifts a little further into the direction of attributing the poor with agency. Firstly, it is stated that social and economic inequalities can inhibit aggregate optimal economic growth and development (World Bank 2006:21). Secondly, it is claimed that 'specific types of redistribution' can alleviate these inequalities by empowering the poor to make investments and contribute to the economy (102). Cash transfers, especially conditional cash transfers are later named as one such instrument of redistribution (148–155), in spite of remaining concerns that they may cause dependency (149).

In sum, the 2006 report implies that it is not only possible to foster agency in the poor, but that it is also a necessary prerequisite for growth and development. The argument is further sharpened in the 2008 flagship publication *For Protection and Promotion*. As the title indicates, 'safety nets', including cash transfers, are attributed with a 'promotive function' besides protection from risk (World Bank 2008:25): 'They also promote independence, allowing households to invest and thereby improve their livelihoods [...]'. Comparable to the case of HelpAge, the perception that cash transfers may cause dependency is strongly qualified. The authors rather state that cash transfers promote agency and can lift people to a threshold of economic independence. This shift in ideas on the poor seems to have stabilised. The concept of a 'promotive' function of social protection and cash transfers is still present in current Bank publication, including the second Social Protection Sector Strategy (World Bank 2012:3).

Nevertheless, the World Bank still voices concerns that badly designed schemes may cause dependency or inhibit agency (World Bank 2012:25). I argue that the World Bank has not shifted as far as other organisations in attributing the poor with agency. While the assumed relationship between redistribution and growth is supported by statistics, the role of economically active poor remains rather implicit and is given no specific proof (World Bank 2006:85–87, 98). Notably, World Bank publications contain only very few examples of narratives that HelpAge, for instance, used to illustrate the agency of the poor (see the example mentioned earlier and World Bank 2008:18).

The ILO provides a further example of shifting concepts on agency and the poor. Early documents on social security and cash transfers by the ILO staff recognise the poor as those 'who cannot be reached

by policies for productive employment', that is, those without sufficient agency, as the target group of 'social assistance' (van Ginneken
1999:52). Publications in the following years generally emphasise that
social protection will 'enhance individual autonomy' (ILO 2001:68)
but do not focus on the poor and their potential contributions to
development.

Concepts on agency and the poor perceptibly begin to change with
the introduction of the 'global social floor'. The ILO publications now
pointed out that a coherent system of cash transfers facilitates the stability
and social peace which people needed to maintain their economic
productivity, as well as a feeling of security which promotes the taking
of economic risks (ILO 2005:1, 4–5, 2006a:9, 2009b:1, 20, 36). Again, the
poor are not the explicit focus here, even though it is mentioned that
cash transfers will not cause dependency, but will instead support the
uptake of new economic activities (ILO 2009b:20). In short, it is implied
that all forms of social protection, including cash transfers, will facilitate
the agency of beneficiaries – including the poor.

All in all, the ILO does not talk about a threshold of agency or of
contributions by the poor to development. However, I assert that the
overarching argument of the ILO that social protection contributes to
economic growth by increasing productivity includes potential contributions by the poor. It should also be noted that the work of the ILO
on social protection is not limited to basic social protection and the
global social floor, but encompasses research on a wide range of social
protection systems, including social insurance and social services.
This includes ground-breaking research on the affordability of social
protection in developing countries and the positive effects of social
protection systems on economic growth that helped to establish the
idea that social protection is an economic investment, not a cost (ILO
2004c) – greatly increasing the overall legitimacy of all kinds of social
protection.

Last but not least, a similar shift of ideas can be observed in DFID
publications. As seen earlier, early DFID (1997:12) publications already
emphasised that the poor would use resources and opportunities in an
economically productive manner. The 2005 practice paper on social cash
transfers expanded this idea by claiming that the poor could contribute
to growth and would use cash transfers to make economic investments
(DFID 2005:5, 17). A 2011 'evidence paper' on cash transfers repeats
these arguments and states that cash transfers 'are one part of a broader
strategy to achieve economic and social development' (DFID 2011:1).
Later, the text clarifies that the poor can contribute to economic growth

in the long-term, provided that they can 'cross critical thresholds for participation in markets', for example, achieve agency via cash transfers (35, 37).

All in all, the similar shifts of ideas within different organisations demonstrate that the global discourse on poverty did change considerably to increasingly attribute the poor with agency. I propose that this long-term shift towards agency was caused by an interaction between the global discourse on poverty and the practice of development policy. As indicated earlier, the first steps towards attributing the poor with agency were taken after the strongly market-based development policies of the 1980s were criticised for causing poverty in the Global South. While this led policy actors to focus on supporting the agency of the poorest, the idea that the poor could actually contribute to development was evidently accelerated by experiences with cash transfers in developing countries. Notably, many of the narratives and examples used in the publications which I analysed earlier refer to the effects of actual cash transfers on beneficiaries in the Global South to illustrate that such benefits actually enable the poor to contribute to the economy.

In the end, global policy actors widely constructed the poor as potential contributors to the economy and legitimised cash transfers as an instrument to facilitate these contributions. Crucially, this indicates that cash transfers are currently legitimised by a strongly economic rationale that portrays them as an instrument of economic growth. The following analysis of development discourse illustrates that this may be a consequence of long-standing ideas that have characterised development policy from its very beginnings.

4.2   Development: the individualisation of progress

Even though cash transfers are regarded as social policy in the Global North, they have been taken up by global organisations that regard themselves as makers of development policy. Therefore, a global discourse on development as an idea and a practice has had significant impact on the career of cash transfers as policy models.

In consequence, the guiding questions of this chapter are: in how far traditional ideas of development policy have influenced the up-take of cash transfers by policy actors and in what way development discourse has shifted in order to legitimise cash transfers? Looking at changes in development discourse will also provide an answer to one of the major questions of this book: Is the legitimisation of cash transfers part of a development revolution or more indicative of a gradual change in development policy?

I find that development discourse has shifted significantly during the 1990s: initially, only nation states were recognised as units and agents of development. With the emergence of human development, individuals and their capabilities were increasingly constructed as units and agents of social progress, including the poor. In keeping with this, cash transfers have retained on feature of traditional social policy because they are targeted on individuals, not communities or nation states.

However, I also find that two traditional ideas of development discourse have equally shaped the up-take of cash transfers. Firstly, development discourse is based on a long-term perspective on social progress that has also shaped cash transfers – the main goal is not to alleviate poverty in the short term, but to enable people to climb out of poverty in the long-term. Secondly, fostering economic growth has remained a major goal of development policy, in spite of the emergence of human development as a strong idea. In consequence, development discourse tends to emphasise the economically productive effects of basic social protection.

In the following, I first analyse the phenomenon structure of development discourse which consists of four categories: process, goals, means and agents (see Table 4.2). Secondly, I trace shifts in the discourse historically.

4.2.1   Process

At its core, the concept of development is constructed as constant process of social change towards a final state, which is regarded as natural, inevitable and irreversible (Rist 2006:25–46, 69–79). Modern development policy is further based on the assumption that social process can and should be directed, at least to a certain extent.

In contrast to older concepts of development, it is now widely recognised that individual nation states will necessarily follow different paths of development, depending on their specific geographic and social context (e.g., Keeley 2012:3; UNDP 2010:45, 54). Nevertheless, it is still expected that these different paths will converge on the same end result, namely, catching up to standard of living in the Global North (e.g., ILO 2009a:169; UNDP 2010:143–146). What is more, countries are also often put into different categories which imply different stages of development that also involve a clear ranking (e.g., ILO 2009a:118; ILO and OECD 2011:2). In addition, specific countries are occasionally used as

Table 4.2   Phenomenon structure of development discourse

Category	Content
Process	Development is perceived as a teleological process of social progress in nation states, taking countries of the Global North as the benchmark. Even though it is now widely accepted that each country follows an individual path, certain results are still expected. • Countries are seen at different 'stages' of development and are occasionally ranked according to various criteria (e.g., 'low', 'middle' and 'high income' countries). • Certain countries are presented as models for specific aspects of development (Brazil, South Africa).
Goals	An improvement of human life around the world, leading to a convergence between countries. It comprises quantitative and qualitative changes in several dimensions: • improvement of living standard (poverty reduction); • increased economic efficiency and growth; • greater resilience against crises and shocks (sustainability); • peace and political stability; and • expansion of human capabilities (autonomy, empowerment).
Means	Development is to be mostly achieved by indirect means, based upon a long-term perspective: • creating a stable social and political environment that facilitates growth and enables long-term planning; • investing in people – children are defined as the major target group for investment; • sustainable and equitable growth.
Agents	Development is meant to be carried by a mixture of agents from different spheres and levels of society. Responsibility is equally attributed to the state and the private sector: • nation states (conditions, institutions); • markets (growth); • individual citizens, including the poor.

models for specific aspects of development, for example, Brazil, Mexico and South Africa as forerunners of good cash transfer schemes (HAI and IDPM 2003:7).

4.2.2   Goals

The various goals which are set as part of the development process specify what development actually means in different areas of life. The general idea of development is that the natural progress of nation states will lead to an improvement in the quality of human life (e.g., UNDP 1990:41). Development discourse further differentiates the quality of human life according to five particular goals: an improvement in the standard of living, economic growth, increased resilience against risk, increased social stability and increased human agency – because the effects that cash transfers have been attributed with match these goals, they provide a powerful legitimisation for the policy models analysed in Chapter 2.

In addition, there is a marginalised discursive sub-position which constructs development as a process of transformation and thus sets slightly different goals.

The first, most basic goal is still an improvement in the material standard of living, for example, financial income, housing and nutrition (e.g., DFID 2011:47; HAI 2004:17; OECD-DAC 2001:9). In this respect, reaching a minimally adequate standard of living is perceived as a major step for developing countries, usually referring to the UDHR and the ICESCR. This minimum standard is seldom defined in detail, but since poverty is generally seen as a violation of that standard, it can be inferred that it should be sufficient to allow agency and participation in economic growth (Kannan 2004:30–31; Künnemann and Leonhard 2008:15; van Ginneken 2009:239). Naturally, this provides a good legitimisation for cash transfers, who have been constructed as an instrument to alleviate poverty and foster economic growth.

In fact, increased economic growth is constructed as a second key goal of development (DFID 2011:47; HAI 2004:11, 2006a:14; ILO 2009a:xix; UNDP 1990:iii). The progress of countries is still mostly evaluated on the grounds of economic performance, for example, GDP per capita and growth rates (e.g., Künnemann and Leonhard 2008:48).

Why economic growth in particular is the chosen indicator of development can be explained with reference to discursive practices: it is notable that economic growth is easily quantifiable in statistical terms, for example, in the form of GDP. As mentioned in Chapter 1, Heintz (2010) suggests that such easily comparable and depersonalised types of data facilitate the global comparisons and are an especially successful form of communication. In the case of development, indicators like GDP or the Human Development index help to construct the perception that all countries in the world are essentially the same and will follow similar paths of social progress.

Research into the history of development policy (Speich 2011) clearly demonstrates that GDP was quickly picked up by virtually all relevant actors in development policy shortly after the Second World War. As a side effect of the wide usage of GDP as a yardstick of development, development policy remained strongly focused on economic growth in the following decades and, to a certain extent, until today (21, 27).

The focus on economic growth may also help explain why the promotion of human capital has been constructed as an effect of virtually all policy models. Even though the beneficiaries are targeted as individuals or households, a reference to human capital can be used to argue that these policies have a positive impact on overall development in communities and nation states. Evidently, the great importance given to economic growth in development discourse has shaped cash transfers considerably: As analysed in Section 4.1, even the perception that cash transfers reduces poverty is connected to the idea of enabling the poor to participate in markets.

The third goal of development is to increase national resilience against 'risk', 'crises' and 'shocks'. This can be regarded as an outcome of a pervasive global discourse on risks and crises which has established uncertainty as a fundamental constant of our environment which threatens societies globally (see Section 4.3). Since development is defined as social progress, it is logical to construct a reduction of uncertainty as one of its goals. Cash transfers, in turn, have been constructed in a fitting manner. Even though protection against risk was traditionally the role of social insurance while non-contributory schemes functioned as a residual 'safety net' – at least in the welfare states of the Global North (Bahle et al. 2011:23–51) – social cash transfers are now widely held to provide beneficiaries with 'security'. This gives cash transfers legitimacy in development policy because it is assumed that 'security' will enable people to undertake more risky, that is, more profitable economic activities and create a good climate for foreign investment – resulting in higher growth (e.g., DFID 2005:15; ILO 2010a:115; UN 2011:9–10).

The fourth goal of development is highly conflated with the increase of resilience against risk but is often mentioned separately and thus merits specific attention. Development is also constructed as an increase in socio-political stability, resulting in lasting peace (DFID 2006b:45; HAI 2006a:14; ILO 2009a:144; Norton et al. 2001:17). On the one hand, this is understood to be inherently desirable because political instability and war threaten human life. On the other hand, both instability and war are also seen as factors of 'insecurity' and are often mentioned as possible 'shocks' and 'crises'. In consequence, promoting stability and peace will also foster economic growth (e.g., Commission for Africa 2005:33, 133). Cash transfers are perceived as stabilisers because they have been attributed with positive on 'state-building', giving non-contributory benefits further legitimacy from a developmental perspective (e.g., DFID 2011:47).

The fifth goal of development differs from the first four, in so far as it is less focused on economic growth and markets. Many, if not all, policy actors agree that development should first and foremost be an increase in human capabilities and available opportunities, or, in other words, an increase in 'freedom' (DFID 2006b:iv; ILO 2004b:13; Künnemann and Leonhard 2008:16; UNDP 1990:10). I propose that this implies an understanding of development as increasing human agency. Quality of life is defined as the ability to freely choose your goals and to achieve them by your own actions. Such an idea of freedom certainly includes economic opportunities, and growth is constructed as an important part of human development (OECD-DAC 2001:47; World Bank 2006:155).

However, human development is constructed as a departure from the more traditional focus on the economy, in favour of a more holistic approach to development (ILO 2004b:13; UNDP 1990:9; 1994:14). This is to say that human development is also supposed to improve social and political life by tackling discrimination and inequities, particularly the inequality between genders. Education, for instance, is seen as inherently valuable, not just an instrument of economic growth. In addition socio-political 'empowerment', that is, promotion of effective political participation and autonomy by building better institutions emerge as important facets of development (Commission for Africa 2005:213; DFID 201147; HAI 2000: 5; ILO 2009a:124; World Bank 2006:124).

I argue that cash transfers have in fact been constructed in a way that bridges the tension between economic growth and human agency as goals of development – while cash transfers are constructed as instruments of economic growth, they are also widely perceived as an investment into human capabilities that strengthens the agency of beneficiaries.

Crucially, one further aspect of human development has had significant impact and has most likely facilitated the success of cash transfers as a policy model: the term 'human development' in itself implies a shift of the social unit which benefits from development towards individual human beings. As a matter of fact, early proponents of this discursive position, such as the UNDP, explicitly advocated that development should now begin to focus on the well-being and the capabilities of individuals (see UNDP 1990:iii, 9, for an early example). This is a departure from more traditional concepts of development, which see nation states or communities, that is, social collectives, as the beneficiaries of development and thus emphasise more indirect structural policies which have large-scale impact (e.g., Chenery et al. 1975; Cornia et al. 1987; World Bank 1980). In contrast, the focus on individual 'freedom' in human development rather legitimises direct intervention on the level of individuals or households, in order to ensure the promotion of capabilities (e.g., World Bank 2006:102). Redistributive policies like social cash transfers fit these requirements because they are defined as direct transfers to specific beneficiaries.

4.2.3   Means

The means which are expected to achieve social progress can be roughly divided into indirect and direct interventions. On the one hand, development policy is meant to involve the creation of a social and economic environment that is conducive to growth and the flourishing of capabilities. This includes the creation of sound economic and political institutions, as well as the construction of good public infrastructure, including social services like health and education (DFID 1997:15; OECD-DAC 1996:13; UNDP 1990:62, 1994:13; UNICEF 2012:8). On the other hand, concepts of human development legitimise direct investments into the capabilities of people in developing countries, for example, cash transfers.

The point is that the two sets of instruments are perceived as complementary. Ideally, cash transfers are supposed to be embedded into a wider context of public interventions, including other means of social protection, social services and stable political institutions. The impact of conditional cash transfers, for instance, is generally constructed as dependent upon the availability of good social services which ensure that the fulfilment of conditions has an actual impact (e.g., DFID 2006a:4, 2011:85; ILO 2010a:43; Künnemann and Leonhard 2008:20; World Bank 2009a:xii).

Development discourse has gradually moved from indirect, structural policies to direct interventions since the early 1990s. This seems to be an outcome of the debate on human development which emphasised the development of individual capabilities. Indeed, social cash transfers are frequently legitimised in the context of human development or human capital by constructing them as an 'investment' into the personal development of the beneficiaries (e.g., ILO 2009a:118, 124; World Bank 2009a:xiii, 22).

4.2.4   Agents

Since economic growth is perceived as a central aspect of social progress, the importance of markets and the private sector as agents of development is still emphasised. However, purely market-based policies were de-legitimised due to the perceived failure of such strategies in the 1980s. In consequence, the idea that only certain types of growth are beneficial to development established itself as common sense and re-introduced the state as an agent of development. As the analysis of concepts like 'pro-poor growth' has demonstrated, public interventions have been constructed as the appropriate tool to foster this type of development. This does not imply primacy of the state in development since such public interventions are usually meant to create background conditions under which markets will produce the desired types of growth autonomously (e.g., Commission for Africa 2005:33; DFID 2009:18; ILO 2001:42, 2010a:115). In sum, states and markets emerge as equally important drivers of development. Growth is necessary, but it cannot take place without public support.

In respect to cash transfers, a third agent of development is crucial. As analysed in Section 4.1, individual citizens including the poor have been identified as potential contributors of development (e.g., HAI and IDPM 2003:7). The general idea is that able-bodied people, including working age poor, have a responsibility to contribute to development if they want to benefit from it (e.g., ILO 2001:39). In addition, as explained earlier, even the poorest are perceived as potential agents of development given the correct support, legitimising cash transfers from a developmental perspective.

4.2.5 The impact of development discourse on SCT

To conclude the analysis of the phenomenon structure, I summarise to what extent development discourse has influenced the uptake of social cash transfers as a policy model. In short, I propose that the original concept of a social cash transfer as constructed in the Global North has been filtered in terms of well-established ideas in development discourse, since these ideas have shaped the perceptions of global policy actors. As a consequence, the policy models analysed in Chapter 2 share some characteristics, both with classic social policy and traditional development policy but are not reducible to either origin.

The most important idea which filtered the perceptions of policy actors is the inherent long-term perspective of development discourse. In contrast to social policy, development policy is less focused on the immediate fulfilment of needs or the maintenance of a certain living standard and more on future social progress. This long-term perspective has influenced four important characteristics of cash transfers.

Firstly, it may explain why vulnerability has become a major dimension of poverty and why needs are only relevant in the context of human capital. As explained, the dimension of vulnerability implies a clear long-term perspective. Alleviating vulnerability means securing the ability of people to plan for the future by protecting them against contingencies – it is nearly common sense that this will facilitate growth, that is, development.

Satisfying basic needs in contrast, implies the goal of closing the gap to a certain standard of living. While this is certainly compatible with development, it is not in itself enough to legitimise a policy model; the satisfaction of needs had to be associated with a long-term effect on social progress to fit with development discourse, that is, a positive impact on human capital. This has affected how social cash transfers are constructed as policy models. The satisfaction of need is regarded as a rather secondary effect. Policy actors emphasise the reduction of vulnerability and the promotion of human capital as the primary advantages of cash transfers. Fulfilling needs is generally treated as a means to those ends. This is most evident in the case of conditional cash transfers. The conditions indicate that promotion of human capital is the intended outcome, making CCT the most developmental out of the four models. The priority of human capital is less clear in the other cases, but needs are rarely emphasised over developmental goals.

In so far, the characteristic focus on long-term progress may also answer the question on the construction of CCT raised in Section 2.2.2: Why exactly did the World Bank pick up new policy ideas from Latin America and use them to construct the specific model of conditional cash transfers? The basic salience of Bolsa Familia in Brazil and PROGRESA in Mexico to the World Bank can indeed be traced back to discourses on development and poverty. Crucially, both discourses emphasise children as a primary target group, and the indicated transfer schemes were exclusively aimed at children in poor families. What is more, the conditions within the schemes also already aimed at facilitating the usage of health and education services – this conformed with the centrality of human capital in both discourses on poverty and development, as a dimension of poverty and a prerequisite of economic growth. Policies which are perceived to facilitate the accumulation of human capital may thus have been salient because they promised to both reduce poverty and enhance growth in the long term – that is, both help reduce a major social problem and facilitate social progress in the future.

Secondly, the ubiquitous focus on children and the emphasis on benefits with an 'investment character also stem from a strongly developmental rationale (ILO 2006a:33). Naturally, children are also a target group of social policy. Take, for instance, the traditional category of 'deserving poor' or the well-established model of family allowances.

But children also have a specific significance to development: development as a concept revolves around progress and managing growth. Naturally, this suggests children as a target group, since they are at an early point of the life cycle – as one development expert puts it, a common perception is that 'children are the future' (Interview 4). This perception is reinforced by the widespread attitude that development interventions should be as efficient as possible. It is nearly common sense that interventions are more efficient if they take place early in the life cycle, since childhood development strongly influences future potential, particularly in the form of human capital (e.g., DFID 2005:14; Levine 2001:18; World Bank 2009a:55).

The focus on children has had a strong impact on the construction of cash transfers as policy models. Most policy models of cash transfers are legitimised by effects on children, even if they are not the actual target group. Furthermore, the smooth transition of family allowances to the global level may also be a result of the accentuated position of children in development discourse. It is the only policy model which was transported from traditional social policy without significant changes. It is also one of the two policy models which clearly targets children. I have repeatedly mentioned that conditional cash transfers, the other model which targets children, has been heavily criticised from a human rights perspective. The focus on children may well have served to maintain the legitimacy of the model in the face of such criticism. Even actors who are otherwise sceptical of CCT recognise their positive impacts on children, for example, the reduction of child labour (e.g., ILO 2010a:86).

Ultimately, the strong developmental rationale has consequences for the prioritisation of policy models and target groups. As indicated earlier, those models who promise the highest return in long-term economic and social progress are given priority.

Thirdly, the long-term perspective of development has also influenced the construction of poverty reduction as a policy goal. As mentioned, cash transfers are not intended to alleviate poverty immediately and completely. Rather, it is envisioned that cash transfers will enable people to escape from poverty out of their own power in the future. The elimination of 'poverty traps' in particular, that is, the intergenerational transmission of poverty, is a central policy goal (e.g., DFID 2005:17; ILO 2009a:124; Künnemann and Leonhard 2008:14; OECD-DAC 2009:26). Again, this means that the currently poor adults are not expected to escape from poverty. An actual reduction of the poverty headcount is to be achieved by their children, due to the positive impact of cash transfers, especially on human capital. This is a difference to the function which social cash transfers were often accorded in the Global North, namely, to reduce the poverty headcount at present.

Fourthly, development discourse has had an influence on the level of benefits which cash transfers are intended to offer. As analysed in Section 4.1, the public responsibility for financial support only extends as far as the threshold of agency – this matches with the idea that the state should only intervene to create the appropriate conditions for autonomous social progress. Because of these limits to state responsibility, the actual benefit level of cash transfers is often meant to be quite limited (e.g., to a second meal a day, see GTZ 2005:20). In contrast, cash transfers in the Global North are often intended to close the poverty gap entirely and immediately. Transfers, for example, in Germany, are often supposed to provide a minimum standard of living just above the poverty line, which should allow for participation in social life (Huster et al. 2009:3).

However, the preceding analysis should not lead to the conclusion that development policy and social policy do not have any common ground and that the term 'social cash transfers' is merely a term to cover purely developmental policy models. Indeed, social policy in the Global North can also have developmental aspects. Consider, for instance, the increasing prevalence of 'activation' as a policy goal in European welfare states since the early 1990s, which emphasises the role of social policy in facilitating growth (Dingeldey 2005a:4, 2005b:4–5). While social cash transfers are still seen as a tool to maintain a minimum standard of living and reduce poverty, it has gradually become common sense that they should also be designed to promote re-entry into the labour market, or the 'activation' of beneficiaries. Comparable to cash transfers in development policy, the goal is to promote human capital and the willingness to work, that is, agency and economically rational behaviour (Dingeldey 2005a:5, 2005b:14–15). Such pedagogic effects are to be achieved through specific conditions for receipt of the transfers; therefore, conditional cash transfers actually come close to this style of social policy. Interestingly, the careers of 'activating social policy' and social cash transfers as policy ideas ran in parallel to a certain extent, the former becoming established somewhat earlier, in the late 1990s and early 2000s – further research beyond the scope of this book might explore whether there is a connection between national discourses on 'activating social policy' and the rise of cash transfers.

Conversely, development policy also shares some elements with social policy. Reaching and maintaining a minimum standard of living is a stated goal in both fields, and the fulfilment of basic needs does play a role for cash transfers, at least in relation to human capital. Ultimately, this may have eased the uptake of cash transfers by global development actors. It seems likely that the construction of the new policy models began by focusing on those elements which were familiar from development discourse and proceeded by emphasising them over those aspects of cash transfers which belong more to traditional social policy. The end result is a set of policy models which still share the basic design features of cash transfers in the Global North – being regular transfers of cash to people in need – while following different goals. On the level of design features, this has led to variants of cash transfers which primarily target certain categorical groups and offer relatively low benefits, up to a threshold of agency – in contrast to primarily need-oriented assistance to households in Western welfare states.

In sum, the way in which policy actors have taken up cash transfers and filtered aspects of this policy model that stem from social policy also indicates in how far the legitimisation of cash transfers has revolutionised development. My analysis illustrates that cash transfers are not a development revolution in the narrow sense of the term. That is to say, the introduction of cash transfers is certainly not part of a complete upheaval of development policy. After all, traditionally important concepts like economic growth and long-term thinking on social progress have remained in focus and have shaped the way cash transfers were constructed. However, cash transfers have still been part of a change in development policy; if not a revolution, this process of change has gradually introduced new concepts that legitimise cash transfers. The emergence of human development has introduced individuals and their capabilities as units of development and has lifted social policies to a much higher status in development policy. In so far, cash transfers that cater to both traditional ideas of development and more recent concepts of human development provide a compromise to which the majority of policy actors can agree.

4.2.6   Historical analysis

With this, I proceed to the historical analysis of development discourse and ask in how far discursive shifts have prepared the ground for social cash transfers. I find that development discourse was initially focused on economic growth and rather disregarded direct poverty reduction and human development. This changed when many policy actors became disillusioned with market-based policies in the 1980s due to widespread perceptions of rising poverty. Ultimately, this led to a shift in discourse that re-focused development on states and markets as complementary actors in development policy and, crucially, constructed individual human capabilities as a unit of development. Ultimately, this shift towards individuals culminated in the idea that individuals are equally important as actors of development as nation states and markets. This 'individualisation' of development provides a strong legitimisation for cash transfers that were constructed as investment into individuals.

'Development' as a basic concept has a long history in European thinking. According to Gilbert Rist (2006:25–46, 47–68), concepts of human history as constant and teleological social progress can be traced from ancient Greece to 19th-century Europe, culminating in theories of 'social evolution', for example, Karl Marx or Herbert Spencer.

Modern development policy, however, did not emerge until after the Second World War, when an increasing number of colonies became independent and the United States and other developed nations pledged to support the former colonies in closing a perceived gap in wealth and economic growth (Rist 2006:69–79; Speich 2011). Specialised agencies were first set up by the newly founded United Nations, which declared 'development' as one of its key goals. One significant aspect in this historical phase of development is the role of the state. The emerging idea of social progress as a rationally controllable and technocratic process legitimised strong state intervention and central planning, making national governments the central agents of development (Emmerij et al. 2001:16–42).

All in all, economic growth and modernisation theory, based on the idea that developing countries merely needed to copy the historical paths of economic progress in the Global North, dominated development policy until the 1970s (Rist 2006:93–122). Then, concepts of development first began to change. The perception that many people in the Global South were living in deep poverty in spite of economic growth led to the emergence of the 'basic needs' approach, which defined the fulfilment of elementary human needs such as nutrition and housing as a priority of development and first legitimised direct interventions to help the poor (140–170; Emmerij et al. 2001:60–79). Rist points out that even such interventions were legitimised by expected gains in productivity, thus maintaining a strong connection to economic growth – indeed, a small number of publications at this time already mention 'human development' as a productive factor (e.g., World Bank 1980:iii, 1).

As mentioned earlier, the rise of economic liberalism and the success of monetarist theories in economics in the 1980s strongly re-focused development policy on economic growth and led to the disappearance of the 'basic needs' approach. This may well have been caused by the perceived failure of the centralised government planning and interventionist policies of the 1960s and 1970s to facilitate social progress – the resulting state bureaucracies were commonly seen as over-sized and inefficient (Emmerij et al. 2001:183–204). These factors combined to de-legitimise the state as the primary agent of development in favour of free markets. Developing countries began to follow policies of 'structural adjustment' to make their economies more competitive and direct state interventions subsided (Rist 2006:171–196).

These policies were also perceived as failures by the mid- to late 1980s due to a perception of rising poverty in developing countries. This led to a further attempt at re-thinking development (Rist 2006:171–196, 197–210): concepts of human development and social development emerged, advocating a departure from economic growth as the primary indicator of social progress.

In regards to cash transfers, this is the most significant discursive shift because the new focus on human capabilities and the consequences of structural growth policies put individuals in the centre of development (Emmerij et al. 2001:120–145). Consider, for instance, the following quotation from the first human development report (UNDP 1990:9): 'People are the real wealth of a nation'.

Before such ideas were established, the direct transfer of resources to the poor was secondary to structural policies – now, newly emerging goals of poverty reduction, social justice and employment legitimised social policy as an instrument of development. Even central supporters of 'structural adjustment' like the World Bank and the International monetary fund opened up to a broader approach to development. In consequence, human capital and an adequate standard of living were widely recognised as aspects of social progress (Emmerij et al. 2001:120–145). Not least, the poor were increasingly recognised as a primary target of development. Furthermore, discursive positions on the primary agent of development shifted again as human development became more influential. Since both purely governmental and purely market-based policies seemed to have failed, development organisations, for example, the UN, now began to develop hybrid concepts which proposed an 'adaptation' of the state to regulate the production of welfare by markets and balance out market failures (183–204).

In sum, development discourse had basically shifted into the *phenomenon structure* analysed earlier by the late 1990s. Most ideas which are central for the construction of cash transfers as global models were already in place: (1) regulated, 'pro-poor' growth as the central aspect of social progress; (2) states and markets as equally crucial drivers of development; (3) the importance of human capabilities or human capital to development; (4) poverty reduction as a primary goal, including the targeting of children and other categorical groups; and (5) the perception that individuals should be a primary unit of social progress.

I propose that one final discursive shift was necessary to legitimise cash transfers and enable their construction: the identification of individuals, especially the poor, as potential agents of development. As analysed earlier, the poor had already been identified as targets of human development and pro-poor growth during the 1990s. However, they were mostly perceived as passive recipients of the benefits of social progress.

However, as analysed in Section 4.1, the poor were gradually attributed with agency in development processes during the 1990s. In a first step, it was established that development policy should take account of poor people's demands, since they are natural experts regarding their own needs – while the poor were still regarded as more passive beneficiaries of the development process, they now had a voice in the design of development interventions, as individuals who had superior information on their specific livelihoods and needs (UN 1995:43). In a second step, the poor were defined as potential 'means of development' (DFID 1997:12) – this is a major discursive shift, since the position of the poor as a group in relation to social progress changes. Before this point the poor, as individuals, were objects of the actual process of development; now they were perceived as agents of development, on par with other actors like nation states and markets.

In the late 1990s, the idea that the poor may be agents of development was still relatively new and marginal in development discourse. Indeed, no other organisation besides DFID seems to have advocated it explicitly before the construction of cash transfers as policy models. For instance, neither the first Social Protection Strategy of the World Bank nor early ILO documents on the global extension of social security make mention of the poor as agents of development. The four major policy models analysed in Chapter 2, however, are strongly based on the idea that the poor as individuals that participate in society and in markets can and should contribute to development – as long as they receive the necessary support.

I propose that there is a dialectic relationship between the discursive shift towards poor individuals as agents of development and the rise of cash transfers as legitimate policy models. On the one hand, the legitimisation of cash transfers depended on the concept of individuals as potential agents of social progress, since it allowed policy actors to re-interpret cash transfers as instruments of development. On the other hand, the successful construction of policy models on the concept of individuals as agents of development also moved it to the centre of development discourse, nearly giving it an appearance of common sense.

In summary, the preceding analysis demonstrates that the current legitimacy of social cash transfers in development policy is the result of two discursive shifts which took place from the mid-1980s to the early 2000s. The discourse on development redefined individuals, including the poor, as agents of development, and the increase of human capabilities appeared as a new goal of development besides economic growth.

The common denominator of these two shifts is the individualisation of development. The capabilities of individual human beings were constructed both as an end and as a means of development. This increased the general legitimacy of policies which could be interpreted as a direct investment into individuals. In consequence, cash transfers were increasingly perceived as a legitimate instrument of development policy and were actively constructed as an instrument that fostered human capabilities and strengthened the agency of individuals.

4.3   Risk: the discovery of uncertainty

The analysis of policy models and the policy paradigm behind cash transfers has already illustrated that the concepts of risk, shocks, crises and vulnerability are of great importance in legitimising social protection and cash transfers – all types of social protection are frequently constructed as stabilisers that protect beneficiaries from all sorts of hazards, from unemployment to natural catastrophes.

I assert that the ubiquity of this language of vulnerability is the result of a global discourse on risks and crises that first emerged in the 1970s and has strongly shaped the positions of policy actors on social protection. Following initial debates on environmental problems and 'limits to growth', this discourse shifted to construct natural disasters as a threat to development. During the 1990s, this was gradually complemented by the perception that economic crises are similarly becoming a threat. Ultimately, this led to the emergence of the idea of *uncertainty*, a highly influential scheme of interpretation that established the perception that a high, and rising, frequency is an environment constant that always threatens development. Social protection and cash transfers were then constructed as instruments that could mitigate *uncertainty* to an extent that stabilises development at an acceptable level.

Again, in order to support this observation, I first analyse the *phenomenon structure* which consists of five categories: environmental constant, causes, consequences, victims and solutions (see Table 4.3). Secondly, I trace discursive shifts since the 1970s in order to specify their impact on the legitimisation of social cash transfers.

4.3.1   Environmental constant

The fundamental scheme of interpretation in the discourse is risk is uncertainty, which is constructed as an environmental constant. Policy actors perceive our natural and social environment as fundamentally insecure and unpredictable.

This is based on two assumptions: firstly, that the environment which we live in is nearly unpredictable and that unforeseen hazards – that is, natural disasters, economic crises and individual hazards in the life cycle – constantly threaten the global population (e.g., DFID 2011:7–9, 2004:4; HAI et al. 2005:2; Holzmann and Jorgensen 2000:2–3; OECD-DAC 2009:21; UNICEF 2012:13–21; World Bank 2009a:26, 197). These events are normally designated as 'shocks' or 'crises', and encompass both one-time events and long-lasting conditions. They are seen as dangerous because they threaten the livelihoods of their victims and thus impair economic growth and development. It is widely claimed that uncertainty has been increasing in recent decades and has become a defining feature of the modern social and economic order – policy actors often emphasise that the number of 'shocks' and 'crises' has been growing in recent decades and will continue to do so (e.g., ILO 2001:34–35; ILO 2004b:39; World Bank 2009a:xiii; World Bank/Poverty Group 1999:7).

Secondly, that people and societies inherently require some sort of protection against such effects to function normally, due to psychological and social factors, especially feelings of insecurity experienced by those who are affected by risks. These perceptions of insecurity are constructed as a factor that damages social cohesion and inhibits economic activity; thus insecurity is widely regarded as the source of social problems like poverty, social inequities and social disintegration (DFID 2004:4; HAI et al. 2005:2; Holzmann and Jorgensen 2000; ILO 2004b; OECD-DAC 2009:21; UNICEF 2012:13–21).

While these basic assumptions are widely shared within the policy field, there is some variation between the discursive positions of development organisations concerning the spheres of life which are perceived as threatened by uncertainty. The World Bank focuses on economic hazards, while the ILO proposes a holistic concept of uncertainty which pertains

Table 4.3 Phenomenon structure of the discourse on risk and crises

Category	Content
Environmental constant	*Uncertainty* is constructed as a fundamental characteristic of our environment. That is, social and natural events are essentially contingent, making certain hazards a constant threat to human well-being. Historically, a gradual increase of *uncertainty* is perceived. This is compounded by the perception that human beings have a natural need for 'security', that is, to feel safe from such hazards.
Causes	To a large extent, *uncertainty* is perceived as a natural feature – specific causes are not usually given. Its increase, however, is widely attributed to a number of chronic conditions and crises: globalisation, climate change, HIV/AIDS and recurrent economic breakdowns.
Consequences	Unchecked *uncertainty* is thought to be the root cause behind the most pressing social problems, especially in developing countries: • The threat of 'risks' causes behaviour which keeps people from realising their full economic potential. This perpetuates poverty and inhibits growth. • Manifest 'risks' in the form of 'crises' and 'shocks' destroy livelihoods, exacerbating poverty and causing social disintegration.
Victims	Hypothetically, everybody is subject to *uncertainty*, but since the ability to cope with 'risk' is dependent on resources and human capital, certain especially 'vulnerable groups' are identified: • The poor in general are seen as 'vulnerable' due to insufficient resources. Their coping strategies are perceived as circumstantially rational but inefficient, since they perpetuate or deepen poverty. • Categorical groups, specifically children, the elderly, the disabled and women are attributed the highest degree of 'vulnerability', because they cannot earn their livelihood by themselves and/or are socially marginalised.
Solutions	Even though *uncertainty* is defined as a natural constant, it is also perceived as manageable with the appropriate interventions. Generally, preventing the consequences of manifest *uncertainty* ex ante is preferred to mitigating them ex post: • One method is to indirectly mitigate the *uncertainty* of the environment with stabilising measures, which includes transparent and dependable administration, good infrastructure and reliable social services; • A second approach is to support the coping efforts of 'vulnerable groups' directly, by transferring resources and/or promoting human capital.

to all areas of life. These two variants of uncertainty are mirrored by a variation in the terminology. While the term 'risk' is often connected to variations of uncertainty which emphasise economic hazards, 'security', 'insecurity' and 'vulnerability' stand for more holistic approaches to this concept.

The term 'risk' has become widely used in global development policy since the World Bank introduced 'social risk management' as the centrepiece of its first 'Social Protection Sector Strategy' in 2001 (e.g., DFID 2011:7; HAI 2004:2; ILO 2001:46, 2010a:5–9; UNICEF and ODI 2009:12; World Bank 2001a). 'Social risk management' encompasses a variety of strategies which supposedly prepare potential victims for the consequences of manifested risks, which occur in the form of 'shocks' or 'crises' by stabilising their income. The Bank suggests many types of policy but focuses on 'safety nets', that is, short-term transfers of goods or cash which mitigate the worst consequences of manifested risks (e.g., World Bank 1990:90–102, 2008:11–44). The World Bank variant of the term 'risk' thus circumscribes a rather technocratic and residual approach to uncertainty which focuses more on the first element, that is, the impact of unpredictable hazards, and less on the second element, which deals with human psychology in the face of risk. The World Bank version of risk is also distinct because it mostly revolves around the impact of unpredictable events on economic activity. Unprotected exposure to risks is perceived to decrease the willingness of people to exploit economic opportunities and undertake profitable investments, as well as damaging to human capital (e.g., World Bank 2001a:146, 2006:148).

Other policy actors do not necessarily share this assessment and emphasise 'social risks' that stem from social inequities and long-standing structural factors – in consequence, the effects of risk and vulnerability on social relations and individual well-being are regarded equally important as economic effects (e.g., Devereux and Sabates-Wheeler 2004:6–7). In accordance with this argument, other policy actors, for example, the ILO, often criticise the World Bank for using an obfuscating terminology which wrongly focuses attention on 'extraneous' events and individual strategies of managing them without paying sufficient attention to the social context out of which both the risks and strategies are born (ibid.; ILO 2010c:16; UNICEF 2012:13–21). Indeed, the ILO favours a different terminology which rests on the dichotomous terms of 'insecurity' and 'security'. The 2004 publication *Economic Security for a Better World* explicitly develops these two terms from a critique of 'social risk management' (see ILO 2004b:3–17).

This is strongly based on the earlier concept of 'human security' which was introduced as a new perspective on 'human development' in the Human Development Report 1994 (UNDP 1994). This variant of uncertainty defines 'human security' as 'first, safety from such chronic threats as hunger, disease and repression. And second [...] protection from sudden and hurtful disruptions in the patterns of daily life-whether in homes, in jobs or in communities' (23). Terminology aside, the concept seems highly similar to 'social risk management'.

The major difference is that both the UNDP and later the ILO, further differentiate security into several more dimensions besides 'economic security'. The list varies between different actors, but besides 'economic security', 'health', 'food' and political representation are frequently named as further dimensions of security (e.g., ILO 2004b:viii–xi; UNDP 1994:24–25; UNICEF 2011). Furthermore, the ILO tends to see the need for security in these dimensions as a fundamental anthropological constant – lack of fulfilment, or 'insecurity' is perceived to cause 'socially irresponsible behaviour' and inhibit economic productivity (ILO 2004b:3, 2010a:5–6, 9, 115). Such 'insecurity' is also attributed to 'risks' – this term is picked up from the World Bank, in spite of criticism. More precisely, the International Labour Office distinguishes between 'hazards' as possible negative events and 'risk' as the probability of such events, claiming that there should be a clear terminological distinction between these two aspects (ILO 2010c:16).

To summarise, the usage of the terms 'security' and 'insecurity' implies a more holistic approach to the concept of uncertainty than 'risk', as they emphasise social conditions and the threat of destabilisation in non-economic spheres of human life.

However, the spread of the term 'risk' in global policy indicates that the concept of 'uncertainty' is currently centred on issues of 'economic security', that is, the impact of hazards on human capital and productivity. I posit that the influence of World Bank terminology and thinking was caused by the wide reception of the first Social Protection Sector Strategy of 2001, as 'social risk management' has become a staple of the debate on social protection (e.g., DFID 2011:6; HAI 2004:32). Even organisations like the ILO who also employ the term 'security' tend to copy the World Bank's terminology of 'risk' – critical engagement of 'social risk management' evidently forces other policy actors to partially adopt the Bank's terminology and thinking.

Terminological conflicts aside, all variants of uncertainty help to construct social cash transfers as policy models. I indicated in Chapter 2 that the regularity and predictability of cash transfers is widely perceived as one of their most defining and important characteristics. In fact, social protection and social security in general are regarded as 'stabilizers' in case of shocks and crises (e.g., ILO 2010a:23). Naturally, this strongly applies to social insurances, which transfer cash in case of certain events that are commonly seen as a risk, for example, unemployment, but rather cater to beneficiaries above the poverty line.

Cash transfers play a similar role for policy actors: even in the absence of social insurance, they are thought to secure the absolute minimum level of resources necessary for human welfare against the manifold 'shocks' and 'crises' (e.g., DFID 2011:6). Furthermore, the ILO points out that the existence of such transfers gives potential beneficiaries a feeling of 'security' which supports well-being and economic activity (e.g., ILO 2009a:86). As pressing social problems like poverty, social inequities and social disintegration are thought to be at least partially caused or exacerbated by the unmitigated impact of manifested risk and feelings of insecurity are expected to inhibit growth and social cohesion, the definition of cash transfers as regular and predictable stabilisers suggests them as an adequate solution.

Interestingly, the terminology of 'risk', 'crises' and 'shocks' which is used to describe the different hazards which are connected to uncertainty ultimately constructs both natural disasters and 'man-made' events like economic crises as part of the same category – this is illustrated by frequently depicted matrices of 'risk' that contain both sorts of events (e.g., Devereux and Rachel Sabates-Wheeler 2004:13; World Bank 2001a:12; UNICEF and ODI 2009:13). I argue that this facilitates the legitimisation of certain policies like cash transfers as universally applicable models, as long as they can be defined as tools to combat uncertainty. The connection to uncertainty constructs them as the solution to a wide variety of problems, as they also deal with the universal cause behind different types of hazards.

In sum, I assert that uncertainty as a scheme of interpretation is ambiguous and connected to a variety of overlapping terms but that it justifies social cash transfers as a feasible model of global policy in any case. The major difference between different variants of uncertainty is that they lead to an emphasis on different effects of cash transfers. Proponents of the economic variant connected to 'social risk management' rather emphasise that a mitigation of uncertainty via cash transfers will facilitate economic growth. In contrast, proponents of a more holistic position on uncertainty emphasise that cash transfers will improve the general well-being of the beneficiaries and prevent social problems.

4.3.2   Causes

The perceived causes behind *uncertainty* are important because they also shape perceptions of appropriate solutions. Interestingly *uncertainty* in itself is essentially regarded as natural and inevitable. While it is seen as the cause behind various social problems, no causal factors behind *uncertainty* are named. Ultimately, a central rationale for social protection has emerged from global discourse without being supported by hard data, in contrast to the ubiquitous usage of scientific evidence in current development policy. The claim that *uncertainty* is a natural phenomenon seems to eliminate the need for an elaborate justification.

However, the assumed increase in uncertainty in the recent past is generally attributed to four causal factors. First and foremost, globalisation is perceived to facilitate the transmission of events and conditions which increase uncertainty between different nation states and world regions (DFID 2011:8; ILO 2001:46, 2009b: 27; OECD-DAC 2009:132; World Bank 2011:1). This is a logical result of the common definition of globalisation: a gradual intensification of international and global interdependence through trade relations and other social connections.

Secondly, climate change is seen as the cause behind an increase in a specific aspect of uncertainty, that is, the rising number and intensity of natural disasters in the last few decades (e.g., DFID 2011:9–10, 45–46; ILO 2009a:125, 2011:15–16; OECD-DAC 2009:168, 178; World Bank 2001c:37). This increase in disasters is seen as continuous and inevitable, since climate change is perceived as a chronic condition.

Thirdly, HIV/AIDS is frequently named as a chronic condition of insecurity which harms livelihoods by decreasing labour power and causing social stigmatisation (e.g., ILO 2009a:125, 2009b: 53; Levine 2001; OECD-DAC 2009:18; World Bank 2009a:7).

Fourthly, recurrent global economic crises are identified as a major cause of rising uncertainty, as they are seen to cause sudden and drastic drops in income and growth on a global scale, thus deepening poverty and inhibiting development. Indeed, the 'Asian Crisis' of the late 1990s and the 'global financial crisis' which began in 2008 were used to justify the introduction of social protection and the need for a 'global social floor' – see later (Holzmann and Jorgensen 2000:5; ILO 2010a, 2010b:v; World Bank 2001a, 2009a:xi).

The attribution of causes to uncertainty has shaped cash transfers in so far that their effects have been constructed as tools that can mitigate these causes. Cash transfers are perceived as an instrument to shape a 'fair globalisation' to reduce the impact of natural catastrophes that stem from climate change and to stabilise livelihoods during economic crises (see Chapter 2).

4.3.3   Consequences

Crises and shocks also play a significant role as consequences of uncertainty. In general, policy actors differentiate between three main consequences:

Firstly, 'crises' and 'shocks' are generally defined as harmful events because they force people into negative coping strategies (e.g., DFID 2011:7; ILO 2010a:6; World Bank 2006:148, 2009a:1). Because poor people do not have many resources in any case, potential drops in welfare are perceived to force them into inefficient and ultimately damaging behaviour to maintain an acceptable standard of living, for example, selling off assets or putting their children to work (e.g., Holzmann and Jorgensen 2000:7, 17; OECD-DAC 2009:21; World Bank 2001a:33, 2008:17–19). This results in further loss of resources and human capital, lowering the potential to escape poverty and to contribute to development.

Secondly, there perceived to be a psychological component which operates even in the absence of manifest 'shocks'. The knowledge of potential hazards supposedly motivates people to adopt livelihoods which are relatively safe but also less profitable. A widely used example is that farmers in developing countries will plant less valuable crops which offer a dependable harvest instead of more delicate cash crops because they fear droughts or other natural catastrophes (e.g., DFID 2011:35; ILO 2009a:123). Again, this lowers the economic potential of people, possibly keeping them in poverty and inhibiting their contribution to development.

Thirdly, uncertainty is directly connected to the problem definition of social disintegration. The constant threat of 'crises' and 'shocks' is perceived to lower social solidarity and trust in the state, which damages social networks and decreases the capacity for public reform, as analysed earlier (Holzmann and Jorgensen 2000:23; ILO 2001:42, 2009b:7; OECD-DAC 2009:18; World Bank 2008:431).

The attribution of causes has also had a direct impact on the construction of cash transfers. Non-contributory benefits are generally constructed as instruments that give beneficiaries sufficient security via regular income to prevent negative coping and instil the psychological security that maintains economic security and social networks (see Chapter 3).

4.3.4   Victims

The fourth discursive category specifies the victims that are subject to *uncertainty* and its consequences. At first glance, this category may seem fairly broad – since *uncertainty* is perceived as an environmental constant, it should logically affect the entire global population equally.

At second glance, however, a distinction between different groups emerges. Vulnerability is constructed as an outcome of individual or group-specific resources and livelihoods. Accordingly, the poor and categorical groups like children and older people are identified as more vulnerable – this justifies the design of different policies for different target groups. In this respect, harmful strategies for coping with uncertainty also play a role. Vulnerable groups are further marked by the unavailability of efficient means to deal with risk and consequently by reduced contributions to development (e.g., World Bank 2008:346) – as a result, they are constructed as especially deserving of support.

I argue that the construction of vulnerable groups as a preferred target of policy has one paradox effect: it glosses over potential differences between the categorical groups which are designated with this term. Women, children, the older people and the disabled and the poorest of the poor are all defined as vulnerable groups. Furthermore, especially vulnerable sub-categories like widows or 'orphans and vulnerable children' are also mentioned (e.g., Levine 2001). It could be plausibly argued that each of these groups has highly specific needs and should thus be targeted with tailored policies. After all, the set of sub-groups is fairly heterogeneous, containing life-cycle groups like children and the older people, women as a particular gender and the disabled with a specific health disadvantage. In other words, the term 'vulnerable groups' subsumes people who might hypothetically be faced with very different problems and may not live under comparable conditions.

Nevertheless, the idea that all of these groups are especially 'vulnerable' allows policy actors to characterise them as part of a single category, facilitating the construction and legitimisation of policies. Since they all belong to one category, any policy that can be constructed as an instrument to reduce vulnerability can then be portrayed as a benefit to a wide variety of heterogeneous target groups – most of which are given priority as 'deserving poor'.

I posit that this happened in the case of cash transfers. Non-contributory benefits were attributed with traits that define them as a tool against vulnerability, thus making them equally beneficial to all vulnerable groups. If 'needs' instead of uncertainty was the guiding idea in social protection policy, it may well have been more difficult to legitimise a single policy model as a catch-all solution. As indicated, 'needs' are usually perceived as group-specific, making highly focused policy models more plausible. In contrast, uncertainty, the basic concept behind 'vulnerable groups', is defined as a general environmental constant and enables the construction of universally applicable models which can serve different groups.

4.3.5   Solutions

These policy models can be circumscribed as solutions to *uncertainty*. It should be emphasised that *uncertainty*, in spite if being an environmental constant, is actually perceived as a manageable phenomenon, if not entirely removable, as it is regarded as an essential characteristic of our environment.

The World Bank's prevalent 'social risk management' framework best exemplifies this aspect of the discourse on risk. Policy is supposed to protect from the harmful consequences of *uncertainty* without keeping people from high risk, high return activities (Holzmann and Jorgensen 2000; World Bank 2001a). Social risk management also illustrates that both indirect and direct interventions are constructed as solutions to uncertainty, as it includes both structural policies and 'safety nets'. Policy actors see the creation of a stable and predictable environment in terms of 'good governance' and good social services as an indirect way to mitigate uncertainty (e.g., World Bank 2001a:15). This is supposed to facilitate the coping strategies of 'vulnerable people' and to mitigate the psychological aspect of uncertainty by giving them the feeling that help is available in the case of 'crises' and 'shocks' (e.g., ILO 2010b:14).

Furthermore, the direct transfer of resources to vulnerable groups is also legitimised, both to support coping in the case of manifest risk and to support more resilient and profitable livelihoods in advance of potential hazards (e.g., HAI 2004:29). This explains why the regularity and predictability of cash transfers is emphasised to such an extent – attributing cash transfers with the ability to stabilise livelihoods constructs them as an instrument to manage uncertainty and thus legitimises them in terms of the discourse on risks and crises.

A common feature of both direct and indirect interventions to mitigate uncertainty is that policy actors prefer them to be preventive of harmful consequences rather than ex post attempts to mitigate their impact (e.g., World Bank 2008:18–20). This is not surprising in itself, since uncertainty is mostly deemed harmful due to the social problem that it causes via manifest 'shocks' and 'crises'; therefore, it makes sense to alleviate vulnerability by supporting livelihoods and coping strategies before such events take place.

It is, however, surprising, that cash transfers are today perceived as preventive measures. During the 1990s the early 2000s they were rather perceived as residual benefits to cushion the worst impact of 'shocks' and 'crises' – the World Bank's 'safety nets' approach to cash transfers which essentially compromises this position was dominant in global development policy (World Bank 2001a:13–14). During the phase of policy development (see Chapter 3) this changed: I propose that the increasing attribution of the poor with agency, as analysed in Section 4.1, also changed the perception of cash transfers. Whereas such transfers had originally been conceptualised as non-productive support of living standards, they were now seen as investments. In other words, before the crucial shift regarding agency in the discourse of poverty, cash transfers were constructed as instruments to mitigate the consequences of high vulnerability – afterwards, their assumed impact on human capital and economic activity helped to construct them as a tool that actually lowered vulnerability, at least in the long term.

4.3.6 Historical analysis

With this, I move to the historical analysis of shifts in the discourse on risk and their impact on cash transfers. I argue that the current discourse on risks and crises is an outcome of the global debate on environmental protection and climate change that newly emerged from the 1970s onwards. While risks and crises were not initially important concepts in development policy, they quickly emerged as influential ideas after global debates on the environmental impact of economic growth and sustainable development began. However, the concept of *uncertainty* only emerged fully in the late 1990s when the 'Asian crisis' focused the attention of policy actors on the impact of economic crises. Social protection, but not cash transfers specifically, was quickly picked up as stabilisers that could mitigate economic crises. Cash transfers were then gradually legitimised with reference to *uncertainty* during the 2000s, when non-contributory transfers were constructed as an instrument that could reduce vulnerability ex ante.

Early global policy documents until the 1970s did not refer to 'crises', 'risk' or 'vulnerability' to a significant extent. What is more, even barring the absence of such terms, closer analysis does not reveal *uncertainty* as a relevant scheme of interpretation (e.g., Chenery et al. 1975; ILO 1972, 1944, 1952). Experienced development experts report that social progress was regarded as certain and unproblematic in this phase. More specifically, it was expected that some policies, for example, mass education, would automatically set developing countries on a path to progress (Interview 4).

This begins to slowly change in the late 1970s: the 1979 OECD study *Facing Futures* is one of the first policy documents in the field of development which indicates the emergence of a global discourse on risk and crises. The purpose of the study was to prognosticate long-term economic developments, in order to facilitate policy-making in the face of new social problems like unemployment and low growth rates (1–2). Interestingly, a main point of the study is that future paths of development are contingent, since 'more or less abrupt changes in direction are conceivable' due to the uncertain effects of policy (65). Even though the likelihood of several different growth scenarios is calculated, the contingency of their realisation due to potential 'breaks' in the development process, for example, political revolutions or economic recessions, is emphasised (95–96). This is perceived as a sign that both developing and developed societies are 'vulnerable' to the 'risk of a major crisis', as various social, environmental and economic problems interact with each other (ibid.).

I propose that this was a first step in the development of uncertainty as a scheme of interpretation: both the perception of an unpredictably hazardous environment and the terminology of 'crisis', 'risk' and 'vulnerability' are present in rudimentary forms. Significantly, environmental pollution and climatic changes are identified as one major source of risks that may threaten growth (OECD 1979:56–61) – this corroborates the hypothesis that such problem definitions are at the root of the discourse on risk. What is more, the study already emphasises two points regarding climate change which currently characterise uncertainty as a scheme of interpretation: (1) that climatic systems are so complex that future events are barely predictable, and (2) that climate has become more unstable in the recent past, increasing the frequency of harmful fluctuations (59). Notably, a direct relationship between such events and social problems like poverty is not yet defined – this only changed in the late 1980s, when the global discourse on poverty grew more important.

Policy documents in the early 1980s, however, rarely mention 'risks' or 'crises' and do not seem to contain any references to uncertainty. Significantly, this also applies to documents which are tied to the first debate on social cash transfers in between 1985 and 1990 (e.g., Schubert and Balzer 1990:I). This indicates that the discourse on risk and crises was still in its early stages, that is, not joined by a sufficiently large number of actors to influence policy to a large extent. This may also help to explain why the first attempt to construct cash transfers as a global policy model ultimately failed. With *uncertainty*, a crucial legitimisation for cash transfers was yet lacking.

The idea of environmental and social risks and crises as a constant threat gained further influence on development policy during the 1980s in the context of 'sustainable development'. In the wake of a global debate on natural limits to economic growth in the 1970s, set, for example, by scarce resources and pollution, the term 'sustainability' emerged in an attempt to promote a more stable path of social progress which does not damage its own social and natural base (see Grober 2007).

Interestingly, the uptake of 'sustainable development' by the United Nations in the 1980s heavily relied on these terms like 'risk' and 'crisis'. The final report of the UN World Commission on Environment and Development, published in 1987, emphasises that social progress is threatened by an 'interlocking crisis' and 'global risks', that is, unforeseen changes and events in the natural environment as well as new social and economic problems (WCED 1987). These crises and risks are perceived as eroding the base of development; accordingly, the concept of 'sustainable development' is presented as an attempt to find a more stable solution.

All in all, the report does not refer to uncertainty in its current form: it is not emphasised as an environmental constant, and the suddenness and unpredictability of hazardous events is only mentioned implicitly. The focus is more on chronic crises and 'stress' stemming from environmental degradation than on sudden, one-time shocks. An encompassing matrix of different 'risks' is not yet constructed. What is more, references to 'vulnerable groups' are missing. Nevertheless, there are some indications that uncertainty as a fundamental concept was taking root. As mentioned, both the basic idea of destabilising and unpredictable environmental hazards and the terminology of 'crisis' and 'risk' first appear in a central policy document. Not least, the report also mentions that there is a 'rising incidence of disasters', that is, that the frequency of natural catastrophes has strongly increased since the 1960s (WCED 1987:31). It is further claimed that 'the impoverished in poor nations' suffer particularly, as they are more 'vulnerable' because their living conditions leave them more exposed (ibid.) – that is, the poor were first identified as specific victims of 'crises' and a relationship to the social problem of poverty was constructed.

During the 1990s, the discourse on risk and crises grew more elaborate and also began to influence the new debate on human development. Many policy documents between 1990 and 1999 refer to the particular 'vulnerability' of the poor to 'shocks', while women and children are now singled out as specific 'vulnerable groups' – this includes the Human Development Report 1997 and the report of the World Summit for Social Development (UN 1995:5, 7–8; UNDP 1997:61; World Bank 1990:iii, 38; World Bank/Poverty Group 1999:5–8, 12–13). In this phase, the participatory poverty research of the World Bank Poverty Group first emphasised the psychological stress or which 'insecurity', that is, the threat of 'shocks', caused the poor (World Bank/Poverty Group 1999). Even though all organisations still emphasised natural disasters as the primary hazards, they also identify a growing number of sources of uncertainty, for example, violent conflict, loss of earning power or life-cycle events like the death of a family member (UN 1995:8; van Ginneken 1999:53). In addition, the exacerbation of poverty is now explicitly perceived as a primary consequence of 'crises' and 'shocks', due to the inability of the poor to cope properly (Scoones 1998; World Bank/Poverty Group 1999:12–13). Significantly, social disintegration is now also mentioned as a social problem that may be caused by 'shocks' or 'crises' (e.g., UNDP 1997:66). Last but not least, both globalisation and HIV are first made out as sources of rising uncertainty, on par with environmental degradation, in the late 1990s (65). In so far, many ideas that came to legitimise basic social protection were already established in global policy.

However, the turning point in the discourse on risks and crises that led to the legitimisation of cash transfers was the period between 1999 and 2001. In the wake of the Asian crisis in 1999, *uncertainty* was increasingly perceived as a basic feature of modern society and was explicitly used to legitimise social protection as an instrument of development policy. As mentioned earlier, the World Bank published its first Social Protection Sector Strategy (SPSS) in 2001, making 'social risk management' the centrepiece of Bank policy. The uptake of social protection policies is justified in reference to the economic crisis in Asia, which is taken as a sign that any gains in development and poverty reduction are vulnerable to unforeseen and inevitable events (Holzmann and Jorgensen 2000:2–3; World Bank 2001a:ix).

The strategy introduced the now familiar terminology of 'risks', 'vulnerability', 'shocks' and 'crises' and was one of the first publications to define an encompassing matrix of different types of 'risk', which are defined as a constant global threat, especially to poor people (World Bank 2001a:x, 12, 2001c:161–162). Furthermore, globalisation was clearly identified as a factor which increased uncertainty by creating stronger trade connections between countries (Holzmann and Jorgensen 2000:5). As mentioned earlier, the first SPSS is also important because it focused social protection policy on the poor; indeed the poor are clearly identified as 'the most vulnerable in a society', both because they cannot cope with risk and because the psychological component of uncertainty keeps them from exploiting economic opportunities (8–9).

The 'social risk management' strategy also establishes the distinction between direct and indirect interventions to counteract uncertainty and the preference for preventive instruments (Holzmann and Jorgensen 2000:14–15, 17; World Bank 2001c:141, 159). Here, the main point is that cash transfers are not yet recognised as a preventive intervention, but are categorised as an instrument of ex post, coping to handle 'repeated or catastrophic risk'. Ex ante intervention is limited to indirect, structural policies which improve the functioning of markets and facilitate employment.

The ODI report on the DFID 'inter-agency workshop' in March 2000 (see Chapter 3) indicates that the increasingly elaborate discourse on risk and crises was taking hold with global organisations besides the World Bank. The contribution of DFID to the workshop points out that the 'Asian crisis' has demonstrated a need to secure developmental gains against 'risks' and further economic crises and identify social protection as the appropriate instrument, also because it facilitates the taking of positive economic risk by the poor (Conway et al. 2000:1–5, 9, 40, 58).

In addition, globalisation is identified as a factor which increases the 'risk' of hazardous events in the future (Conway et al. 2000:9, 62). Interestingly, the ILO also agrees on globalisation as a major factor of uncertainty in its contribution, even though it uses the term 'income insecurity' and draws different conclusions (22–23). The condition of 'insecurity' is mostly seen to affect 'informal sector workers', not the poor in general, due to the lack of appropriate insurance systems. In consequence, the global extension of social security is advocated, in order to alleviate poverty and facilitate economic growth. In other words, the problem definition of the 'coverage gap' here emerges in the context of a debate on uncertainty. Not least, publications on the workshop also emphasise 'social disintegration' as a consequence of 'crises' and thus uncertainty (10; Norton et al. 2001:43).

I argue that one crucial shift in the discourse on *uncertainty* within the debate surrounding the World Bank's social protection strategy concerns the types of risk that were recognised as manifestations of *uncertainty*. Policy actors now began to design encompassing matrices of risks in order to legitimise policy interventions. Notably, these matrices not only included natural disasters, but also economic risks. I would argue that the global recognition of the 'Asian crisis' as an *economic* crisis with worldwide repercussions helped to add new categories to the concept of risk. Initially, it had been limited to natural disasters and the like, stemming from the early debate on environmental pollution and climate change. In the 1990s, the list of potential 'risks' and 'shocks' had widened, but natural events remained the primary category. Now, in the wake of the 'Asian crisis', economic risks were perceived as equally important.

To summarise, the debate on social protection around 2001 seems to have established *uncertainty* as a global phenomenon in the perception of development organisations, and social protection was taken up as a solution since it could both prevent and mitigate manifest 'risks'. Social cash transfers, however, had not yet been recognised as an appropriate policy because they were widely regarded as ex post interventions.

This began to change in the following years, as some publications began to emphasise the preventive impact of cash transfers and the psychological component of *uncertainty*.

Stephen Devereux's (2001:50) paper *Social pensions in Namibia and South Africa*, for instance, emphasises that social pensions protect beneficiaries from risk because their 'regularity and reliability [...] facilitates access to credit and provides non-covariate buffers against livelihood shocks'. This is a clear difference to the categorisation of cash transfers as 'coping' instruments in 'social risk management'. Indeed, even World Bank papers begin to advance the idea of psychological ex ante effects of cash transfers around this time, pointing out that they provide a sense of security and thus facilitate the taking of economic risks which may increase welfare, that is, resistance to 'shocks' (Tabor 2002:7).

The psychological component of uncertainty which is implied in both of these documents was expanded upon by ILO publications. For example, *Economic Security for a Better World* (ILO 2004b) elaborated the terminology of 'security' and 'insecurity' in great detail, as an explicit critique of 'social risk management'.

On the one hand, *Economic Security for a Better World* reproduces central aspects of discourse encompassed by the World Bank strategy. Globalisation, for example, is identified as a factor of increasing global 'insecurity', and 'risk' is defined both as the threat of hazardous events and a prerequisite of economic growth. It is stated that a certain level of 'insecurity' is actually necessary for societies to develop and adapt (ILO 2004b:17, 19).

On the other hand, as mentioned earlier, the need for 'security' is explicitly defined as an anthropological constant, and lack of fulfilment is perceived as a direct cause of social disintegration (ILO 2004b:3–4, 9, 12). Indeed, the provision of 'basic security' is identified as a prerequisite for development, especially human development in the sense of increasing agency and freedom (15). The concept of 'basic security' includes 'basic income security', and a rights-based 'universal floor' is suggested as the appropriate solution (ibid.). Significantly, the authors later argue that regular cash transfers are 'the least costly and most rapid way of helping people in times of crisis' and are more efficient than other interventions because they reduce risk 'ex ante' by alleviating poverty (ILO 2004a:387). All in all, this is one of the first documents that explicitly constructs cash transfers as a preventive intervention against uncertainty.

Furthermore, the concept of a 'global social floor' also emerged from perceptions of increasing uncertainty. In early ILO (2004a) publications on the floor, globalisation is perceived to cause 'sudden change' which forces societies and individuals to cope – this is constructed as problematic because of the 'coverage gap', as mentioned earlier (109–110). Accordingly, it is claimed that '[a] certain minimum level of social protection needs to be accepted and undisputed as part of the socio-economic floor of the global economy' (110). Cash transfers, however, are not mentioned in this particular document – apparently, the discursive shift which constructed them as preventive measures was not complete.

Indeed, some actors, for example, DFID (2004:4), still defined cash transfers as residual coping instruments for categorical groups outside the labour market. However, the idea of increasing uncertainty and the construction of social protection, including cash transfers as stabilising measures which can counteract this development is found in ILO publications after 2004 (e.g., ILO 2006a). I would argue that the promotion of these ideas by one of the largest and most influential IOs facilitated their spread, especially since the 'global social floor' provided a powerful symbol that gained legitimacy after the financial crisis of 2008.

Meanwhile, other, coterminous shifts in discourse were strengthening the legitimisation of cash transfers. The concept of 'vulnerable groups', for instance, was becoming more important and the life cycle was established as its base. In fact, Hoogeven (2004:25–30) and his co-writers suggest that the identification of 'vulnerable groups' should be the first step in setting up 'social risk management' policies and claim that 'the life cycle approach is commonly used to identify different vulnerable groups and to prioritize amongst them'.

All in all, it can be stated that the discourse on risk and crisis was sufficiently established to legitimise cash transfers by the mid-2000s. This is reflected in policy documents in the following years (e.g., HAI et al. 2005:2; ODI and GTZ 2005). Indeed, even the World Bank gradually changed the policy idea of 'safety nets' by recognising that cash transfers could have a preventive effect via the psychology of beneficiaries.

Consider the following quotation from the flagship publication *For Protection and Promotion* (World Bank 2008:19): 'Some safety nets can provide an insurance function to help households avoid taking ex ante risk management decisions that lower their incomes. If households could know that in the event of a bad year they would have reliable access to a safety net program, they could make their income and investment decisions based more on return and less on security'.

While the rest of the document mostly defines cash transfers as residual mechanisms to mitigate the impact of uncertainty (World Bank 2008:267, 335), the quotation indicates that their re-categorisation as preventive measures was becoming common sense. I argue that the construction of this effect as a consequence of the psychology of individual beneficiaries is most likely a major cause of this development. The idea that transfers might affect individual perceptions of risk and thus change economic behaviour matches well with the increasing emphasis on individuals in both the discourses on development and poverty, as analysed earlier. Not least, *For Protection and Promotion* illustrates that the construction of certain categorical groups as 'vulnerable groups' had been linked to cash transfers by 2008. Both social pensions and family allowances are legitimised as specific safety nets for elderly and children in a chapter entitled 'Assisting Traditionally Vulnerable Groups' (346–372).

The final shift in the discourse on risk and crises, however, took place in 2008 and 2009, as the global financial crisis was employed to further legitimise social protection and cash transfers. Publications on cash transfers from 2008 onwards frequently argue that they are the best tool to reduce vulnerability ex ante and to mitigate crises ex post, referring to the financial crisis as an indicator for increasing uncertainty. The regularity and predictability of cash transfers from the perspective of the beneficiaries is usually mentioned to legitimise this assertion (e.g., ILO 2009b:3, 32; OECD-DAC 2009:11, 17, 20–23, 45; World Bank 2009a:xi–xiii, 123).

What is more, the 'global social floor' was officially recognised by the United Nations as part of an initiative to counteract the global financial crisis (UN-CEB 2009). That is to say, without the widespread perception of a new global crisis, a category constructed in this discourse, the crucial symbolical recognition of cash transfers as a universally applicable tool of protection may not have come to pass. Indeed, the official publication of the UN Chief Executive's board exemplifies how cash transfers are legitimised in terms of the discourse on risk and crises. It is first claimed that action against a global crisis, perceived as the result of strong globalisation, is necessary because it exacerbates poverty and social disintegration (3, 5). A 'social protection floor' is then constructed as an appropriate countermeasure since 'social security benefits and public health services act as social, health and economic stabilizers' by alleviating poverty and supporting economic demand (20). Cash transfers in particular are advocated as a potential tool to empower people and strengthen their human capital, thus increasing resistance against future crises (19). Here, 'stability' emerges as the defining characteristic of a 'global social floor', mirrored in the common emphasis of regularity in the case of cash transfers – both traits legitimise these policies as protection against uncertainty. These arguments are essentially repeated in later ILO (2010a:1, 5, 45, 104–105) publications which elaborate on the concept of the 'global social floor', predominantly *Extending Social Security to All*, which also emphasises the need for security as an anthropological constant.

In the wake of the official recognition of the 'global social floor', other organisations such as DFID (2011:5–10), who had rarely framed cash transfers in terms of risks, also began to legitimise them as tools to decrease vulnerability and advocated social protection measures as 'automatic stabilisers' in the current times of crisis. This supports the hypothesis that the adoption of the 'floor' by the UN had a significant impact on the level of ideas by strengthening existing arguments for cash transfers that had not been widely accepted before.

The spread of these arguments may have been reinforced by further UN (2011) publications, for example, *The Global Social Crisis*, which emphasised the global character and disastrous social impact of the crisis and constructed social protection and a social floor as necessary countermeasures (9–10). Further evidence for the increased strength of the discourse on risk can be found in the new social protection strategy published by UNICEF in 2012. The document defines social protection as a set of instruments which reduces vulnerabilities and justifies it by claiming that increasing 'volatility', manifested in more numerous crises, has become a fundamental feature of human life (UNICEF 2012:5–6, 14, 23).

In all of these cases, the idea of a 'social floor' is referenced in some form – indeed, the UNICEF strategy is centred on its implementation. Even though the second Social Protection Sector Strategy of the World Bank does not refer to a 'social floor', it also reproduces central elements of the discourse on risk, including the idea that 'volatility' and 'risk' are inevitable features of modern life and that social protection and cash transfers can both cushion the impact of crises and help people build more resilient livelihoods by giving them a feeling of security (World Bank 2012:1, 14, 24).

To summarise, I have illustrated how the emergence of the discourse on risks and crises from debates on environmental problems in the 1970s has contributed to the construction and legitimisation of cash transfers as a policy model. In short, starting in the 1970s, policy actors increasingly perceived uncertainty as a natural background condition that threatens development. During the 1990s, uncertainty was also constructed as a common cause behind social problems like poverty and finally connected to social cash transfers after the 'Asian Crisis'. From 2000 onwards, cash transfers were more and more constructed as preventive solutions to uncertainty because regularity was emphasised as a key characteristic of non-contributory benefits.

4.4   Human rights: the rise of social rights

My analysis has repeatedly demonstrated that human rights have played a central role in the emergence of cash transfers as legitimate development policy. Non-contributory benefits are widely regarded as an instrument to fulfil different human rights, including the right to social security and the right to an adequate standard of living. In so far, cash transfers are strongly legitimised by *social* rights. However, social rights were long under-emphasised in global human rights discourse, in favour of civil and political rights.

I assert that since the 1980s, human rights discourse has undergone two major shifts that have legitimised cash transfers. Firstly, human rights in general first gained importance in development policy starting in the 1970s, after having been mostly peripheral to global policy since their inception in 1948. In the 1990s, the increasing influence of human rights culminated in the idea that fulfilling these rights should be a major goal of development, preparing the ground for the construction of new policies. Secondly, starting in the 1980s, the relative importance of social rights compared to civil and political rights grew significantly, until policy actors perceived the fulfilment of social rights as a central goal of development policy. This shift specifically facilitated the construction of new policies that could be argued to promote social rights, such as cash transfers.

Again, I follow the structure established in the previous sections. In the first step of analysis, I delineate the phenomenon structure of human rights discourse (see Table 4.4). In the second step, I move on to

Table 4.4 Phenomenon structure of human rights discourse

Category	Content
Moral code	Human rights are widely defined as a universally applicable code of ethics and rules which specify ideal conditions of human existence. Two overlapping justifications for their universality and appropriateness are usually given: • human rights are a natural moral imperative, founded on the inherent dignity of human beings and • they have been officially approved by a majority of the world's states in binding legal treaties. This is complemented by the assertion that the realisation of human rights will also have positive effects on economic and social development.
Policy imperative	In consequence of their claim to universal applicability, the realisation of human rights is widely taken for granted as a goal of global policy. From the perspective of human rights discourse, every intervention should be designed to facilitate their fulfilment. A minimum level of rights that every person should enjoy is constructed as the first step towards realisation. This includes the right to basic necessities like housing, food and clothing but also a minimum of social protection.
Claimants	Human rights are constructed as legal guarantees to every individual human being. Therefore, everybody is perceived as a potential claimant. However, people whose rights are not fulfilled are given priority. The concept of rights as individual entitlements implies that mechanisms for making individual claims are necessary.
Social responsibility	The concept of human rights as entitlements necessitates the definition of actors who are responsible for their realisation. In general, nation states are identified as the primary guarantors of human rights. However, their fulfilment is also thought to be part of the mandate of some international organisations.
Obstacles	Several conditions are seen as impediments to the realisation of human rights and the making of claims by individuals: • First and foremost, poverty is seen as a violation of human rights in itself because it implies a failure to fulfil minimum standards. • The 'structural problems of social security' is seen as a specific obstacle to the right to social security. • A lack of 'good governance', that is, transparency and accountability of government and administration, is thought to hinder the making of claims.
Instruments	Two broad categories of instruments to achieve the realisation of human rights are specified: • firstly, the *creation of structures* that allow people to claim rights are advocated, for example, human rights courts, ombudsmen and 'good governance'; • secondly, policies to *directly facilitate the realisation of rights* are suggested, that is, the provision of the necessary goods and services. This includes financial assistance, for example, SCT.

a historical analysis of discursive shifts towards a greater importance of human rights.

4.4.1   Moral code

I designate the most basic category of human rights discourse as 'moral code'. This circumscribes the construction of a set of rules which specify the ideal, morally appropriate conditions of human life. The specific feature of human rights is that they are constructed as universally applicable due to two overlapping arguments.

Firstly, human rights are regarded as a quasi-natural moral imperative because they are perceived to protect the inherent dignity of human beings. Secondly, in a legalistic interpretation, human rights are treated as universal because they have been put into international treaties which have been signed by a majority of nation states (see Munro 2010:30–31; e.g., DFID 2006b:73; ILO 2004b:5, 2009b:1, 9–10, 2010a:10; van Ginneken 2009:230; also see references in Chapter 3.2.2).

However, policy actors in the field of cash transfers rarely discuss human rights in great detail. The two foundations identified earlier are often only implied in policy documents – especially the justification by natural law is only rarely found in the form of brief appeals to the moral value of rights (e.g., ILO 2009b:1). The justification via legal treaties is mentioned more frequently and is perceive as the sign of a global consensus on the necessity and appropriateness of human rights.

The original Universal Declaration of Human Rights of 1948 and the two international Covenants on Civil and Political, as well as on Economic, Social and Cultural Rights (ICCPR and ICESCR) ratified in 1976, are regarded as the primary sources of the universal moral code – these documents are the foundation of the legalistic justification for the universality of human rights. In respect to social cash transfers, only a small part of the declaration and the treaties is used as legitimisation. Mostly the UDHR (Articles 22 and 25) and the ICESCR (Articles 9 and 11) are used to advocate social protection and cash transfers – that is, they are legitimised purely in terms of social rights. Cash transfers are thus intended to contribute to the realisation of the rights to social security and an adequate standard of living, which are commonly constructed from these articles (e.g., HAI 2004:23; ILO 2001:56; Künnemann and Leonhard 2008:29–30).

However, this is not a given, as the articles in question are vaguely formulated. The primary source of human rights, the UDHR, does not specify what instruments social security actually encompasses and only lists a number of basic needs and risks that need to be covered to achieve an 'adequate standard of living' (UN 2012b). Even though the ICESCR was intended to translate the general ideas of the UDHR into a more specific programme of action, it remains similarly open (Craven 1995; e.g., van Ginneken 2009:230). The only significant difference is that 'social insurance' is named as part of the right to social security (UN 2012c).

To reiterate from Chapter 3, the essential human rights documents do not establish a specific right to basic social security in the form of non-contributory transfers. In this respect, it is notable that many policy documents on cash transfers mention human rights only as a brief introduction and/or in graphically separated 'boxes' besides the main text and immediately move on to describe the positive, utilitarian impact of transfers (e.g., DFID 2005:6–7). It seems that the perceived universal and natural character of human rights makes a detailed discussion of their precise relation to cash transfers in policy documents unnecessary in the eyes of policy actors – the fact that such benefits are commonly classified as sub-type of social security is apparently sufficient.

I argue that this supports the categorisation of human rights as a frame in the case of social cash transfers. They provide a universalistic background of legitimacy and authority, but the actual design of policy follows technocratic and utilitarian criteria (i.e., quantifiable benchmarks like the MDGs). Indeed, some development scholars criticise the incorporation of human rights into development policy as pure rhetoric, with little impact on actual practice (e.g., Uvin 2010). In the particular case of cash transfers, human rights serve to frame them as entitlements, which does have consequences for their perceived status in relation to other forms of poverty alleviation and aid.

The specific case of cash transfers further illustrates that the assumed moral appropriateness of human rights is often complemented by the assertion that their realisation also facilitates economic and social development (e.g., HAI 2006a:5, 2006b:3; ILO 2005, 2010c:v, 2011:22; Keeley 2012:131; UNICEF 2012:5). At first glance, this seems to be a puzzling inconsistency, since the universality of these rights should logically make any further arguments unnecessary. It should, however, be kept in mind that development organisations are essentially interested in the creation of tangible social progress, preferably in economic terms due to the nature of development discourse. In light of this, it appears consistent that even human rights require additional justification in utilitarian terms – especially since human rights were only weakly connected to development policy until the 1990s, as explained later.

4.4.2 Policy imperative

The second discursive category circumscribes the consequences of the construction of a universal moral code. The existence of universal, quasi-natural rights is perceived to simultaneously create the moral duty to realise those rights – they thus become a policy imperative. Even though human rights do not seem to have an impact on the design of policy models, their realisation is frequently mentioned as a goal. Most policy actors agree that development should encompass the gradual realisation of human rights (e.g., DFID 1997:17, 19; HAI 2004:23; OECD-DAC 2001:10; UN 2012:9–10; UN-CEB 2009:6). Social cash transfers are generally perceived as an appropriate means to this end. Firstly, they are normally categorised as a form of social security and therefore realise the right to social security. Secondly, since they are designed to improve the material well-being of beneficiaries and contribute to their health and education, they are also thought to realise a number of other rights, including the rights to an adequate living standard, food, health and education (e.g., GTZ 2005:3).

It is commonly recognised that the full realisation of human rights is a demanding task in terms of necessary resources and state capacity. In consequence, the concept of 'progressive realisation' has gained global legitimacy since its adoption in the ICESCR (Article 2.1; see Craven 1995; e.g., ILO 2010a:16; Künnemann and Leonhard 2008:25; UNICEF 2012:24). It prescribes that the obligated state parties have the duty to realise human rights only in so far as they have the necessary resources to do so but are then obligated to employ these resources fully.

However, as mentioned earlier, the treaties neither specify measures nor their acceptable cost. It is a strongly debated issue in human rights discourse, which measures poor developing countries are actually obligated to implement. In recent years, concurrent with the increased global consensus on cash transfers, the idea of a minimum of social rights as a first step towards full realisation has emerged with the 'global social floor'. Because the 'floor' is intended to realise social rights through basic social protection, it legitimises cash transfers as essential policies in terms of a guaranteed minimal set of human rights (see ILO 2010a; UNICEF 2012:23; van Ginneken 2009:236). The adoption of the latest ILO recommendation on 'national social protection floors' has thus greatly increased the symbolic status of cash transfers. Not least, calculations made by the ILO statistics department in the mid-2000s suggested that basic social security measures were affordable to developing countries at their current level of economic resources (ILO 2004c). This also justifies cash transfers, to the extent that 'progressive realisation', that is, lack of sufficient resources, can no longer be taken for granted as an argument against transfers.

It should be noted that the minimal set of human rights guarantees contained in the global social floor is not specified in quantitative terms – it remains similarly vague as the minimal threshold of agency analysed in Section 4.1. At most, policy actors indicate that the most basic rights, such as the right to food, should be satisfied by social cash transfers and that such levels have to be calculated locally (e.g., Künnemann and Leonhard 2008:24). This is connected to another internal contradiction of human rights discourse: even though human rights are supposed to be a universal moral code, their implementation is regarded as a purely national task, out of respect for local conditions and cultural variations – this includes the concept of a 'global social floor' (see ILO 2010a). Indeed, the final recommendation was modified to advocate the promotion of 'national social protection floors' (ILO 2012a). The shift in terminology, which emphasises national specificity and the possibility of different variants of the original concept, indicates that the ILO member states were unable or unwilling to agree on a definite quantitative minimum. In respect to cash transfer, this makes it very likely that associated ideas of a global social minimum will retain their mostly symbolic character.

4.4.3 Claimants

Since this discourse constructs a moral code in terms of rights, it needs to also define claimants to whom those rights apply. Since human rights are constructed as universal, every individual human being is seen as entitled to their fulfilment. In consequence, it is claimed that every individual should have opportunity to complain about the violation or non-fulfilment of human rights and to make binding claims of realisation (e.g. ILO 2009b: 38, 2011:131; Künnemann and Leonhard 2008:5; van Ginneken 2009:230).

However, there are some internal contradictions in human rights discourse concerning the position of individuals as the primary legal subjects. Many organisations, especially those which advocate the interests of categorical groups, for example, HelpAge International and UNICEF, refer to group-specific human rights in order to strengthen their arguments (e.g., HAI 2004; UNICEF 2012). In respect to cash transfers, the 'rights of children' and 'the rights of older people' are employed to promote policy models which rely on categorical targeting, that is, social pensions and family allowances. Indeed, a special UN convention on the rights of children exists, and HAI (2012) is lobbying for the creation of an equivalent document for older persons. What is more, social protection in general is often expected to promote the specific rights of women, as enshrined in the Convention on the Elimination of all Forms of Discrimination against Women (CEDAW; e.g., Devereux and Sabates-Wheeler 2004:24). From a standpoint of simple logic, this is not compatible with the very core idea of human rights found in article 2 of the UDHR: that one single moral code applies to every individual human being regardless of age, gender, nationality or other ascribed characteristics (UN 2012d). It should therefore be asked why the rights of categorical groups are an established idea in the discourse, even though their existence contradicts the essential ideas of human rights.

On the one hand, the rights certain groups were recognised early in the history of human rights (Normand and Zaidi 2008:247–288). Even though the Universal Declaration of human rights focuses on individual rights, both the rights of women and children received first attention before human rights even became important to public discourse in the 1970s. Women's rights were already mentioned in the United Nations charter of 1946, which also established a commission on the rights of women that led a successful campaign for the creation of CEDAW between 1968 and 1979. Children's rights were first taken account of by the creation of UNICEF in 1946, and a first declaration on the rights of children was adopted by the UN in 1959. There may be various reasons why group rights played such an early role in spite of the inherent individualism of human rights. In the case of children, for instance, the catastrophic after-effects of the Second World War on their well-being seems to first have motivated action (ibid.).

On the other hand, there may have been a crucial interaction with the other three global discourses which I analysed earlier. Each of these discourses constructs preferred target groups of policy in some form: the 'deserving poor','vulnerable groups', and children as future drivers of development. Note that children and older persons are thus especially legitimate target groups in most discourses. Since human rights discourse only gained significant influence on development policy after the other three (see later), it seems plausible that legitimising policy in terms of rights was easier if it referred to pre-established target groups.

In addition, specific target groups may also be a better match with the principles of cost-efficiency that pervade cash transfer policy (see Chapter 2). These principles prescribe that policies should be well-targeted in order to achieve the best results. This may well make it more difficult to legitimise policies which do not have a clear target group and thus poorly calculable costs. I assert that it would be more difficult to promote cash transfers that actually express the core idea of human rights and target individuals, irrespective of ascribed characteristics. Note that the policy model of general household assistance, which fits this description, is the least legitimate. In contrast, social pensions, CCT and family allowances have fairly limited target groups, each of which is also justifiable in terms of group-specific rights, 'deserving poor' and 'vulnerable groups'.

4.4.4   Social responsibility

Because the discourse on human rights constructs a universal set of rights, it not only has to create a category of claimants, but also needs to specify which social actors are obligated to fulfil the entitlements of these claimants. Comparable to the discourse on poverty, this can be circumscribed with a discursive category of social responsibility that identifies those social actors who are legally obligated to fulfil human rights.

In general, nation states are identified as the guarantors of human rights, since they are the signatories of the UDHR and ICESCR (e.g., Künnemann and Leonhard 2008:5). Some international organisations, for example, the ILO, also perceive the realisation of human rights as part of their mandate, but states are attributed with the actual legal responsibility and are thus susceptible to binding claims and accusations of violation (e.g., ILO 2011:10–13).

In this respect, human rights discourse most likely has a strong influence on the discourse on poverty, as indicated earlier. The main difference is that the concept of 'social responsibility' in human rights discourse does not seem to be qualified by the idea of agency – nation states are obligated to fulfil human rights to their full extent, barring the principle of 'progressive realisation'. However, human rights are sufficiently vague to allow for the specific concept of 'social responsibility' in poverty discourse. While the human rights treaties do specify that people have, for example, the right to an adequate living standard, they do not prescribe a particular way to reach that goal. In so far, it is entirely within the scope of human rights discourse if nation states manage to fulfil human rights by lifting people up to a threshold of agency and then rely on the assumed ability of markets to increase welfare. This is further evidence for the status of human rights as a frame in the case of cash transfers. They construct nation states as responsible social actors but do not clarify the exact nature of that responsibility – this is done in other discourses which specify social problems like poverty.

4.4.5   Obstacles

In spite of the strong policy imperative and the identification of clear target groups, the discourse on human rights does not construct their realisation as an inevitability. Indeed, as the discursive category of obstacles circumscribes, the fulfilment of rights is perceived as a complex and demanding process. A variety of global conditions are identified as impediments to the progressive realisation of rights – the discourse thus contributes to the definition of several social problems. Firstly, poverty in itself has been identified as a violation of human rights, as explained in Chapter 3. Because it can be framed as a failure to fulfil various rights, for example, the right to an adequate living standard, poverty is identified as an obstacle to the global realisation of human rights in general (HAI 2000:5; OECD-DAC 2001:46; UNDP 1997:106; van Ginneken 2009:239). Secondly, 'structural problems of social security', particularly the 'coverage gap', are perceived as specifically hindering the realisation of the right to social security, as they imply a lack of appropriate policies. Last but not least, many actors complain that mechanisms which would allow people to claim their rights are not sufficiently implemented: clear, transparent administrative structures and legal procedures which would allow people to identify violations and file a complaint are supposedly lacking in developing countries (e.g., Künnemann and Leonhard 2008:23). In light of this, the process of realisation is slowed, since the obligated state parties can rarely be sanctioned for violations.

4.4.6   Instruments

The identification of obstacles shapes the final discursive category of instruments, that is, the means which are expected to facilitate the process of progressive realisation. All in all, two sub-categories of instruments can be distinguished.

Firstly, the implementation of structures which indirectly facilitate the making of rights claims is advocated; as mentioned earlier, this encompasses better administration or 'good governance', as well as actual legal structures, for example, human rights ombudsmen, specialised courts and legislation that allows direct claims (Keeley 2012:127–134; Künnemann and Leonhard 2008:23; OECD-DAC 2001:19; van Ginneken 2009:241). Secondly, direct interventions to realise rights are demanded, which primarily means the transfer of resources and/or the provision of social services (e.g., HAI 2006b:15, 2004:10, 23; ILO 2010a:17, 46; Künnemann and Leonhard 2008:5, 21–22).

Cash transfers have been constructed as direct interventions to realise rights because they are thought to have a positive impact on a number of social rights. Since cash transfers are defined as a direct transfer of resources to households or individuals, it is claimed that they contribute to the fulfilment the right to food and the right to an adequate living standard by alleviating poverty (Künnemann and Leonhard 2008:5, 21–22). Naturally, cash transfers are also defined as an inherent part of the right to social security, having been identified as an affordable and effective type of social security in developing countries within other discourses.

This gives cash transfers a specific status in comparison to other forms of poverty alleviation which is generally used to emphasise their innovative character and superiority. More traditional forms of aid to the poor are often constructed as 'charity', that is, as entirely dependent on the goodwill of the donor, thus making the poor dependent (e.g., HAI et al. 2005:55; ILO 2004b:5–7; Künnemann and Leonhard 2008:27; OECD-DAC 2001:47; van Ginneken 2009). Cash transfers, in contrast, because they are defined as one component of the right to social security, are seen as an individual entitlement. In consequence, the hypothetical ability that makes a legal claim to a cash transfers is perceived to empower the poor because it lays binding obligations on governments.

In sum, cash transfers thus appear as appropriate interventions from the perspective of human rights discourse, with two caveats. On the one hand, they are not expected to fulfil human rights entirely, but are only seen as a first step in the process of realisation. As indicated earlier, cash transfers are thought to be part of an obligatory rights minimum, but this implies that they have to be complemented by other instruments of social protection to fulfil human rights, for example, social services and ultimately social insurance (see the ILO principle of the social security staircase which defines the floor as a first step in the progressive extension of social security; e.g., ILO 2010a).

On the other hand, the case of conditional cash transfers demonstrates that not all models of cash transfers are necessarily legitimised by human rights. As mentioned, the conditions which are at the heart of CCT as a policy model are being heavily criticised by policy actors who emphasise the importance of human rights. However, this second caveat concerns only CCT, who have a strong alternative legitimisation in terms of developmental goals via their perceived impact on human capital.

Before I proceed with the historical analysis of human rights discourse, I answer one outstanding research question on universalism, a concept which plays a central role in global discourse on human rights.

As explained in Section 2.2.4, Leisering (2008) suggests that a spread of universalism in global ideological discourses has prepared the rise of cash transfers because conflicting ideological discourses in global policy were now able to support non-contributory benefits. In turn, I assert that this hypothesis needs to be qualified since it does not fit with the low recognition of general household assistance by policy actors. To be more precise, it can be observed that global policy is not perfectly universalistic regarding cash transfers, since working-age poor are under-emphasised as a target group and are covered by other means of basic social protection.

However, the preceding analysis of human rights discourse indicates that Leisering's hypothesis is basically correct. Human rights discourse has indeed achieved significant influence on global policy actors since the early 1990s. This has certainly led to a pervasion of development policy by universalism – with the exception of the Bretton Woods institutions, virtually all policy actors agree that everybody is entitled to social protection and that human rights proscribe global extension of coverage.

However, the preceding analysis has also illustrated that universalism in the shape of human rights alone was not sufficient to legitimise cash transfers and was accompanied by shifts in three other global discourses, some of which had a non-universalistic character. First and foremost, the global discourses on poverty and risks and crises have established the categories of 'undeserving' and 'deserving poor' and 'vulnerable groups'. As analysed earlier, the construction of these target groups shapes how social responsibility and, in turn, universalism are constructed.

The result is a position which can be circumscribed as *categorical universalism*: only specific priority groups like older persons and children are meant to receive unconditional benefits as fulfilment of their rights, since they lack agency. From a moral standpoint they are therefore classified as 'deserving' and from a technocratic assessment of risks as 'vulnerable'. Because working-age poor are attributed with sufficient agency to support themselves, they are preferably targeted by other means of basic social protection. As indicated earlier, universalism in the form of cash transfers applies to them in so far as they drop below the critical threshold of agency, for example, in cases of extreme poverty – then cash transfers may be an option. Otherwise, support is conditioned and functions according to principles of reciprocity, as in the case of public employment programmes, which are still a preferred policy for this target group.

4.4.7 Historical analysis

With this, I proceed to the historical analysis of human rights discourse and look for discursive shifts which have helped to legitimise cash transfers as global policy models. The two primary shifts in this discourse are (1) the uptake of human rights as an operating principle by development policy, starting in the 1990s; and (2) the gradually increasing importance of social rights.

The historical origins of human rights discourse are beyond the scope of this book and have been well documented by other scholars (Irie et al. 2012; Ishay 2008; Moyn 2010; Normand and Zaidi 2008). In respect to basic social protection, the most pertinent historical observation is that social rights, in contrast to civil and political rights, were not in the foreground of discourse in 1948, when human rights were first codified in the Universal Declaration of Human Rights. Civil and political rights were generally regarded as more fundamental than social rights among the nation states who participated in the drafting of the UDHR (Moyn 2010:44–83; Normand and Zaidi 2008:188–193). In short, two main reasons were given for the primacy of civil and political rights (Craven 1995:9–14, 128–134; Normand and Zaidi 2008:209): (1) that they have historical priority, having been created with the destruction of the feudal order in the 18th century, while social rights were regarded as an outcome of industrialisation in the 19th and early 20th century; (2) that civil and political rights were easier to realise, since they were 'negative rights', that is, could be granted simply through appropriate legislation and respect of government power for individual freedoms through inaction. Social rights, in contrast, were framed as 'positive rights', that is, it was thought that their realisation necessitated a prolonged expenditure of resources. In the opinion of the influential nation states of the global North, civil and political rights were thus both more important than social rights from the perspective of legal tradition and less expensive.

Nevertheless, there was no political conflict on the inclusion of social rights in the UDHR, in spite of their assumed secondariness to civil and political rights. In the wake of the Second World War there was a basic consensus that market forces needed to be regulated to stabilise post-war order, and economic and social rights were taken for granted as a 'stage in development' by the draft commission (Moyn 2010:44–83; Davy 2013). However, this consensus did not extend to the actual formulation of social rights in the UDHR. The participating nation states had to find a compromise between their differing conceptions of social rights, which led to the relatively vague formulations mentioned earlier – the United

States, in tandem with the European countries, specifically rejected the inclusion of clear state duties (Davy 2013). Ultimately, such conflicts about the practical consequences of human rights led the member states of the newly founded UN to place their actual legislation into a binding form into separate treaties, giving the UDHR a mostly symbolic character (Moyn 2010:44–83; Normand and Zaidi 2008:139–242).

Because of this vague and non-binding character of the UDHR, human rights in general, and social rights in particular, failed to have significant influence on global politics and policy in the immediate post-war era (Moyn 2010:44–83). The United Nations, international law and global social movements rather focused on decolonisation and emphasised state sovereignty as a major principle (ibid.). This was not compatible with the idea of human rights as a universal moral code which transcended state authority. In consequence, they were widely regarded as pure rhetoric with no bearing on Cold War politics and their focus on military security. Development discourse and policy at the time focused on aggregate economic growth and the idea of 'trickle down'. Universal human rights and associated individual entitlements were not a central issue.

In fact, in the early years of the United Nations, up until the 1970s, very few NGOs focused on human rights and attempted to lobby for them on the global level (Moyn 2010:120–175). This may be explained by a lack of opportunities because human rights structures within the UN remained weak and did not offer much political leverage. The High Commission on Human Rights, for instance, had decided that it did not possess the mandate to consider individual petitions in 1947, even before the UDHR was ratified (Normand and Zaidi 2008:143–176) – an interesting contradiction to the supposedly individual character of human rights which greatly de-powered them.

According to Samuel Moyn, this only changed in the late 1960s and 1970s when the popular political ideologies of the time, for example, socialism, started to lose public support. It can be argued that human rights began to fill the resulting ideological vacuum as they were re-interpreted as a universal ideology which transcended politics and could be used to criticise the actions of national governments (Moyn 2010:120–175). At the same time, civil society, frustrated with the unresponsiveness of the UN, began to develop new forms of 'grass-roots' activism that employed human rights, predominantly symbolic activism to publicly shame nation states for their actions. Amnesty International in particular was successful with this strategy and significantly helped to popularise human rights as a universal moral code in public discourse – not least by being awarded with the Nobel peace prize in 1977. At the same time, the number of NGOs with a focus on human rights began to grow. It is, however, notable that Amnesty International was founded to promote civil and political rights and did not extend its mandate to economic, social and cultural rights until 2001 (Amnesty 2013) – the re-interpretation of human rights still neglected the aspect of economic and social rights. All in all, the salience and popularity of human rights, both in public discourse and specialised fields like international law, started to grow significantly since the 1970s (120–211).

In addition, two events in human rights discourse within the same time frame both began to increase the relative importance of social rights and strengthened the connection between human rights and development policy.

Firstly, the two binding human rights treaties that had been planned since the 1940s were finally adopted by the General Assembly of the UN in 1966 and came into force in 1976, after being ratified by a sufficient number of countries (Craven 1995). One of the treaties, the International Covenant on Economic, Social and Cultural Rights was specifically intended to promote these types of rights, including the right to social security. However, the political conflict between the UN member states about the specific content of human rights and mechanisms of implementation had not been solved (Normand and Zaidi 2008:197–243). Since the more powerful nations wished to avoid interference with their internal affairs, only a reporting mechanism without sanctions was established, consisting of regular state party reports to an observing body. This proved to be especially problematic in the case of the ICESCR – it did not receive an effective observing body until the Committee on Economic, Social and Cultural Rights was created by the UN Economic and Social Council in 1986. In short, the impact of the ICESCR on global policy was initially limited, even though it began to increase in the early 1990s.

Secondly, the debate on a 'right to development' within the UN emphasised economic and social rights and their potential role in development policy. The idea of a right to development emerged from the attempt of the developing countries to reform the global economy within the framework of the United Nations (Normand and Zaidi 2008:289–315). The original goal was to seek financial reparations for Northern colonialism in order to facilitate socio-economic development in the Global South. Because the developed countries remained staunchly opposed to any attempts to institutionalise such global redistribution in the UN, the developing countries switched tactics. Starting around 1967, they began to use the human rights system to advance their agenda, after gaining a numerical majority in the Commission on Human Rights (CHR), the main UN body for human rights questions (Normand and Zaidi 2008:298–303). In 1976, the CHR began to debate the creation of 'solidarity rights', that is, 'collective rights of peoples that require international as well as national efforts for their realization' (299) – the agenda for global redistribution was being translated into human rights terms. In short, the developing countries tried to tie the fulfilment of economic and social rights to reforms in the global economy, referring to the 'just international order' promised in the UDHR. Crucially, this included the argument that the traditional priority of civil and political rights was erroneous because the realisation of social and economic rights is a prerequisite for their fulfilment (300).

Ultimately, the developed countries rejected the suggested collective 'right to development', both because they did not want to de-legitimise the global economic order and because it clashed with the emphasis on individual civil and political rights in their legal traditions (Normand and Zaidi 2008:303–310). In the end, the UN (2013a) only adopted a non-binding resolution in 1986, which finally defined the right to development as the right of peoples 'to participate in, contribute to, and enjoy economic, social, cultural and political development, in which all human rights and fundamental freedoms can be fully realized' but did not mention global redistribution. Nevertheless, the declaration specifically emphasised social and economic aspects of development (ibid.). What is more, it can be argued that the debate on this right reduced the distance between human rights and development policy. Indeed, innovations of the 1990s such as Amartya Sen's capabilities approach and 'human development' first began to apply human rights as a principle of development (Normand and Zaidi 2008:312–313).

To recapitulate, in between 1948 and the late 1980s, human rights did not play a significant role in development policy, and social rights were long regarded as secondary and difficult to realise. In fact, none of the policy documents from that timespan which were analysed for this book make any mention of human rights. Interestingly, this includes those documents which were published in the context of the first debate on social cash transfers in between 1984 and 1990. Neither Bernd Schubert nor any other participant of the debate utilises human rights to legitimise cash transfers, nor to de-legitimise them. At this point the arguments for cash transfers were predominantly technocratic, referring to the lack of appropriate policies for the poorest of the poor. This changed in the second debate on cash transfers in the early 2000s and may well have contributed to their success.

The dissolution of the Soviet Union and the resulting changes in global politics around 1990 mark a turning point for human rights discourse. As mentioned, they had gradually become more salient in public discourse and specialised discourses, for example, within the United Nations system. But after the end of the Cold War and the accompanying further decline of political ideologies, the importance of human rights increased exponentially, both in terms of NGO activism and the specialised discourse of global development organisations (Normand and Zaidi 2008:316–342).

Indeed, the policy documents analysed here first begin to mention human rights in the early 1990s. Social rights, however, are rarely mentioned. As indicated earlier, human development was one of the first concepts to insert human rights into development policy. The first Human Development Report in 1990 clearly identifies human rights as part of the new approach to development in the second part of the official definition, 'but human development does not end there. Additional choices, highly valued by many people, range from political, economic and social freedom to opportunities for being creative and productive, and enjoying personal self-respect and guaranteed human rights' (UNDP 1990:10).

The quotation indicates that human rights, as 'additional choices', are still secondary to 'essential choices' mentioned before, for example, a long and healthy life or a decent standard of living (UNDP 1990:10). Nevertheless, the reference to 'political, economic and social freedom' implies that the authors of the report perceived the whole range of rights as part of human development, not just political and civil rights.

The status of human rights within the concept of human development increased markedly from this point. Reports from the early to mid-1990s mention human rights only selectively, for example, by defining an index for the measurement of political freedom based government respect for human rights or by emphasising the specific rights of women (UNDP 1992, 1995). This changes in the late 1990s. The Human Development Report 1998 states that 'human development leads to the realisation of human rights – economic, social, cultural, civil and political' (14) – explicitly rejecting a focus on civil and political rights.

Finally, the Human Development Report 2000, entitled 'Human Rights and Human Development' puts the relationship between the two concepts at the centre: 'Human rights and human development share a common vision and a common purpose – to secure the freedom, well-being and dignity of all people everywhere' (1). What is more, it is claimed that 'human development is essential for realizing human rights, and human rights are essential for full human development', again referring to a common goal of 'human freedom' (2). Here, human rights and human development are essentially presented as two overlapping approaches to social progress. Again, both civil and political as well as social and economic rights are defined as equally important – their respective realisation is even seen as constitutionally interdependent (9). In addition, poverty is framed as a problem in terms of human rights, as it is thought to 'limit human freedom' (73) – this may well be one of the first steps in the construction of the human rights facet of poverty as a social problem.

The emergence of human rights – including social rights – as a major objective of development can also be observed in other policy documents from 1995 onwards. The report of the World Summit for Social Development mentions human rights extensively, stating early that the 'vision of social development' is based on human rights (UN 1995:9). Their realisation, however, is not explicitly defined as a main goal of development, in contrast to the Human Development Report 2000. 'Sound' development policy is rather supposed to 'respect' human rights, that is, is not to lead to their violation and should help to 'promote' them (5, 10–11, 37–38) – in terms of policy, this translates into demands for 'rule of law' in developing countries. The report also emphasises the importance of the 'social aspect of human rights' but only refers to the 'right to development' (129). This indicates that the debate on the right to development during the 1970s and 1980s had lasting influence on development policy by emphasising social and economic rights.

Notably, DFID (1997) also included human rights in the white paper *Eliminating World Poverty*, which encompasses the development strategy of the then-new organisation. The document clearly affirms that DFID follows a 'commitment to human rights' and mentions that 'all states have committed themselves to respect, protect and realise human rights (16–17). Furthermore, 'good governance and the realisation of human rights' are also identified as an instrument for the elimination of poverty (19). This supports the observation that the human rights facet of poverty as a social problem was emerging in the late 1990s – even though it is only implied in this particular case. The DFID white paper is also one of the earliest cases in which social protection, human rights and development are mentioned together.

However, human rights became even more strongly connected to social protection and social security between 2000 and 2005, leading up to the recognition of cash transfers as a global policy model. The publications and activities of several organisations illustrate this.

Firstly, HelpAge International: in 2000, this organisation published *The Mark of a Noble Society*, which affirms human rights as the base of global values and demands the fulfilment of older people's rights through development – poverty is also recognised as a key impediment to human rights progress (1–5). Significantly, social protection or social pensions are not mentioned here. Conversely, the 2003 study on 'non-contributory pensions' mentioned before does not refer to human rights at all (HAI and IDPM 2003). This changes with *Age and Security*, HelpAge International's 2004 flagship publication. Protection against poverty in old age and social protection are now explicitly named as human rights with reference to the UDHR and the human rights treaties (10, 23–24). The appropriateness and growing importance of social pensions in developing countries is justified by their status as a 'key element' of social protection and the increasing prevalence of 'rights-based approaches' to development within the UN system. It is also notable that the characteristic pattern of a combined moral and utilitarian argumentation emerges here. Human rights are also advocated because their realisation is perceived to facilitate older people's contributions to development (HAI 2000:4).

Secondly, the ILO: during the 1990s, the International Labour Organisation did not publish any significant work on human rights and social protection or development. However, the new campaign for the global extension of social security, started in 2001, was essentially based on human rights. The mandate to advocate a global extension of social security is justified by its status as a right within the UDHR, the accompanying treaties, as well as ILO conventions (ILO 2001:1, 56). Following the start of the campaign, most ILO policy documents begin by justifying the need for social security in terms of human rights (e.g., ILO 2005:1, 2006a:1, 5). As analysed earlier, the problem definition of a global 'coverage gap' was also constructed in the context of this campaign, mostly referring to the human right to social security.

Thirdly, as mentioned earlier, the DFID (2005:6–7) practice paper on 'social transfers' of 2005 clearly advocates them with reference to human rights, specifically the right to social protection in the UDHR and the ICESCR. It should be emphasised that the first comprehensive policy document on cash transfers practically takes their appropriateness in terms of human rights for granted and does not elaborate on exact connections or potential problems. This supports the observation that human rights function as a frame in development policy. Apparently, human rights had already become recognised as a universal moral code in development policy by this point, so that it sufficed to symbolically place cash transfers in their context via reference to the recognised human rights treaties.

In short, human rights were immediately used as a frame to legitimise social cash transfers as policy models. Conditional cash transfers are the sole exception. Neither the World Bank nor the Inter-American Development Bank, the two major organisations behind their construction as a policy model, have ever justified them with reference to human rights. Indeed, it is notable that the Bretton Woods institutions, including the World Bank, are the sole organisations within the UN system that have generally refused to employ human rights ideas (Normand and Zaidi 2008:313).

The status of human rights as a normative frame did not change significantly after 2005, even as social cash transfers gained increasing recognition as policy models. The reference to human rights is still used to construct the essential moral appropriateness and necessity of social cash transfers – or the inappropriateness of specific model, as in the case of CCT.

Nevertheless, on more important discursive shift took place with the creation and widespread recognition of the 'global social floor'. As mentioned, the ILO began to re-emphasise human rights, specifically the right to social security, in 2001. The idea of a 'global social floor' emerged from this renewed interest in human rights. The final report of the ILO World Commission on the Social Dimension of Globalisation is generally accepted as the first publication to officially use the term 'social floor' (e.g., ILO and WHO 2009b:4). The document in general criticises the negative consequences of globalisation, such as insecurity and poverty, naming the neglect of human rights as one aspect of such problems. Consequently, the realisation of human rights is defined as part of a solution, that is, a 'social dimension of globalization' (ILO 2004a:2, 5).

The 'floor' is introduced as part of this process of realisation (ILO 2004a: 5): 'The essentials of this social dimension include: [...] An international commitment to ensure the basic material and other requirements of human dignity for all, enshrined in the Universal Declaration of Human Rights. The eradication of poverty and the attainment of the Millennium Development Goals (MDGs) should be seen as the first steps towards a socio-economic "floor" for the global economy'. The authors of the report later specify that 'a certain minimum level of social protection needs to be accepted and undisputed as part of the socio-economic floor of the global economy' because 'basic security' has been recognised as a human right (109–110).

Even though the term later changed from 'socio-economic floor' to 'global social floor', the essential idea of a necessary minimum level of social protection is clearly present. The point is that it emerges directly from the new assertion that there are certain minimal human rights obligations that extend to social protection – in the form of the 'international commitment to ensure the basic material and other requirements of human dignity' and the right to 'basic security'. Notably, social cash transfers are not yet mentioned here. Even though the basic idea of a social floor as a human rights obligation is established, it lacks specific policy models.

This changed in the following years. ILO papers begin to mention specific components of a 'socio-economic floor' as early as 2006, including 'minimum pensions' and 'cash grants for primary education', that is, CCT (ILO 2006a:23). That is, the discursive link between social cash transfers and human rights grew stronger, since they were gradually constructed as part of a minimum human rights obligation – an assertion which was increasingly shared by other organisations besides the ILO (e.g., HAI 2006a:31; Künnemann and Leonhard 2008).

Finally, in 2009, the joint paper of the ILO and the WHO on the 'social protection floor' as an official UN initiative against the global financial crisis explicitly states that 'the term "social floor" can correspond to the existing notion of "core obligations", to ensure the realization of, at the very least, minimum essential levels of rights embodied in human rights treaties' (ILO and WHO 2009b:4) – 'essential services' and 'social transfers' are named as the two main components (5). In the wake of the official recognition of the 'floor' by the UN, the ILO continued this line of argumentation and therefore presented social cash transfers as the realisation of 'basic social rights' and as individual entitlements (e.g., ILO 2010a:10, 17, 2011:10–11, 22, 131). As mentioned earlier, the 'global social floor' has been symbolically accepted by a significant number of other organisations, giving cash transfers a strong legitimisation in human rights terms from circa 2009 onwards (e.g., UNICEF 2012).

The emerging connection between human rights and cash transfers may be explained in several ways. Firstly, human rights had become taken for granted as a principle of development policy by the time that cash transfers were constructed as policy models in the early 2000s. From this perspective, it was simply necessary to frame cash transfers in terms of human rights in order to legitimise them as appropriate development policy – the policy models were shaped by pre-existing discursive structures.

Secondly, following the creation of the Committee on Economic, Social and Cultural Rights as the new observing body of the ICESCR in 1985, there were advances in specialised legal discourse on global social rights. On the one hand, an analysis of the state party reports to the Committee over time indicates that social rights have become increasingly important to national governments since the ratification of the ICESCR in 1976 (Davy 2013:11–13). Both the length of the reports and the quality of the information therein have improved considerably over the years. What is more, since circa 1993, the content of the reports has also changed: the original focus on development and economic growth has been replaced by an emphasis on the realisation of social rights through poverty alleviation (ibid.).

On the other hand, the Committee itself has fleshed out social rights by releasing official interpretations of the often vague ICESCR articles in the form of General Comments, starting in 1989 (UN 2013b). In 2008, General Comment No. 19, on the right to social security was released (UN 2013c). Crucially, the Committee here specifies that state parties to the ICESCR should implement both social insurance and non-contributory benefits, that is, cash transfers, in order to 'guarantee all peoples a minimum enjoyment of this human right' – notably, the original ICESCR article 9 on social security only mentions social insurance. In short, the gradual specification of social rights in specialised legal discourse on human rights has also changed discursive structures to accommodate the new policy models. Notably, the authors of General Comment No. 19 refer to an ILO publication which advocates the extension of social security via a 'global social floor' in order to support their arguments, indicating that innovations on the level of policy may have influenced more abstract human rights discourse (ILO 2006a).

To summarise, a series of shifts in human rights discourse over several decades has prepared the ground for the construction of social cash transfers as a legitimate policy model. Since their first codification in the UDHR, human rights have gradually become more important to development policy and social rights have significantly increased in importance. I posit that a strong global human rights discourse was necessary to provide a moral justification for cash transfers.

A comparison between the first debate on cash transfers in the 1980s and current global policy supports this argument. At first glance, it is surprising that the rationale for cash transfers in the first debate was purely technocratic, being based on new target groups and the efficient alleviation of gaps in development policy. In contrast, cash transfers were immediately framed as the fulfilment of universal human rights when the second debate began in the early 2000s. Since the rational and technocratic arguments for cash transfers have remained essentially the same, if more elaborate, the inclusion of human rights provided the additional moral legitimisation which was necessary to create widespread acceptance for the new policy models.

Indeed, current human rights discourse complements and reinforces the rational justification for cash transfers which results from the other discourses in a number of ways. First and foremost, the categorical groups which are defined both as 'deserving poor' and as especially 'vulnerable' in the discourses on poverty and risk are also attributed with group-specific rights. Cash transfers to children and the older persons are therefore not only feasible from a technocratic rationale which emphasises the efficient alleviation of social problems, but also a strong legal and moral obligation. Secondly, the idea of social responsibility in poverty discourse is strongly related to a similar idea in human rights discourse. In fact, the basic idea that national governments are obligated to offer a minimal standard of living seems to be rooted in human rights. However, the two discourses on poverty and rights offer two different and complementary definitions of this 'social minimum': the minimum which is set in poverty discourse is rather rational and technocratic, as it lies at the threshold of agency. Conversely, the 'social minimum' in human rights discourse is a moral minimum, set at the minimal standard of living necessary to preserve human dignity. Ultimately, both social minima are vague discursive categories, since they do not specify the amount of resources at which agency and dignity are secured – they remain mostly symbolic ideas.

4.5   Discourse coalitions and discursive practices

An overview of the analysis of global discourses also permits me to answer two open research questions: firstly, whether there are discourse coalitions in the field of cash transfers, and secondly, whether specific discursive practices characterise the global discourses analysed earlier.

Firstly, discourse coalitions: there are surprisingly few conflicting sub-positions within global discourses which might indicate the existence of discourse coalitions. Policy actors subscribe to the same basic schemes of interpretation but in slightly different versions. Still, observable differences in the global discourses on poverty, risk and human rights show a clear pattern: one group of actors rather emphasises problems of economic development, while a second group promotes a more holistic concept of human development.

In the discourse on poverty, some actors, like the UNDP, emphasise that individual capabilities are inherently valuable while others, like the World Bank, treat human skills and abilities as an economic factor, that is, as human capital – but virtually all actors still adhere to the basic idea that lack of capabilities or human capital is an important dimension of poverty as a major social problem.

In the case of the discourse on risk, there is a similar division between actors, as some, like the World Bank, emphasise economic risks as a major threat, while others, like the ILO, explicitly include social risks in the list of important hazards. However, all actors seem to be equally influenced by *uncertainty* as a basic scheme of interpretation.

The strongest divide between policy actors, however, concerns the global discourse on human rights. As indicated, the Bretton Woods institutions, most notably the World Bank, selectively ignore human rights in most, if not all, of their work. In so far, only the other policy actors in the field of cash transfers are influenced by the strong moral code which the discourse on human rights constructs.

All in all, the different positions in these three discourses signify the existence of two discourse coalitions in the field of cash transfers, based on different ideas of development. On the one hand, there is a set of actors that emphasises 'human development' and 'social development' alongside or even over economic development – here designated as the 'human development coalition'. This coalition includes a wide variety of policy actors: NGOs like HelpAge International and FIAN; UN sub-organisations like UNICEF, the UNDP or the ILO; academic think tanks like the IDS; and bilateral development agencies like DFID or GIZ. These policy actors generally adhere to human rights as a universal moral code and use them to legitimise or criticise policy. In terms of policy, the human development coalition tends to prefer non-conditioned benefits and tends to advocate universal transfers to 'vulnerable groups' like older people and children. On the other hand, there is an 'economic development coalition' which emphasises economic growth as the core process of development and mostly ignores human rights – as implied earlier, it is centred on the World Bank, but it also includes the other international development banks like the IADB and the ADB, as well as associated think-tanks like the IFPRI. In terms of policy, this coalition strongly prefers conditional cash transfers for their supposed effect on economic growth but also advocates social pensions to older persons or the disabled to support groups which can no longer contribute significantly to the economy.

It should be noted that these two coalitions are purely analytical divisions which focus on the most central positions of policy actors. Some organisations like DFID and the ILO demonstrate such broad and vague ideas on issues like the development and economic growth that they cannot be clearly assigned to the human development coalition. I suggest that these organisations may function as brokers between the two discourse coalitions. Indeed, both the ILO and the DFID are notable for their extensive cooperation with a variety of policy actors and their support for a wide variety of policy models – for instance, both organisations recognise human rights-based criticism of CCT but do not reject this policy model completely.

Secondly, discursive practices: two distinctive discursive practices can be identified in the four global discourses analysed here, with implications for speaking positions within global discourses. The major discursive practice which is used in all discourses is the presentation of scientific evidence, usually in the form of statistical data and statistical comparisons, as repeatedly emphasised earlier. This conforms with expectations derived from theory: apparently, global organisations do rely on the impersonal and objective perception of statistical data to construct social problems and policy models (see Chapter 1). This implies that scientific experts occupy privileged speaking positions in global discourses since they have the necessary qualifications and skills which allow them to produce statistical data which are recognised as objective representations of reality. Consider, for example, the impact of statistical studies like 'Non-contributory pensions and poverty prevention' have had on the legitimisation of cash transfers as policy models (HAI and IDPM 2003).

The second relevant practice is the usage of short narratives on the lives of the poor to illustrate poverty as a social problem, as well as the impact of certain policies like cash transfers. I would argue that this complements the usage of statistical data within global discourses because it is evidently a strongly personalised way of presenting information. As noted earlier, such narratives are often told from the perspective of the poor and may include verbatim quotations. This indicates that the poor were thus also given a speaking position in global discourses, implicitly justified by their status as victims of major social problems. The utilisation of narratives which established this speaking position coincides with the attribution of the poor with agency in the late 1990s and early 2000s. It cannot be clearly determined whether the use of narrative is a cause or a consequence of this process of attribution. Ultimately, it seems likely that the introduction of the practice and emergence of the agency of the poor on the level of ideas are causally interdependent and have mutually reinforced each other – making it impossible to say which came first.

Conclusion

At the beginning of this book, I set out to provide a comprehensive analysis of the career of social cash transfers in global policy. Two major questions have guided this analysis: Firstly, in how far cash transfers have been part of a 'development revolution', and secondly, whether cash transfers are connected to a wider model of social protection that has implications for the future of social policy in the Global South.

In order to answer these questions, I checked if cash transfers have become recognised as policy models that are legitimised by a policy paradigm and overarching global discourses. My analysis illustrates that four variants of cash transfers – family allowances, conditional cash transfers, social pensions and general household assistance – have indeed been institutionalised as global models and are embedded into a global paradigm of social protection based on four discourses (see Figure C.1).

An overview of policy models, paradigms and discourses indicates that cash transfers are legitimised by a mixture of economic, social and rights-based rationales that combine traditional ideas of development policy with concepts that have emerged more recently. Evidently, the one legitimisation for cash transfers that a majority of policy actors can agree on is that such benefits facilitate economic growth, if in the long term. Virtually all variants of non-contributory benefits are attributed with the ability to strengthen the human capital of beneficiaries and enable them to participate in markets. The strong reliance on economic growth indicates that cash transfers have not been part of a thorough development revolution because development policy has been charac-terised by a focus on growth since its very inception.

However, the type of economic growth and the role that beneficiaries of cash transfers are expected to play also point to innovative concepts

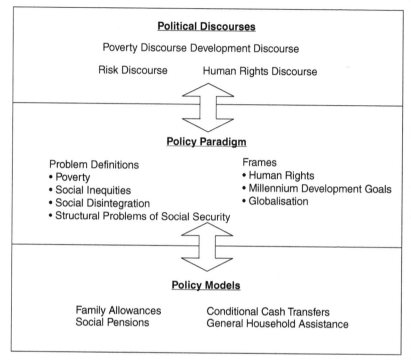

Figure C.1   The discursive background of social cash transfers

that have legitimised non-contributory benefits in development policy. Currently, growth is widely expected to be 'pro-poor'. The idea of 'pro-poor growth' basically indicates that the poor should benefit more directly from growth. It is also connected to a shift in perceptions on the agency of the poor. Fostering the human capital of the poor has become a major goal of development policy because the poor were constructed as potential agents of development during the 1990s. Cash transfers were then legitimised as an instrument that could help the poor to unlock their economic potential and include them as active participants of markets. In comparison to development policy before the emergence of social protection as a paradigm, the innovation of cash transfers is that the poor are now given an active role in economic growth, in contrast to their passive role in long-standing ideas of 'trickle down' growth.

While ideas of pro-poor growth also provide an economic rationale for cash transfers, the shifts in the global discourses on poverty and development that led to a focus on the poor as active individuals with economic potential also caused the emergence of a powerful social rationale for basic social protection. As human capital or human capabilities gained the attention of policy actors, they were constructed as the goal of development in and of themselves. The individual welfare and condition of the poor became benchmarks of social progress, and individuals became units of development on par with nation states and communities. In consequence, the alleviation of social problems like poverty, social inequities and social disintegration became an important legitimisation for policy due to their perceived impact on individual welfare.

Last but not least, the economic and social rationales for social protection and cash transfers were complemented by a strong rights-based rationale during the 1990s and early 2000s. The resurgence of interest in human rights in general in combination with the increasing importance of social rights led policy actors to perceive cash transfers as an entitlement that nation states are obligated to provide to their citizens, irrespective of economic or social concerns.

All in all, an analysis of the discourses that legitimise cash transfers thus demonstrates that the emergence of non-contributory benefits as development policy, if not a 'revolution', is part of a gradual change towards a more holistic concept of development that complements economic growth with other forms of social progress and social rights, the fulfilment of which does not need to have economic utility. There may have not been a revolution of development, but cash transfers can certainly be said to be part of diversification of development policy that has opened the way for new policies which cater to more than just growth – indeed, cash transfers are attributed with a wide variety of effects ranging from economic growth to preventing social disintegration and are advocated by a range of issue communities that represent different target groups. In sum, cash transfers are now an established part of global development policy under the umbrella of social protection as a more general paradigm. Indeed, I argue that the debate on cash transfers has not moved much since a wide consensus on social protection was reached around 2010 (see Chapter 3, especially Section 3.3) – the basic arguments for and against certain types of cash transfers and certain design features such as targeting and conditions have essentially remained the same.

Looking at the established ideas that legitimise cash transfers also helps to answer the question whether non-contributory benefits to the poor are embedded in a wider model of social protection that has implications for future social policy in the Global South. I assert that cash transfers are, in fact, part of a developmental model of social protection strongly focused on the assumed ability of social protection measures to foster and stabilise economic growth.

As explained throughout my analysis, policy actors widely agree that basic social protection should be implemented in developing countries to foster growth and social progress and to fulfil human rights. However, cash transfers and basic social protection are not intended to support all target groups equally or indefinitely. Support is meant to be extended up to the point where the poor cross the threshold of agency that allows them to participate in the economy, so that they can contribute to society and exit poverty out of their own power. This shapes the way in which the extension of basic social protection in the Global South is conceptualised. Priority in the provision of cash transfers is given to groups that are either mostly unable to contribute to the economy and deserve support – older persons – or groups where a transfer of resources is perceived as an investment into future economic potential – children. Working-age poor, in contrast, are attributed with sufficient economic agency to contribute without much support, so that policies like public employment programmes that combine social protection with economically productive outcomes are preferred over cash transfers. Hence, the model of social protection behind cash transfers is developmental because it prioritises economic growth as the goal that shapes the provision of cash transfers.

However, this is not to say that this model of social protection is purely residual and that policy actors only intend to provide cash transfers to the poor in order to alleviate the worst forms of poverty and include the poor in markets. Two aspects of the current model of social protection illustrate that it is indeed a model of complementary social responsibility shared by states and markets that aims to cover wide range of social problems and life risks, both for the poor and non-poor. Firstly, as exemplified by the widely supported concept of a 'global social floor', basic social protection is commonly envisioned as a complementary set of different instruments, including cash transfers and similar instruments like public employment programmes to different target groups, as well as basic social services like healthcare that benefit children, older persons and working-age poor equally, even if they are not poor. In so far, even basic forms of social protection are not meant to be focused on a residual safety-net approach that provides cash to ensure existential survival.

Secondly, the 'global social floor' also demonstrates that basic social protection is widely perceived as a first step towards the implementation of advanced forms of social protection. While a minimal set of social protection guarantees that alleviates poverty and other social problems is widely regarded as a necessity that should be implemented as soon as possible, the ILO is strongly advocating the future extension of social protection to the non-poor as soon as the 'floor' is established – this would include all common forms of social insurance that cover risks from unemployment, to old age, to health.

In sum, the model of social protection that most global development organisations support in conjunction with cash transfers thus implies a state that takes considerable social responsibility for its citizens by protecting and supporting the poor and mitigating common risks for the entire population but with the stated intention of fostering markets and economic growth as much as possible while doing so. In the end, this developmental model of social protection differs only gradually from the way social protection has traditionally been legitimised in the Global North. Here too, fostering economic growth has always been a goal of social protection measures, for example, by maintaining the labour power of the population in times of market decline, even if maintaining a certain standard of living may have been an equally or more important goal in many strongly institutionalised welfare states in the recent past (e.g., Kaufmann 2006). Indeed, the trend towards policies of activation that pervades welfare state reform in Europe in the recent past emphasises the need to strengthen economically productive effects of social protection and may signify that social protection policies in the Global North and the Global South are converging.

That said, while the model of social protection behind cash transfers appears to be fairly comprehensive conceptually, and the debate on cash transfers has not changed much since a stable consensus was reached around 2010 (see Chapter 3), is the implementation of social protection in the Global South actually following these ideas? In the case of basic social protection, the implementation of global ideas on the national level might be complicated by the vagueness of some fundamental concepts.

My analysis illustrates that policy actors, while generally agreeing on the necessity and utility of cash transfers to the poor, are reluctant to specify the level of benefits that is needed to provide essential social protection – the lowest common denominator is that cash transfers should lift the poor to the threshold of economic agency. In so far, the minimum level of social protection embodied by cash transfers has a rather symbolic character that developing countries are able to interpret quite differently according to their given needs and capabilities. Recent developments in global social protection policy reinforce the impression that the quality of basic social protection may greatly vary between nation states of the Global South in the future, first and foremost the change in terminology from 'global social floor' to 'national floors of social protection' in ILO Recommendation No. 202. Even though this terminological change suggests a departure from the strongly universalistic concept of a *global* social floor first suggested by the ILO, I argue that this should not be seen as a weakening of the original intent to extend social protection as comprehensively as possible on a global scale.

The shift towards national floor of protection can be regarded as an attempt to ease the adaptation of universal and abstract ideas of social protection to local circumstances that does not necessarily weaken the global consensus that social protection should be extended. In fact, social protection is playing a significant role in the suggestions given by the global policy community for 'sustainable development goals' that are to replace the Millennium Development Goals after 2015. The first proposal for new development goals given by a United Nations Open Working Group clearly advocates the implementation of social protection floors on a global scale in order to counteract poverty and inequality (UN 2014). As it seems, the global consensus to extend social protection and cash transfers remains an influential factor, even though it remains to be seen in how far such policies will become part of the finalised post-2015 development agenda.

But the potentially bright future of social protection policies on the global scale aside, what has actually been done in developing countries to lay the ground for the future extension of social protection, especially in terms of cash transfers? It should not be assumed that the policies advocated by global organisations will be perfectly implemented by nation states in the Global South, as research into education policy, for instance, has provided firm evidence of decoupling between the stated goals of global organisations, the legislation of developing countries and what is actually done in practice (see Meyer et al. 1997).

In the case of cash transfers, there is in fact some evidence that the ideas held by global organisations and the type of scheme implemented on the national level differ to some extent. Available studies do indicate that cash transfer programs have spread considerably throughout developing countries but that not all types of cash transfers are equally common and that the growth in cash transfer programs is not evenly distributed between countries (Weible forthcoming).

Preliminary overviews of the global spread of cash transfers in the Global South indicate that the number of cash transfer programmes in the Global South has been growing since the early 2000s and that social pensions and conditional cash transfers are the most common forms of cash transfers in this expansion, mirroring the priority of children and older people as target groups in global discourses (Weible forthcoming). However, even though general household assistance is not a favoured model of cash transfer in global policy, anecdotal evidence indicates that many African countries have implemented schemes that conform to this type (see Chapter 2; Interview 6; Bernd Schubert, personal communication): the Maputo 'food subsidy scheme', originally implemented in the early 1990s, still exists and covers 372,000 households, as does the original Kalomo pilot project in Zambia, started in the early 2000s. Bernd Schubert has personally participated in setting up similar pilot projects that follow the model of general household assistance in ten further African countries, for example, a UNICEF-financed project in Zimbabwe in 2011. The fact that UNICEF, an organisation that officially favours family allowances, finances general household assistance implies that there may in fact be significant differences between global policy discourses and practice on the ground.

Besides, it should be noted that not all cash transfers that have been implemented recently are strongly institutionalised on the national level: many countries have first implemented pilot programs or are only slowly extending the coverage of more permanent cash transfer schemes that start out with a small number of beneficiaries due to financial and administrative reasons. Only few countries in the Global South have systems of several complementary cash transfers programs to different target groups that approach the idea of a social floor, such as South Africa – and even in this case benefits are generally set at a level that only alleviates poverty and does not cover the entire living expenses of beneficiaries (Weible and Leisering 2012).

All in all, the extension of cash transfers in the Global South is still in its early stages, and it remains to be seen whether the idea of a global social floor can be realised in the near future. In times of fiscal austerity and continuing welfare state retrenchments in the Global North, the international political climate seems to be full of obstacles that promise to slow down the implementation of basic social protection in the Global South, let alone the introduction of more advanced forms of social protection like social insurance. However, as the recognition of cash transfers as policy models for the Global South indicates, even strong and long-standing obstacles will not stop policy change, even if it seems unlikely initially. Much has happened in terms of ideas on social protection on a global scale since the turn of the previous millennium, and as much may happen in terms of practice if the global consensus on cash transfers remains strong.

List of Sources

References

Amnesty International. 2013. http://www.amnesty.org/en/who-we-are/history, date accessed 8 January 2013.

Asian Development Bank (ADB). 2008. *Conditional Cash Transfer Programs: An Effective Tool for Poverty Alleviation?*, Manila: ADB.

Bahle, Thomas, Vanessa Hubl and Michaela Pfeifer. 2011. *The Last Safety Net. A Handbook of Minimum Income Protection in Europe*, Bristol: Policy Press.

Barrientos, Armando. 2010. 'Protecting Capability, Eradicating Extreme Poverty: Chile Solidario and the Future of Social Protection'. *Journal of Human Development and Capabilities*. 11:579–597.

Barrientos, Armando and Jocelyn DeJong. 2004. *Child Poverty and Cash Transfers – CHIP Report No.4*, London: Childhood Poverty Research and Policy Centre (CHIP).

Barrientos, Armando and Peter Lloyd-Sherlock. 2002. *Non-contributory Pensions and Social Protection*, Geneva: ILO.

Basic Income Earth Network (BIEN). 2012. http://binews.org/2011/09/india-basic-income-pilot-projects-are-underway/ and http://binews.org/2012/04/basic-income-pilot-project-in-india-makes-progress/, date accessed 1 October 2012.

——. 2014. http://www.basicincome.org/bien/aboutbien.html#history, date accessed 17 September 2014.

Basic Income Grant Coalition (BIG Coalition). 2009. *Making the Difference! The BIG in Namibia – Basic Income Grant Pilot Project Assessment Report, April 2009*, Windhoek: BIG Coalition.

Beattie, Roger. 2000. 'Social Protection for All: But How?'. *International Labour Review*. 139:129–148.

Béland, Daniel. 2005a. 'Ideas and Social Policy: An Institutionalist Perspective'. *Social Policy & Administration*. 39:1–18.

——. 2005b. 'Insecurity, Citizenship, and Globalization: The Multiple Faces of State Protection' *Sociological Theory*. 23:25–41.

——. 2009. 'Ideas, Institutions, and Policy Change'. *Journal of European Public Policy*. 16:701–718.

Berner, Frank. 2009. *Der hybride Sozialstaat. Die Neuordnung von öffentlich und privat in der sozialen Sicherung*. Vol. 69, Frankfurt am Main: Campus Verlag GmbH.

Blyth, Mark. 2001. 'The Transformation of the Swedish Model: Economic Ideas, Distributional Conflict, and Institutional Change' *World Politics*. 54:1–26.

——. 2002. *Great Transformations. Economic Ideas and Institutional Change in the Twentieth Century*, New York: Cambridge University Press.

Boli, John (ed.). 1999. *Constructing World Culture. International Nongovernmental Organizations since 1875*, Stanford, CA: Stanford University Press.

Bouillon, César Patricio and Luis Tejerina. 2006. *Do We Know What Works? A Systematic Review of Impact Evaluations of Social Programs in Latin America and the Caribbean*, Washington D.C.: Inter-American Development Bank.

Bourguignon, Francois, Francisco H.G. Ferreira and Phillippe G. Leite. 2002. *Ex-ante Evaluation of Conditional Cash Transfer Programs: The Case of Bolsa Escola*, Washington D.C.: The World Bank.

——. 2003. 'Conditional Cash Transfers, Schooling and Child Labor: Micro-simulating Brazil's Bolsa Escola Program'. *The World Bank Economic Review*. 2:229–254.

Bryant, Antony and Kathy Charmaz. 2007. *The SAGE Handbook of Grounded Theory*, Los Angeles: London: SAGE.

Camargo, José Márcio and Francisco H.G. Ferreira. 2001. *O Benefício Social Único: Uma Proposta de Reforma da Política Social no Brasil (Discussion Paper 443)*, Rio de Janeiro: Department of Economics PUC-Rio.

Campbell, John L. 1998. 'Institutional Analysis and the Role of Ideas in Political Economy'. *Theory and Society*. 27:377–409.

——. 2002. 'Ideas, Politics, and Public Policy' *Annual Review of Sociology*. 28:21–38.

Case, Anne. 2001. *Does Money Protect Health Status? Evidence from South African Pensions (NBER Working Paper 8495)*, Cambridge, MA: National Bureau of Economic Research.

Chenery, Hollis, Montek S. Ahluwalia, C.L.G. Bell, John H. Duloy and Richard Jolly. 1975. *Redistribution with Growth*, London: Oxford University Press.

Commission for Africa. 2005. *Our Common Interest – Report of the Commission for Africa*, http://www.commissionforafrica.info/wp-content/uploads/2005-report/11–03–05_cr_report.pdf.

Conway, Tim, Arjan de Haan and Andy Norton (eds). 2000. *Social Protection: New Directions of Donor Agencies*, London: ODI.

Cornia, Giovanni Andrea, Richard Jolly and Frances Stewart. 1987. *Adjustment with a Human Face – Volume 1: Protecting the Vulnerable and Promoting Growth*, Oxford: Clarendon Press.

Craven, Matthew C.R. 1995. *The International Covenant on Economic, Social and Cultural Rights. A Perspective on Its Development*, Oxford: Clarendon Press.

Davy, Ulrike. 2013. 'Social Citizenship Going International: Changes in the Reading of UN-Sponsored Economic and Social Rights'. *International Journal of Social Welfare*. 22, issue supplement S1:15–31.

Del Ninno, Carlo, Kalanidhi Subbarao and Annamaria Milazzo. 2009. *How to Make Public Works Work*, Washington D.C.: The World Bank.

Department for International Development (DFID). 1997. *Eliminating World Poverty: A Challenge for the 21st Century – White Paper on International Development*, London: DFID.

——. 2004. *How to Accelerate Pro-poor Growth: A Basic Framework for Policy Analysis (Pro-poor Growth Briefing Note 2)*, London: DFID.

——. 2005. *Social Transfers and Chronic Poverty: Emerging Evidence and the Challenge Ahead*, London: DFID.——. 2006a. *Using Social Transfers to Improve Human Development (Social Protection Briefing Note Series, Nr. 3)*, London: DFID.

——. 2006b. *Eliminating World Poverty – Making Governance Work for the Poor*, London: DFID.

——. 2009. *Eliminating World Poverty: Building Our Common Future*, London: DFID.

——. 2011. *Cash Transfers Evidence Paper*, London: DFID.

Devereux, Stephen. 2001. *Social Pensions in Namibia and South Africa (IDS Discussion Paper 379)*, Sussex: Institute of Development Studies.

Devereux, Stephen and Rachel Sabates-Wheeler. 2004. *Transformative Social Protection*, Sussex: Institute of Development Studies.

Devereux, Stephen and Colette Solomon. 2006. *Employment Creation Programmes: The International Experience*, Geneva: ILO.

Dingeldey, Irene. 2005a. *Wandel von Governance im Sozialstaat. Zur Implementation aktivierender Arbeitsmarktpolitik in Deutschland, Dänemark und Grossbritanien.* https://www.econstor.eu/dspace/bitstream/10419/28262/1/497813483.PDF date accessed (21 November 2012).

——. 2005b. *Welfare State Transformation between 'Workfare' and an 'Enabling' State. A Comparative Analysis.* http://www.econstor.eu/dspace/bitstream/10419/2827 1/1/49782261X.PDF, date accessed 21 November 2012.

Dureya, Suzanne and Andrew Morrison. 2004. *The Effect of Conditional Transfers on School Performance and Child Labor: Evidence from an Ex-post Impact Evaluation in Costa Rica*, Washington D.C.: Inter-American Development Bank (IDB).

Eberlei, Walter. 2012. 'Armut als globale Herausforderung'. 725–740, in *Handbuch Armut und Soziale Ausgrenzung*, edited by E.-U. Huster, J. Boeckh and H. Mogge-Grotjahn. Wiesbaden: VS Verlag für Sozialwissenschaften.

Emmerij, Louis, Richard Jolly and Thomas G. Weiss. 2001. *Ahead of the Curve? UN Ideas and Global Challenges*, Bloomington [u.a.]: Indiana University Press.

Foucault, Michel. 1974. *Die Ordnung des Diskurses (L'ordre du discours, dt.). Inauguralvorlesung am Collège de France- 2. Dezember 1970*, München: Hanser.

Freeland, Nicholas. 2007. 'Superfluous, Pernicious, Atrocious and Abominable? The Case against Conditional Cash Transfers'. *IDS Bulletin*. 38:75–78.

Garnier, Philippe. 1982. *Introduction to Special Public Works Programmes*. Geneva: ILO.

Gaude, J., Guichaoua, A., Martens, B. and Miller, S. 1987. 'Rural Development and Labour-Intensive Schemes', *International Labour Review*. 126:423–446.

Gesellschaft für technische Zusammenarbeit (GTZ). 1989. *Kaufkrafttransfer an die Ärmsten – Irrweg oder neuer Ansatz?*, Eschborn: GTZ.

——. 2005. *Social Cash Transfers – Reaching the Poorest: A Contribution to the International Debate Based on Experience in Zambia*, Eschborn: GTZ.

——. 2006. *Social Cash Transfers for the Poor in Developing Countries – A New Strategy of Development Policy?*, Eschborn: GTZ.

Grober, Ulrich. 2007. *Deep Roots. A Conceptual History of 'Sustainable Development' (Nachhaltigkeit)*. http://skylla.wzb.eu/pdf/2007/p07–002.pdf, date accessed 5 December 2012.

Grow up free from poverty coalition (GFP). 2012. http://www.grow-up-free-from-poverty.org.uk/, date accessed 20 September 2012.

Hall, Peter A. 1993. 'Policy Paradigms, Social Learning, and the State: The Case of Economic Policymaking in Britain'. *Comparative Politics*. 25:275–296.

Hanlon, Joseph, Armando Barrientos and David Hulme. 2010. *Just Give Money to the Poor. The Development Revolution from the Global South*, Sterling, VA: Kumarian Press.

Heintz, Bettina. 2010. 'Numerische Differenz. Überlegungen zu einer Soziologie des (quantitativen) Vergleichs'. *Zeitschrift für Soziologie*. 39:162–181.

Heintz, Bettina and Jens Greve. 2005. 'Die "Entdeckung" der Weltgesellschaft. Entstehung und Grenzen der Weltgesellschaftstheorie'. 89–119, in *Zeitschrift für Soziologie, 34.2005, Sonderheft, Weltgesellschaft. Theoretische Zugänge und empirische Problemlagen*, edited by B. Heintz. Stuttgart: Lucius & Lucius.

HelpAge International (HAI). 2000. *The Mark of a Noble Society: Human Rights and Older People*, London: HAI.

——. 2002. *State of the World's Older People 2002*, London: HelpAge International.

——. 2004. *Age and Security – How Social Pensions Deliver Effective Aid to Poor People and Their Families*, London: HAI.

——. 2006a. *Social Cash Transfers for Africa – A Transformative Agenda for the 21st Century*, London: HAI.

——. 2006b. *A Transformative Agenda for the 21st Century – Examining the Case for Basic Social Protection in Africa*, London: HAI.

——. 2006c. *Why Social Pensions Are Needed Now*, London: HAI.

——. 2012. http://www.helpage.org/download/4c3cfa0869630, date accessed 18 December 2012.

HAI and Institute of Development and Policy Management (IDPM). 2003. *Non-contributory Pensions and Poverty Prevention – A Comparative Study of Brazil and South Africa*. Manchester: Institute of Development and Policy Management.

HAI, Save the Children and Institute for Development Studies (IDS). 2005. *Making Cash Count Lessons from Cash Transfer Schemes in East and Southern Africa for Supporting the Most Vulnerable Children and Households*, London: HAI.

Holzmann, Robert and Steen Jorgensen. 2000. *Social Risk Management: A New Conceptual Framework for Social Protection and Beyond*, Washington D.C.: World Bank.

Hoogeven, James, Emil Tesliuc and Renos Vakis. 2004. *A Guide to the Analysis of Risk, Vulnerability and Vulnerable Groups*, Washington D.C.: World Bank.

Hulme, David. 2010. *Global Poverty. How Global Governance Is Failing the Poor*. Vol. 44, New York: Routledge.

Huster, Ernst-Ulrich, Jürgen Boeckh, Kay Bourcade and Johannes D. Schütte. 2009. *Analysis of the Situation in Relation to Minimum Income Schemes in Germany. A Study of National Policies*. http://www.google.de/url?sa=t&rct=j&q=analysis%20 of%20the%20situation%20in%20relation%20to%20minimum%20inc ome&source=web&cd=1&cad=rja&ved=0CDoQFjAA&url=http%3A%2F %2Fwww.peer-review-social-inclusion.eu%2Fnetwork-of-independent-experts%2Freports%2F2009-first-semester%2Fgermany-1–2009&ei=ayCuUK7F LJGLswbwhYDYDQ&usg=AFQjCNGu24KjtWzhJDvoyRY7KOCed_0CDw, date accessed 22 November 2012.

Institute for the Study of Labor (IZA). 2014. http://www.iza.org/en/webcontent/ personnel/vitae/5801_cv.pdf, date accessed 16 September 2014.

Inter-American Development Bank (IDB). 2001. *Targeted Human Development Programs: Investing in the Next Generation*, Washington D.C.: IDB.

International Labour Organisation (ILO).1944. *Declaration Concerning the Aims and Purposes of the International Labour Organisation*, Adopted at the 26th Session of the ILO, Philadelphia, 10 May 1944, Philadelphia: ILO.

——. 1952. *Social Security (Minimum Standards) Convention*, Geneva: ILO.

——. 1972. *Employment, Incomes and Equality – A Strategy for Increasing Productive Employment in Kenya*, Geneva: ILO.

——. 1999. *Social Security for the Excluded Majority – Case Studies of Developing Countries*, Geneva: ILO.

——. 2001. *Social Security: A New Consensus*, Geneva: ILO.

——. 2004a. *A Fair Globalization: Creating Opportunities for All*, Geneva: ILO.

———. 2004b. *Economic Security for a Better World*, Geneva: ILO.

———. 2004c. *Financing Social Protection*, Geneva: ILO.———. 2005. *Social Protection as a Productive Factor*, Geneva: ILO.

———. 2006a. *Social Security for All: Investing in Global Social and Economic Development – A Consultation* (Issues in Social Protection, Discussion Paper 16), Geneva: ILO.

———. 2008. *ILO Declaration on Social Justice for a Fair Globalisation*, Geneva: ILO.

———. 2009a. *Building Decent Societies – Rethinking the Role of Social Security in Development*, Basingstoke: Palgrave Macmillan.

———. 2009b. *Social Security for All – Investing in Social Justice and Economic Development*, Geneva: ILO.

———. 2010a. *Extending Social Security to All – A Guide through Challenges and Options*, Geneva: ILO.

———. 2010b. *Effects of Non-contributory Social Transfers in Developing Countries: A Compendium*, Geneva: ILO.

———. 2010c. *World Social Security Report 2010/11 – Providing Coverage in Times of Crisis and Beyond*, Geneva: ILO.

———. 2011. *Report VI – Social Security for Social Justice and a Fair Globalization*, Geneva: ILO.

———. 2012a. *International Labour Conference – Provisional Record, 101st Session, Geneva, May–June 2012 – Fourth Item on the Agenda: Elaboration of an Autonomous Recommendation on the Social Protection Floor*, Geneva: ILO.

———. 2012b. http://www.ilo.org/global/standards/introduction-to-international-labour-standards/conventions-and-recommendations/lang—en/index.htm, date accessed 29 August 2012.

———. 2014a. http://www.ilo.org/global/standards/introduction-to-international-labour-standards/conventions-and-recommendations/lang—en/index.htm, date accessed 16 September 2014.

———. 2014b. http://www.ilo.org/dyn/normlex/en/f?p=NORMLEXPUB:12100:0:: NO::P12100_INSTRUMENT_ID:3065524, date accessed 18 September 2014.

———. 2014c. http://www.ilo.org/global/about-the-ilo/who-we-are/ilo-director-general/former-directors-general/WCMS_192716/lang—en/index.htm, date accessed 23 September 2014.

ILO and OECD. 2011. *Towards National Social Protection Floors – A Policy Note for the G20 Meeting of Labour and Employment Ministers*, Paris, 26–27 September 2011. http://www.oecd.org/els/48732216.pdf, date accessed 16 November 2012.

ILO and World Health Organisation (WHO). 2009a. *Social Protection Floor Initiative – Manual and Strategic Framework for Joint UN Country Operations*, Geneva: ILO.

———. 2009b. *The Social Protection Floor – A Joint Crisis Initiative of the UN Chief Executives Board for Co-ordination on the Social Protection Floor*, Geneva: ILO.

Irie, Akira, Petra Goedde and William I. Hitchcock. 2012. *The Human Rights Revolution. An International History*, Oxford: Oxford University Press.

Ishay, Micheline. 2008. *The History of Human Rights. From Ancient Times to the Globalization Era*, Berkeley, London: University of California Press.

Kannan, K.P. 2004. *Social Security, Poverty Reduction and Development – Arguments for Enlarging the Concept and Coverage of Social Security in a Globalizing World*, Geneva: ILO.

Kaufmann, Franz-Xaver. 2006. *Varianten des Wohlfahrtsstaats. Der deutsche Sozialstaat im internationalen Vergleich*. Vol. 2301, Frankfurt am Main: Suhrkamp.

Keeley, Brian. 2012. *From Aid to Development: The Global Fight against Poverty (OECD Insights)*, Paris: OECD Publishing.

Keller, Reiner. 2008. *Wissenssoziologische Diskursanalyse. Grundlegung eines Forschungsprogramms*, Wiesbaden: VS Verlag für Sozialwissenschaften | GWV Fachverlage GmbH Wiesbaden.

———. 2009. 'Der menschliche Faktor'. 69–107, in *Diskurs, Macht und Subjekt. Theorie und Empirie von Subjektivierung in der Diskursforschung*, edited by R. Keller, W. Schneider and W. Viehöver. Wiesbaden: VS Verlag für Sozialwissenschaften.

———. 2012. *Doing Discourse Research: An Introduction for Social Scientists*, London: Sage.

Kingdon, John W. 2003. *Agendas, Alternatives, and Public Policies*, New York: Longman.

Korpi, Walter and Joakim Palme. 1998. 'The Paradox of Redistribution and Strategies of Equality'. *American Sociological Review*. 63:661–687.

Künnemann, Rolf and Ralf Leonhard. 2008. *A Human Rights View of Social Cash Transfers for Achieving the Millennium Development Goals*, Bonn/Stuttgart: Brot für die Welt and evangelischer Entwicklungsdienst.

Lal, Radhika, Steve Miller, Maikel Lieuw-Kie-Song and Daniel Kostzer. 2010. *Public Works and Employment Programmes: Towards a Long-Term Development Approach*, Brasilia: UNDP.

Leisering, Lutz. 2008. 'Social Assistance in the Global South. A Survey and Analysis'. *Zeitschrift für ausländisches und internationales Arbeitsrecht*. 22:1–143.

———. 2009. 'Extending Social Security to the Excluded: Are Social Cash Transfers to the Poor an Appropriate Way of Fighting Poverty in Developing Countries?' *Global Social Policy*. 9:246–272.

———. 2010. *Social Assistance in Developed and Developing Countries. A Case of Global Social Policy?* http://www.floorgroup.raumplanung.tu-dortmund.de/FLOOR_Working_papers/FLOOR_WP004_Leisering_Social_assistance_in_developed_and_developing_countries_%282010%29.pdf, date accessed 14 September 2010.

Levine, Anthony. 2001. *Orphans and Other Vulnerable Children: What Role for Social Protection* (Social Protection Discussion Paper Series, No. 0126), Washington D.C.: The World Bank.

Lieuw-Kie-Song, Maikel and Kate Phillip. 2010. *Mitigating a Jobs Crisis: Innovations in Public Employment Programmes (IPEP)*, Geneva: ILO.

Maier-Rigaud, Remi. 2009. 'In Search of a New Approach to Pension Policy: The International Labour Office between Internal Tension and External Pressure'. 165–189, in *The Role of International Organizations in Social Policy. Ideas, Actors and Impact*, edited by R. Ervik. Cheltenham: Elgar.

Maluccio, John A. 2003. *Education and Child Labor: Experimental Evidence from a Nicaraguan Conditional Cash Transfer Program*, Washington D.C.: International Food Policy Research Institute (IFPRI).

Mehta, Jal. 2011. 'The Varied Roles of Ideas in Politics: From "Wether" to "How"'. 23–46, in *Ideas and Politics in Social Science Research*, edited by D. Béland and R.H. Cox. Oxford, New York: Oxford University Press.

Meyer, John W., John Boli, George M. Thomas and Francisco O. Ramirez. 1997. 'World Society and the Nation-State'. *The American Journal of Sociology*. 106:144–181.

Michael Leutelt. 2012. *HelpAge's Involvement in Spreading Social Pensions in the Global South: Slow and Steady Wins the Race?*. http://www.floorgroup.raumplanung.tu-dortmund.de/FLOOR_Working_papers/FLOOR_WP016_Leutelt_HelpAge_social_pensions_global_South.pdf, date accessed 11 January 2013.

Midgley, James. 1995. *Social Development. The Developmental Perspective in Social Welfare*, London [u.a.]: SAGE.

Ministry of Community Development and Social Services (MCDSS) and GTZ. 2004. *The Incapacitated Poor in Zambia*, Lusaka: GTZ Social Safety Net Project.

Ministry of Law and Justice (New Delhi, India). 2005. *The National Rural Employment Guarantee Act*. http://nrega.nic.in/rajaswa.pdf, date accessed 22 October 2014.

Moyn, Samuel. 2010. *The Last Utopia. Human Rights in History*, Cambridge, MA: Belknap Press of Harvard University Press.

Munro, Lauchlan T. 2010. 'Risks, Needs and Rights: Compatible or Contradictory Bases for Social Protection'. 27–46, in *Palgrave Studies in Development, Social Protection for the Poor and Poorest. Concepts, Policies and Politics*, edited by A. Barrientos and D. Hulme. Basingstoke, Hampshire: Palgrave Macmillan.

Noël, Alain. 2006. 'The New Global Politics of Poverty'. *Global Social Policy*. 6:304–333.

Normand, Roger and Sarah Zaidi. 2008. *Human Rights at the UN. The Political History of Universal Justice*, Bloomington: Indiana University Press.

Norton, Andy, Tim Conway and Mick Foster. 2001. *Social Protection Concepts and Approaches: Implications for Policy and Practice in International Development*, London: ODI.

Nullmeier, Frank. 2006. 'Politikwissenschaft auf dem Weg zur Diskursanalyse'. 287–313, in *Handbuch sozialwissenschaftliche Diskursanalyse*, edited by R. Keller, Wiesbaden: VS Verl. für Sozialwiss.

ODI and GTZ. 2005. *Cash Transfers in the Context of Pro-poor Growth*, Eschborn: GTZ.

ODI and World Vision. 2008. *Cash Transfers in Emergencies – A Synthesis of World Vision's Experience and Learning*, London: ODI.

Orenstein, Mitchell A. 2008. *Privatizing Pensions. The Transnational Campaign for Social Security Reform*, Princeton, NJ: Princeton University Press.

Organisation for Economic Cooperation and Development (OECD). 1979. *Facing Futures – Mastering the Probable and Managing the Unpredictable*, Paris: OECD.

OECD/Development Assistance Committee (OECD-DAC). 1996. *Shaping the 21st Century: The Contribution of Development Cooperation*, Paris: OECD.

——. 2001. *The DAC Guidelines – Poverty Reduction*, Paris: OECD.

——. 2009. *Promoting Pro-poor Growth – Social Protection*, Paris: OECD.

Peters, Brainard G. 2005. *Institutional Theory in Political Science. The 'New Institutionalism'*, London [u.a.]: Continuum.

Powell, Martin A. 1999. 'Introduction'. 1–28, in *New Labour, New Welfare State? The 'Third Way' in British Social Policy*, edited by M. A. Powell. Bristol: Policy.

Ranis, Gustav. 2005. 'The Evolution of Development Thinking: Theory and Policy'. 119–140, in *Annual World Bank Conference on Development Economics 2005. Lessons of Experience*, edited by François Bourguignon and Boris Pleskovic. Washington D.C.: The World Bank.

Ravallion, Martin. 1991. 'Reaching the Rural Poor through Public Employment', *The World Bank Research Observer*. 6:153–175.

Rawlings, Laura B. 2004. *A New Approach to Social Assistance: Latin America's Experience with Conditional Cash Transfer Programs* (Social Protection Discussion Paper Series, No. 0416), Washington D.C.: The World Bank.

Rawlings, Laura B. and Bénédicte de la Brière. 2006. *Examining Conditional Cash Transfer Programs: A Role for Increased Social Inclusion?* (Social Protection Discussion Paper Series, No. 0603), Washington D.C.: The World Bank.

Reutlinger, Shlomo. 1988. 'Efficient Alleviation of Poverty and Hunger: A New International Assistance Facility'. *Food Policy*. 13:56–66.

Rist, Gilbert. 2006. *The History of Development. From Western Origins to Global Faith*, London: Zed Books.

Roddis, Suzanne and Zafiris Tzannatos. 1999. *Family Allowances* (Social Protection Discussion Paper Series No. 9814), Washington D.C.: The World Bank.

Schäfer, Gerhard K. 2012. 'Geschichte der Armut im abendländischen Kulturkreis'. 257–278, in *Handbuch Armut und Soziale Ausgrenzung*, edited by E.-U. Huster, J. Boeckh and H. Mogge-Grotjahn, Wiesbaden: VS Verlag für Sozialwissenschaften.

Schmidt, Vivien A. 2002. *The Futures of European Capitalism*, Oxford: Oxford University Press.

——. 2008. 'Discursive Institutionalism: The Explanatory Power of Ideas and Discourse'. *Annual Review of Political Science*. 11:303–326.

——. 2011. 'Reconciling Ideas and Institutions through Discursive Institutionalism'. 47–64, in *Ideas and Politics in Social Science Research*, edited by D. Béland and R.H. Cox, Oxford, New York: Oxford University Press.

Schmidt, Vivien A. and Claudio M. Radaelli. 2004. 'Policy Change and Discourse in Europe: Conceptual and Methodological Issues'. *West European Politics*. 27:183–210.

Schubert, Bernd. 1985. 'Reformvorschläge für die Entwicklungshilfe – Eine Rente für die Ärmsten', *ZEIT*, 04.10.1985.

——. 1987. 'Cash Transfers to the Poorest – New Instruments for a Poverty-Oriented Development Aid Approach', *Food Policy*. 12:2–4.

——. 1990. *Transfers for Survival – Assessment of the Food Subsidy Scheme as Part of the Social Security System in Mozambique*, Eschborn: GTZ.

Schubert, Bernd and Ivonne Antezana. 1991. *Targeting Cash Transfers to the Urban Destitute of Mozambique – Assessment and Reorganization of the FOOD-SUBSIDY-SCHEME*, Eschborn: GTZ.

Schubert, Bernd and Geert Balzer. 1990. *Soziale Sicherungssysteme in Entwicklungsländern – Transfers als sozialpolitischer Ansatz zur Bekämpfung überlebensgefährdender Armut*, Eschborn: GTZ.

Scoones, Ian. 1998. *Sustainable Rural Livelihoods – A Framework for Analysis*, Sussex: Institute for Development Studies.

Skoufias, Emmanuel and Susan W. Parker. 2001. *The Effect of Conditional Transfers on School Performance and Child Labor: Evidence from an Ex-post Impact Evaluation in Costa Rica*, Washington D.C.: IFPRI.

Speich, Daniel. 2011. 'The Use of Global Abstractions: National Income Accounting in the Period of Imperial Decline'. *Journal of Global History*. 6:7–28.

Standing, Guy. 2013. 'India's Experiment in Basic Income Grants', *Global Dialogue*. 3:24–26.

Standing, Guy and Michael Samson. 2003. *A Basic Income Grant for South Africa*, Lansdowne: University of Capetown Press.

Subbarao, K., Aniruddha Bonnerjee, Jeanine Braithwaite, Soniya Carvalho, Kene Ezemenari, Carol Graham and Alan Thompson. 1997. *Safety Net Programs and Poverty Reduction – Lessons from Cross-Country Experience*, Washington D.C.: The World Bank.

Sugiyama, N.B. 2011. 'The Diffusion of Conditional Cash Transfer Programs in the Americas'. *Global Social Policy*. 11:250–278.

Tabor, Steven R. 2002. *Assisting the Poor with Cash: Design and Implementation of Social Transfer Programs*, Washington D.C.: The World Bank.

United Nations. 1995. *Report of the World Summit for Social Development*, New York: United Nations.

——. 2011. *The Global Social Crisis – Report on the World Social Situation 2011*, New York: United Nations.

——. 2012a. http://www.un.org/millenniumgoals/, date accessed 29 August 2012.

——. 2012b. http://www.un.org/en/documents/udhr/index.shtml#a22, date accessed 13 December 2012.

——. 2012c. http://www2.ohchr.org/english/law/cescr.htm, date accessed 13 December 2012.

——. 2012d. http://www.un.org/en/documents/udhr/index.shtml#a2, date accessed 17 December 2012.

——. 2013a. http://www.un.org/documents/ga/res/41/a41r128.htm, date accessed 8 January 2013.

——. 2013b. http://www2.ohchr.org/english/bodies/cescr/comments.htm, date accessed 11 January 2013.

——. 2013c. http://daccess-dds- ny.un.org/doc/UNDOC/GEN/G08/403/97/PDF/G0840397.pdf?OpenElement, date accessed 11 January 2013.

——. 2014. http://sustainabledevelopment.un.org/focussdgs.html, date accessed 9 October 2014.

United Nations Children's Fund (UNICEF). 1997. *State of the World's Children 1997*, New York: Oxford University Press.

——. 2000. *Poverty Reduction Begins with Children*, New York: UNICEF.

——. 2006. *The Malawi Social Cash Transfer Pilot Scheme – Preliminary Lessons Learned*, New York: UNICEF.

——. 2007. *The Impact of Social Cash Transfers on Children Affected by HIV and AIDS – Evidence from Zambia, Malawi and South Africa*, Esaro: UNICEF.

——. 2011. *Escalating Food Prices – The Threat to Poor Households and Policies to Safeguard a Recovery for All*, New York: UNICEF.

——. 2012. *Integrated Social Protection Systems – Enhancing Equity for Children*, New York: UNICEF.

UNICEF and ODI. 2009. *Child Poverty: A Role for Cash Transfers – West and Central Africa*, New York: UNICEF.

UNICEF, DFID, The World Bank, HAI, IDS, ILO, ODI, Save the Children UK, UNDP, Hope & Homes for Children. 2009. *Advancing Child-Sensitive Social Protection*. http://www.beta.undp.org/content/dam/aplaws/publication/en/publications/poverty-reduction/poverty-website/advancing-child-sensitive-social-protection/CSSP%20joint%20statement%208%2020%202009.pdf, date accessed 2 December 2011.

UNICEF, UNAIDS, USAID, The World Bank, Measure DHS, Family Health International, Save the Children. 2005. *Guide to Monitoring and Evaluation of the National Response for Children Orphaned and Made Vulnerable by HIV/AIDS*, New York: UNICEF.

United Nations Development Programme (UNDP). 1990. *Human Development Report 1990*, New York/Oxford: Oxford University Press.

——. 1992. *Human Development Report 1992*, New York/Oxford: Oxford University Press.

——. 1994. *Human Development Report 1994*, New York/Oxford: Oxford University Press.

——. 1997. *Human Development Report 1997*, New York/Oxford: Oxford University Press.

——. 1998. *Human Development Report 1998*, New York/Oxford: Oxford University Press.

——. 2000. *Human Development Report 2000*, New York/Oxford: Oxford University Press.

——. 2010. *Human Development Report 2010 – The Real Wealth of Nations: Pathways to Human Development*, New York: Palgrave Macmillan.

United Nations System Chief Executives Board for Coordination (UN-CEB). 2009. *The Global Financial Crisis and Its Impact on the Work of the UN System*, New York: UN.

——. 2012a. http://www.unsceb.org/ceb/home, date accessed 18 September 2012.

——. 2012b. http://www.unsceb.org/ceb/brochure/overview/ceb/hlcp, date accessed 18 September 2012.

Uvin, Peter. 2010. 'From the Right to Development to the Rights-Based Approach: How "Human Rights" Entered Development". 163–175, in *Deconstructing Development Discourse. Buzzwords and Fuzzwords*, edited by A. Cornwall and D. Eade. Rugby, Warwickshire: Practical Action Pub.

Van Ginneken, Wouter. 1999. 'Social Security for the Informal Sector: A New Challenge for Developing Countries'. *International Social Security Review.* 52:49–69.

Van Parijs, Philippe. 2000. *Basic Income: A Simple and Powerful Idea for the 21st Century*, Basic Income European Network, Paper to the VIIIth International Congress.

Weible, Katrin. (Forthcoming 2016). *Social Institution Building in the Global South*, dissertation, Bielefeld University, Germany.

Weible, Katrin and Lutz Leisering. 2012. 'South Africa's System of Social Cash Transfers. Assessing Its Social Quality'. 247–270, in *Sozialpolitik in globaler Perspektive. Asien, Afrika und Lateinamerika*, edited by H.-J. Burchardt, A. Tittor and N. Weinmann. Frankfurt, M, New York: Campus-Verl.

World Bank. 1980. *World Development Report 1980*, New York: Oxford University Press.

——. 1988. *The Poor and the Poorest – Some Interim Findings*, Washington D.C.: The World Bank.

——. 1990. *World Development Report 1990 – Poverty*, New York: Oxford University Press.

——. 1994. *Averting the Old Age Crisis – Policies to Protect the Old and Promote Growth*, New York: Oxford University Press.

——. 2001a. *Social Protection Sector Strategy – From Safety Net to Springboard*, Washington D.C.: The World Bank.

——. 2001b. *Orphans and Other Vulnerable Children: What Role for Social Protection?*, Washington D.C.: The World Bank.

——. 2001c. *World Development Report 2000/2001 – Attacking Poverty*, New York: Oxford University Press.

——. 2003a. *Workshop on Conditional Cash Transfer Programs (CCTs): Operational Experiences*, Quito: Ayala Consulting Co.

——. 2003b. *The Contribution of Social Protection to the Millennium Development Goals*, Washington D.C.: The World Bank.

——. 2006. *World Development Report 2006 – Equity and Development*, New York: Oxford University Press.

——. 2008. *For Protection and Promotion – The Design and Implementation of Effective Safety Nets*, Washington D.C.: The World Bank.

——. 2009a. *Conditional Cash Transfers – Reducing Present and Future Poverty*, Washington D.C.: The World Bank.

——. 2009b. *Closing the Coverage Gap – The Role of Social Pensions and Other Retirement Income Transfers*, Washington D.C.: The World Bank.

——. 2011. *Building Resilience and Opportunity – The World Bank's Social Protection & Labor Strategy 2012–2022 Concept Note*, Washington D.C.: The World Bank.

——. 2012. *Resilience, Equity and Opportunity – Social Protection and Labor Strategy*, Washington D.C.: The World Bank.

World Bank/Latin America and the Caribbean Regional Office (World Bank/LACRO). 2001. *Brazil – An Assessment of the Bolsa Escola Programs*, Washington D.C.: The World Bank.

World Bank/Poverty Group. 1999. *Global Synthesis – Consultations with the Poor*, Washington D.C.: The World Bank.

World Commission on Environment and Development (WCED). 1987. *Report of the World Commission on Environment and Development: Our Common Future*, http://www.un-documents.net/our-common-future.pdf, date accessed 5 December 2012.

Interviews

Interview 1: Senior development consultant, German NGO; 28 January 2011, Bielefeld, Germany. Conducted in German, translation by the author.

Interview 2: Senior development scholar and consultant, United Kingdom; 13 May 2011, Bielefeld, Germany.

Interview 3: Former senior UNICEF official and development economist; 30 November 2011, Bielefeld, Germany. Conducted in German, translation by the author.

Interview 4: Senior development expert, HelpAge International; 22 February 2012, London, United Kingdom.

Interview 5: Senior staff member, HelpAge International; 22 February 2012, London, United Kingdom.

Interview 6: Group discussion with Bernd Schubert, development consultant; 7 June 2012, Berlin, Germany. Conducted in German, translation by the author.

Interview 7: Development economist, formerly senior staff at the ILO; 14 September 2012, Munich, Germany

Conferences

1 Workshop 'Entwicklungspolitik in der Krise: Hilfe zur Selbsthilfe oder soziale Grundsicherung'

   Friedrich Ebert Foundation (FES), Bonn, Germany; 13 October 2010

   Comment: Workshop organised by the FES in cooperation with several development NGOs, including HelpAge Germany. Workshop participants debated the characteristics of social cash transfers and their feasibility as development policy.

2 Nachhaltige Grundsicherung Armut lindern – natürliche Lebensgrundlagen erhalten

   Protestant academy Saxony-Anhalt e.V., Wittenberg, Germany; 3–5 December 2010

   Comment: Conference on the feasibility of basic income, focusing on issues of sustainability, environmental protection and climate change. Included a debate on the basic income pilot project in Ocivero, Namibia.

3 Global Consultation on the Second Social Protection and Labor Strategy of the World Bank

   Federal Ministry for Cooperation and Development, Bonn, Germany; 4 May 2011

   Comment: Part of a series of World Bank consultations which offered interested parties the opportunity to comment on the draft note for the second social protection strategy. Included presentations on the new strategy by key World Bank staff.

4 Expert talk 'Soziale Sicherung weltweit'

   Paul Löbe house, Berlin, Germany; 23 May 2011

   Comment: Expert talk on global developments in social security, organised by the German Green party. Included presentations on the global social floor by key ILO staff and a presentation on the basic income pilot in Ocivero.

5 International Labour Conference, 100th session

   Palace of Nations, Geneva, Switzerland; 1–17 June 2011

   Comment: Main annual conference of the ILO. Non-participant observation of public proceedings in the discussion on social security and the global social floor (01.04.06).

6 No Social Justice without Social Protection

   Friedrich Ebert Foundation, Berlin Germany; 5 July 2011

   Comment: Expert conference on the implementation of national social protection floors in the wake of the 100th International Labour Conference. Included presentations by the ILO, the ADB, the GIZ, HelpAge Germany and by representatives from developing countries.

7 Social Protection Conference

Ruhr University Bochum, Bochum, Germany; 20–21 October 2011

Comment: International conference on social protection in developing countries, co-organised by GIZ. Included presentations by the ILO, the World Bank and other major international organisations, by eminent development scholars and by representatives from developing countries.

8 Achieving Income Security in Old Age

Dunford House, Sussex, United Kingdom; 21–23 February 2012

Comment: Conference on social pensions organised by HelpAge International. Included representatives from the World Bank, the ILO and other major IOs.

9 Pathways to a Basic Income: The 14th Basic Income Earth Network Congress

Wolf-Ferrari-Haus, Munich, Germany; 14–16 September 2012

Comment: Major global congress on basic income. Included presentations on new basic income pilot projects in India.

Index

basic income, 64–66, 115

children, 32, 36–38, 42, 48, 86, 107,
111, 114–117, 132–133, 147,
164, 186, 189, *see also* social cash
transfers, family allowances;
uncertainity, vulnerable groups

development policy
development as a concept,
124–137
development policy and social
policy, 131–135
development policy in general, 70,
84, 102–103, 113, 142, 168
human development, 43–44,
90–92, 107, 119, 125, 129–130,
135, 137, 151, 172–174, 180
Millennium Development Goals,
57, 82–83, 188, *see also* ideas,
frames
rights-based approaches to
development, 72, 79, 81–82, *see
also* human rights
social development, *see also*
development policy, human
development
disabled people, 48, 53, 97, 101,
117, 147, *see also* uncertainty,
vulnerable groups
discourse
discourse coalitions, 16, 179–181
discursive practices, 15, 41, 127,
181–182
discursive shifts, 15–16, 22–24, 52,
62, 66, 104
discursive window of opportunity,
66, 89, 91, 93, 96, 99, 103
as a general concept, 9–11, 13–17,
18, 20, 42, 48, 60, 66, 85
narratives, 14, 16, 84, 118, 121,
122, *see also* discourse, discursive
practices

phenomenon structure of
discourse, 14, 106, 126, 141, 158
schemes of interpretation, 14,
20–22, 85, 179–180, *see also*
ideas, frames; ideas, problem
definitions
specialised and public discourses,
14–15, 173

economic growth
in general, 34–35, 42, 71, 73, 75,
76–77, 84–85, 87, 110, 127–128,
140–142
human capital, 35, 38, 42, 71, 84,
105–107, 112, 128, 131–132,
134–135, *see also* development
policy, human development;
poverty, agency of the poor;
social cash transfers, CCT
pro-poor growth, 113–114,
130–131, 137–138, 184–185

global organisations, *see also*
discourse, discourse coalitions;
policy, policy community
DFID, 32, 54, 71, 73, 96–97, 102,
107, 123–124, 174
GIZ/ GTZ, 56–57, 73, 180
Help Age International, 32, 48–52,
72–73, 120–121, 175
IDS, 49, 98, 180
ILO, 32, 38, 42–43, 61–62, 73, 75,
78–80, 122–123, 140–144, 175,
see also social protection, global
social floor
ODI, 40, 96–97
UNDP, 90, 107, 129–130, 143,
see also development policy,
human development
UNICEF, 32, 36–42, 51, 73,
100–101, 164, 189, *see also*
children; social cash transfers,
family allowances

Printed in the USA
CPSIA information can be obtained
at www.ICGtesting.com
LVHW080147221123
764347LV00056B/842

9 781137 505682